THE TRENT AND MERSEY CANAL
A HISTORY

SHARDLOW
14
MILES

PRESTON
BROOK
7⅞
MILES

R & D
STONE
1819

THE TRENT AND MERSEY CANAL

A HISTORY

RAY SHILL

The Crowood Press

First published in 2021 by
The Crowood Press Ltd
Ramsbury, Marlborough
Wiltshire SN8 2HR

enquiries@crowood.com

www.crowood.com

© Ray Shill 2021

All rights reserved. No part of this publication may be reproduced or transmitted in any form or by any means, electronic or mechanical, including photocopy, recording, or any information storage and retrieval system, without permission in writing from the publishers.

British Library Cataloguing-in-Publication Data
A catalogue record for this book is available from the British Library.

ISBN 978 1 78500 856 6

Acknowledgements
Assistance has been provided by the following: the late Harry Arnold, Alan Baker, David Henthorn Brown, Peter Cross-Rudkin, Nigel Crowe, Richard Dean, Tom Foxon, Roger Evans, Christopher Jones, Martin O'Keeffe, Allison Smedley, Howard Sprenger, Steve Wood, David Wooliscoft

Unless otherwise attributed, the images have been provided by Heartland Press or the Ray Shill Collection.

Designed and typeset by Guy Croton Publishing Services,
West Malling, Kent
Cover design by Design Deluxe
Printed and bound in India by Parksons Graphics Pvt Ltd., Mumbai.

Contents

Introduction — 6

Chapter 1: Creation of the Trent and Mersey Canal — 7
Chapter 2: Engineering and Infrastructure — 14
Chapter 3: Building the Branches — 34
Chapter 4: Development and Improvement — 44
Chapter 5: Railways and Railway Ownership — 68
Chapter 6: Facets of Trade — 92
Chapter 7: Canal People — 128
Chapter 8: Decline and Restoration — 136

Bibliography — 157
Index — 159

Introduction

Much of the history of navigable waterways in Great Britain has been written down, but there still remains the chance of previously unpublished sources being discovered. There is also the fact that published works are not always comprehensive and there are gaps where histories have not been published.

For the Trent and Mersey Canal a comprehensive history was produced by David & Charles in 1979, with Jean Lindsay as author. Other accounts have followed, including a detailed study by Peter Lead and a comprehensive account on trade by Tom Foxon. As more information has come to light since, however, a fresh account is needed to cover the modern findings as well as to provide a new understanding of the canal and the pivotal role it played in creating the canal network in Britain.

The Trent and Mersey Canal, as first built, was one of a group of waterways engineered by James Brindley. Uniting the River Mersey and the River Trent, it formed the core of the British canal network and provided the means for the movement of goods and minerals through to the ports of Liverpool and Hull. The Staffordshire and Worcestershire Canal, which joined the Trent and Mersey Canal, created a link with the Severn and the ports of Gloucester and Bristol. These two waterways provided a navigation transport backbone for trading by water.

Both the Severn and the Trent had a natural navigable limit. For the Severn, craft could reach as far as Pool Quay, near Welshpool, although most journeys were confined to trips as far as Shrewsbury, where road carriage was used to reach Chester. Bridgnorth and Bewdley were also convenient transhipment places for the West Midlands. With the Trent, the upper limit gradually moved upstream from Nottingham to Wilden Ferry, where the road from Derby to London crossed. The canal proposal was opposed by a number of alternate schemes. First, for those who preferred river development, there were the examples of the Aire and Calder and Calder and Hebble navigations in Yorkshire, the Mersey and Irwell navigation in Lancashire, and the River Weaver in Cheshire. All of these waterways had been made navigable through short lock cuts and played a vital role in manufacturing, serving cotton mills, woollen mills and the salt works. River development towards the Midlands had reached Burton upon Trent through the Upper Trent Navigation and there were other schemes to extend the river navigation beyond Burton to use the Trent and Tame to reach Tamworth. Most notable of these was that of Henry Bradford.

For this study, history is the starting point. There is much more to the story of the Trent and Mersey Canal, which celebrated 250 years of commercial existence in the year 2020.

CHAPTER I

Creation of the Trent and Mersey Canal

Throughout history, events occur that can shape the future for the common good. In past times the use of water to turn a waterwheel was put to commercial advantage and gradually brought industry to the river side. Managing the water supply to the mill was part of that gradual improvement and the skills in making new water courses formed the bedrock for the construction of artificial waterways.

Eighteenth-century English engineer James Brindley worked first as a millwright before gaining skills in the management of water resources. When navigation to the West Midlands from the Trent began to be considered, the primary question was what type of scheme to pursue. Brindley favoured a navigable canal, where the supply of water could be controlled; navigation that relied on a river could be disrupted by issues of flooding and drought, and any disruption would limit trade. Even in modern times, the power of nature has continued to be potentially extremely destructive, as in the case with Storm Ciara and the damage to the Figure of Three Locks on the Calder and Hebble Navigation, in February 2020.

Early Plans

The growing demands of industry in Birmingham, the Potteries and Wolverhampton led to a pressing need to improve local transport networks. The nearest navigations were the River Severn and the River Trent. Proposals to extend those navigations were considered during the eighteenth century, when the needs of industry and merchants came to have greater influence on transport innovation. In 1755 William Taylor and John Eyes surveyed a navigation route between Liverpool and Hull at the request of a group of Liverpool merchants, and chiefly financed by a Mr Hardman. However, this scheme was overtaken by the Sankey Canal project, which drew the merchants' support – and finance – away from the ambitious Trent and Mersey venture.

In 1758 Thomas Broade suggested a canal to link the Trent with the Mersey. Initially limited to a stretch from Stoke-on-Trent to Wilden on the Trent, it was to be about 40 miles in length, 8 yards wide and 1 yard deep, with locks to pound up the water and make it as dead as the canals in Holland.

With Broade's plan, a canal on to Cheshire was thought to be an 'expence too great'. A very good navigation might be made from Northwich to Lawton-wich, which was 5 miles from Burslem, where this Trent navigation might be easily brought. To link the two navigations, a new road for carriages and horses might be made from Lawton through Harecastle Vale to Burslem.

James Brindley made his first surveys in 1758 for a canal route to link Long Bridge (Longport) with

Kings Mill on the Trent. His second survey was made between 13 December 1758 and 16 September 1759. The surveys were recorded in his 'daylanded book'. The places he mentions in connection with the canal route are Newcastle (under Lyme) (13 December 1758); Lichfield (15 December 1758); Harecastle to Lichfield and Alerwas (Alrewas) Mill (10–17 May 1759); Harecastle to Ape Dale (20 May 1759). According to his book, on 2 September 1759 he 'set out for Lichfield Survey to Tamworth', on 8 September 1759 he 'Surveyed for Wilden', and on 16 September 1759 he 'Returnd.' The result of his labours was the proposed canals from the Trent to Long Bridge and Lichfield.

Later, with John Smeaton, Brindley came up with various improvements to this scheme to Lichfield, Tamworth and the Potteries. At the time, Brindley was working on different navigation schemes, most notably the Bridgewater Canal, which first linked the Duke of Bridgewater's collieries at Worsley Delph with Manchester. This waterway had been the subject of change and alteration. The work was under the supervision of John Gilbert, agent for the Duke, but Brindley was employed on the canal from Worsley to Manchester that involved the crossing of the River Irwell by an aqueduct at Barton. Brindley was then associated with the extension towards the Mersey at the Hempstones, as well as the extension to the terminus at Castlefields in Manchester. There was also an intended canal from Sale Moor to Stockport, but this branch was not made.

The Bridgewater Canal was a project that aimed to create a level waterway through the creation of embankments, aqueducts and cuttings. When completed, the new waterway promised to rival the existing river navigation, the Mersey and Irwell, which served central Manchester and Salford and had provided the first water transport route from the Port of Liverpool. A variety of goods were carried up stream to Warrington and Manchester, but it was cotton, one of the pillars of the industrial revolution, that was the main contributor to the wealth of the region. Hundreds of five-and six-storey factories were built in the region around Manchester and it was the Mersey and Irwell Navigation that had given impetus to that trade. The Bridgewater promised to improve the transport of goods even more, as it would not be limited by flooding or drought, as the river could be.

Pack horse trains crossed difficult terrain moving goods across the country.

By 1765, and as work on the Bridgewater Canal towards the Hempstones proceeded from Manchester, the 1755 canal scheme to unite the River Mersey with the River Trent was revived This concept was much more than a uniting of two ports – it was a cross-country waterway with the potential of serving communities and industry along its course. Uncertain and poor road communications with the Potteries were factors that aided the argument to make the canal. Roads were generally in poor condition and the pack horse was a common means of moving goods. Roads were however being improved through the turnpike system, where tolls provided funds for maintenance and improvement.

Josiah Wedgwood

The innovations in industry that occurred in England in the eighteenth century would have been short-lived had there not been a coincident revolution in transport. As Josiah Wedgwood, potter and entrepreneur of Burslem, observed in his 'Address to the Young Inhabitants of the Potteries', a printed pamphlet designed to answer workers' complaints, the infrastructure needed urgent improvement. It was getting increasingly difficult to travel by road. Strings or trains of pack horses provided the main means of moving raw materials and finished products at the time, but the routes were infested with highwaymen and robbers. At the same time, productivity was increasing and the region needed to develop better connections with the rest of the country and with the expanding foreign market. Josiah was an active supporter and promoter of the turnpike roads, particularly those connecting the Potteries to the ports including Liverpool and Chester via Winsford, and Bristol through Bewdley and Bridgnorth. In a speech to the inhabitants of North Staffordshire at the Town Hall of Newcastle-under-Lyme in 1763, he outlined the advantages of such a road system. Wedgwood went on to enlist the help of Lord Gower, a local landowner and Staffordshire Member of Parliament, in seeing the new Turnpike Bill through Parliament. Nine Turnpike Acts were passed in 1766. Later Acts of 1777 and 1783 were specifically aimed at linking the local road system to the main London routes.

The concept of the Trent and Mersey Canal, with a promise to link the Mersey with Hull on the east coast, was developed by some of the most influential industrialists of the age. Josiah Wedgwood's personal involvement in the scheme was substantial. From early meetings with James Brindley to cutting the first section of sod at Middleport, Wedgwood was at the heart of its planning and delivery. He was one of a select group of people who formed the basis of a committee, which was to guide the canal development as well as prevent any monopoly that might arise. They faced a daunting task; there were alternative proposed navigations promoted by influential people who might stop the Trent and Mersey Canal in favour of their own plan. A certain amount of secrecy was required and at first only minimal information about the plans was made public.

Raising Support and Finance

The first meeting of those men interested in and involved with the Trent and Mersey Canal was called on 10 June 1765 at The Crown, a coaching inn in Stone, Staffordshire. Josiah Wedgwood had written to his brother John, on 3 April 1765, stating that this scheme of navigation was undoubtedly the best thing that could possibly be planned for this country, and expressing the hope that there was a great degree of probability of its being carried into execution. Wedgwood's future business partner Thomas Bentley was also a strong advocate of the inland navigation system being proposed. As a Liverpool-based merchant, Bentley had a vested business interest in a canal system that would link the Midlands to the port of Liverpool. Both men played their part in soliciting the various landowners, MPs and authorities in an attempt to gain a support base that would see their proposal as the one to back. One important factor in this plan was a proposed navigation to the developing port of Hull. For Liverpool merchants, the hazardous nature of the shipping route to places such as the Baltic Sea, around Scotland, became a compelling reason for an inland route.

A general meeting, the second one in this regard, was held at the Old Roebuck Inn in Newcastle-under-Lyme on 27 June, to consider an application to Parliament for an Act to make a canal to unite Liverpool with Hull with branches to Lichfield, Birmingham and Newcastle. As this was not the only inland navigation scheme being proposed, it was important that Wedgwood gained the support of those men capable of make his vision come true. Josiah's involvement with the canal scheme was underpinned by a strong belief in the benefits that it would bring to industry. Indeed, such was his faith in it that he offered his services as Treasurer for free, and also became a signatory to a £10,000 indemnity. Wedgwood saw the canal as a valuable resource as his pottery manufacturing company grew in size and popularity. There were financial benefits to be had from an improved system of transport for his bulky raw materials, which included clay and flints. The flints often came by way of the East Coast and the Trent and white clay had to be carried in wagons from the Severn. Travelling in the other direction, the finished pottery goods were susceptible to breakage on their overland journey to Liverpool.

The canal scheme was supported by other like-minded people, including John Sparrow, solicitor of Newcastle-under-Lyme, who would come to play a pivotal role in the promotion of the new canal. The Duke of Bridgewater and his agent John Gilbert had an important influence on the final proposals. The meeting between Wedgwood, Sparrow and the Duke of Bridgewater at Worsley on 6 July 1765 appears to have been a significant step in deciding the layout of the future canal. One decision was the incorporation of a junction between the Bridgewater Canal and the new navigation. For this to happen, the Duke of Bridgewater had to obtain a private Act to alter the route of the Bridgewater through Cheshire. Instead of joining the Mersey at the Hempstones, it would be diverted inland to terminate at Preston Brook, where the junction with the Trent and Mersey would be made. The section of the route between Preston Brook and the Mersey at Runcorn (part of the proposed new navigation) would also become part of the Bridgewater Canal.

A printed notice was published, advocating the general advantages of the new navigation, entitled 'Considerations on the proposal of making a communication between the ports of Liverpool and Hull'. This three-page document acknowledged the Bridgewater Canal and stated that some public-spirited gentlemen had a scheme for opening a communication between Liverpool and Hull by the means of a navigable canal. The advantages of canals over river navigations were discussed. It was observed that it was not unusual on one section of the Mersey and Irwell Navigation near Barton to see seven or eight men labouring to drag a boat along the Irwell, whilst one horse would draw two or three boats at a great rate over the river at that place.

The Duke of Bridgewater had provided the finance for the Bridgewater Canal. As the proposed navigation was a more ambitious scheme, it was suggested that the funds should be raised by the issuing of shares, with interest being paid to shareholders in return for their investment. It was a concept that was to provide the means for the construction of not only this navigation, but also others that were to follow.

Another key step was taken with a meeting held at Wolseley Bridge on 30 December 1765, an event that attracted landowners, gentlemen, traders and manufacturers. The promoters of the Trent and Mersey Canal – sometimes referred to as the Gower-Egerton-Wedgwood Lobby – used this meeting to gain further support. Working on an estimate that £101,000 would be needed to complete the project, they proposed that the cost should be distributed between 505 shares of £200 each. James Brindley had drawn on his previous surveys, alone and with John Smeaton, to come up with a plan for a canal that would be 93½ miles long, passing to the south of the Peak District and piercing the high ridge at Harecastle by a long tunnel, where soughs, or side tunnels, would be cut to serve the Golden Hill coal and mineral mines. It was estimated that some 76 locks would be needed and there would be branches to other important towns.

Subscribers were found to finance the necessary proceedings through Parliament, and a second and larger subscription was begun for the actual construction of the canal. For the second subscription, collectors were appointed in different parts of the country for the collection of money for the shares:

Mr Bentley, Liverpool
Mr Tomkinson, Manchester
James Ford, Town Clerk, Congleton
Mr Sparrow, Newcastle-under-Lyme
Mr Stevenson, Mercer, Stafford
Francis Cobb, Lichfield
Mr Boulton, Birmingham
Mr Willington, Tamworth
Benjamin Molineaux, Wolverhampton
Benjamin Cooper, Walsall
John Finch, Dudley
William Musgrave, Burton
Samuel Crompton, Derby
Abel Smith, Nottingham
Samuel Twentyman, Newark
Mr Maddison, Gainsborough
Isaac Broadby, Hull

Fourteen days were to be allowed for the subscription money to be collected and at the end of that period the funds were to be transferred to John Sparrow at Newcastle. Should the subscription be incomplete, another fourteen days would be allowed.

Opposition and Alternatives

Perhaps inevitably, there were objections to the scheme put forward by Wedgwood and his colleagues, chiefly on the part of promoters of a rival river and canal scheme. This aimed to join the Weaver and use the existing navigation to reach the Mersey. Supporters of the Weaver link included the Corporation of Liverpool, which, according to a letter from Josiah Wedgwood to Erasmus Darwin (10 July 1765), had voted £200 to encourage the scheme for a 'Mersey-Weaver Canal'.

The Weaver had originally been made navigable using locks made of wood, but there had been a programme of replacement using masonry, made possible principally through the efforts of lock designer Robert Pownall (1735–1780). Initial improvements had met with certain structural failure, but, after Pownall's promotion to Director and Surveyor of Works in 1760, new locks and weirs were successfully made that would benefit trade on the Weaver. The making of a navigable branch to Wilton Mill (1764–1765) provided the basis of a junction with the proposed Macclesfield Canal.

One keen supporter of the canal to Macclesfield was Charles Roe, a person of influence who had built up mining and smelting businesses in Scot-

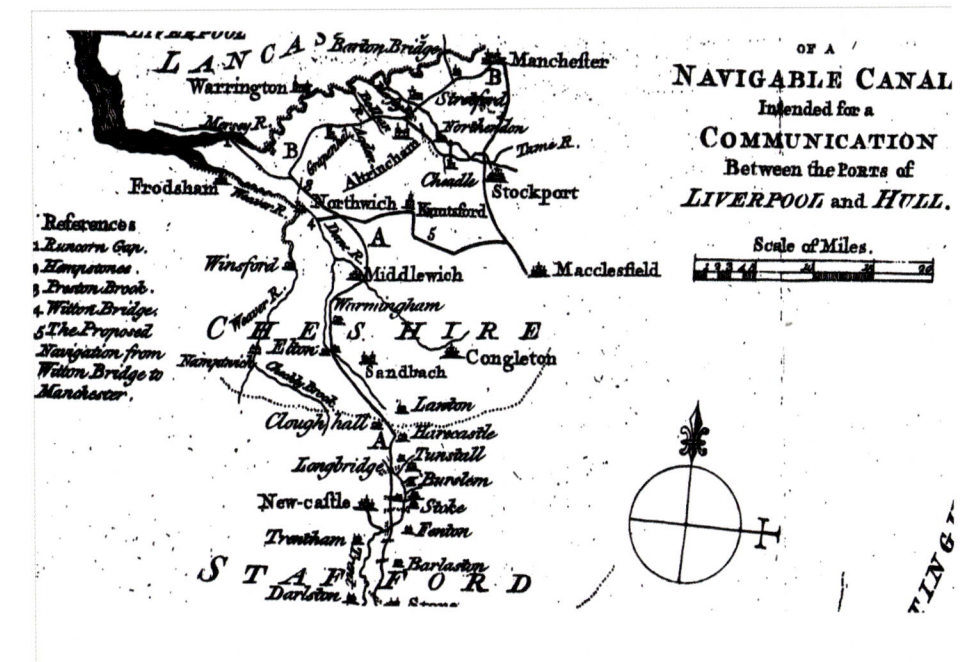

Northern part of the Trent and Mersey Navigation Survey.

land, Wales and Ireland. He wanted the canal for coal supply as the existing coal mines at Macclesfield had been worked out.

Despite the improvement to the Weaver, there was a major obstacle for a junction with the proposed navigation from the Trent to the Mersey. With Manchester traffic being made to lock down to the Mersey and up again into the Bridgewater Canal, it was not viewed as the best option. This became an important factor in determining the canal route to Preston Brook.

There was also the possibility that a junction might be made with the Upper Trent Navigation at Burton. With the Burton trade, the Upper Trent had been made navigable to the Bond End district of that town, with a warehouse made nearby. Those who supported the new navigation from the Trent to the Mersey were not keen on making a junction at Burton; one reason they gave was the imperfect state of the Upper Trent Navigation through the two locks at Kings Mill and Burton Forge. There was another issue in that the former owner of that navigation, Henry Haynes, had opposed other traders on his waterway. By the time plans had been made for the navigation from the Trent to the Mersey, there was a new owner, the Burton Boat Company, which seems to have had a different attitude. However, the legacy of Henry Haynes was such that a decision was taken to locate the junction with the Trent at Derwent Mouth. It was also decided to make the canal bargewidth from Horninglow.

Those who supported a junction with the Weaver were also in favour of a canal proposed to run from the Weaver to Macclesfield and Stockport. Such proposals also included a junction with the Bridgewater Canal near Manchester, but had the potential to divert trade away from the Bridgewater Canal. Furthermore, these supporters devised a totally different plan from the navigation to link the Trent and Mersey, which included a proposed canal from Winsford to the Severn at Tern Bridge and a branch from that to Wilden on the Trent. Such a scheme was equal to whatever the Trent and Mersey Canal could offer; indeed, it could be seen as more favourable, because a canal link to the Severn had still to be decided upon.

The key to both plans was the gaining of parliamentary approval and it was the Macclesfield Canal bill that made more rapid progress through Parliament, reaching the House of Lords in advance of

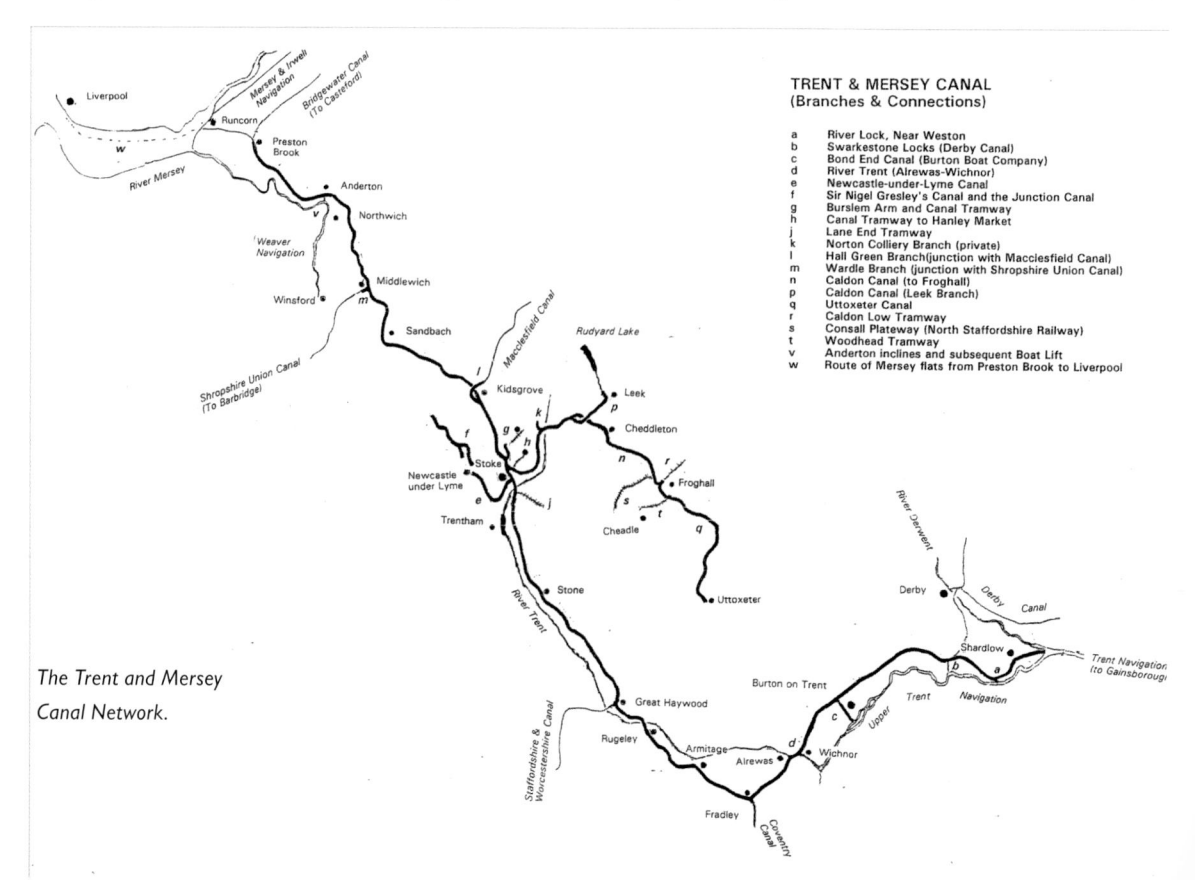

TRENT & MERSEY CANAL
(Branches & Connections)

a River Lock, Near Weston
b Swarkestone Locks (Derby Canal)
c Bond End Canal (Burton Boat Company)
d River Trent (Alrewas-Wichnor)
e Newcastle-under-Lyme Canal
f Sir Nigel Gresley's Canal and the Junction Canal
g Burslem Arm and Canal Tramway
h Canal Tramway to Hanley Market
j Lane End Tramway
k Norton Colliery Branch (private)
l Hall Green Branch (junction with Macclesfield Canal)
m Wardle Branch (junction with Shropshire Union Canal)
n Caldon Canal (to Froghall)
p Caldon Canal (Leek Branch)
q Uttoxeter Canal
r Caldon Low Tramway
s Consall Plateway (North Staffordshire Railway)
t Woodhead Tramway
v Anderton inclines and subsequent Boat Lift
w Route of Mersey flats from Preston Brook to Liverpool

The Trent and Mersey Canal Network.

No	Name	No	Name	No	Name
1	Earl Gower	35	James Falconer	68	John Seaman
2	Duke of Bridgewater	36	John Fletcher	69	William Seaman
3	Reverend William Cotton	37	Samuel Garbett	70	Anna Seward
4	Reverend Mr Martin	38	John Gilbert	71	Thomas Seaward
5	Reverend William Willetts	39	Thomas Gilbert	72	Charles Simpson
6	Ann Abbott	40	Miss Levenson Gower	73	Stephen Simpson
7	Mary Abbot	41	Edward Green	74	Jeremiah Smith
8	Thomas Ames	42	Francis Hickin	75	Ann Sneyd
9	Thomas Anson	43	Richard Hill	76	Edward Sneyd
10	Richard Bailye	44	James Hollingshead	77	John Sneyd
11	John Barker	45	Abraham Hoskins	78	William Strahan
12	Matthew Boulton	46	Charles Howard	79	John Stevenson
13	Samuel Bowyer	47	James Hubbard	80	Thomas Storer
14	John Brindley	48	Richard Kilby	81	Francis Swynfen
15	Isaac Hawkins Brown	49	Francis Laine	82	William Thompson
16	John Bull	50	Abel Colin Launder	83	John Bladon Tinker
17	Cary Butt	51	Robert Lawton	84	William Tomkinson
18	Honora Byrd	52	Samuel Lea	85	James Tunstall
19	John Byrd	53	Edward Leigh	86	George Twemlow
20	Thomas Cartwright	54	Edward Lester	87	Thomas Twemlow
21	George Challoner	55	William Mc Gwire	88	Edward Tyson
22	John Chatterley	56	John Mare	89	William Walsh
23	Francis Cobb	57	Mary Mattock	90	John Wedgwood (Smallwood)
24	Thomas Cobb	58	Ann Mompisson	91	John Wedgwood (Burslem)
25	Henry Copestake	59	Sarah Nixon	92	George Whately
26	Dorothy Cotton	60	Humphrey Palmer	93	George White
27	Elizabeth Cotton, junior	61	Samuel Palmer	94	Snowden White
28	Richard Davenport	62	John Phillips	95	Thomas Whieldon
29	Thomas Deakin	63	Mr Randall	96	Richard Whitworth
30	Joseph Denman	64	Owen Ruffhead	97	Thomas Weston
31	Thomas Dicken Junior	65	Mr Russell	98	Eleanor Wooley
32	Richard Edge	66	Joseph Ryley	99	Richard Wright
33	Nathaniel Edwards	67	Edward Salmon	100	John Yates
34	Samuel Egerton				

the bill relating to the Trent and Mersey Canal. The committee heard the proposals for the Macclesfield Canal and then the objections. One of the principal objectors was of course the Duke of Bridgewater, who was able to benefit from James Brindley's expert evidence and succeeded in having the bill stopped in the House of Lords in May 1766. One factor that came to Brindley's aid was the bill for the Staffordshire and Worcestershire Canal, which was prepared and rushed through Parliament in 1766.

The bill for the Trent and Mersey Canal was presented to Parliament on 18 February 1766 and authorized on 14 May. James Brindley was retained as surveyor, with Hugh Henshall as clerk of works. John Sparrow became clerk to the company, with the task of guiding the project through all the land purchases and the many legal obstacles that might present themselves. The Staffordshire and Worcestershire Canal bill received royal assent on the same day. Together, they provided the means of linking the Mersey, Severn and Trent. James Brindley then went further with two canal schemes, the Coventry and the Oxford, which would join the Trent and Mersey Canal at Fradley with the River Thames at Oxford.

The 1766 Act gave the names of one hundred proprietors who would control the operation, fourteen days from the passing of the act (*see* above).

There was much celebration in the Potteries at the passing of the 1766 Act. The Trent and Mersey Canal was to prove indispensable for Josiah Wedgwood and the Wedgwood Company for over 150 years as its main transport and distribution link. The group of waterways that developed around it were at the core of the British canal network.

CHAPTER 2

Engineering and Infrastructure

Building the Trent and Mersey Canal was the most ambitious navigation scheme undertaken at the time. The project would take eleven years to complete, from Derwent Mouth, on the River Trent, to Preston Brook in Cheshire. When it was first built, it was nearly 94 miles long, a narrow waterway with tight bends and locks that were in need of improvement. The modern canal is now 93½ miles in length. Alterations were made throughout the existence of the canal, with significant changes being proposed by a number of notable engineers.

Early Construction Work

Work started on making Harecastle Tunnel as soon as possible. Contractors began the task of cutting the canal primarily in Staffordshire, with a section between Armitage through Fradley towards Alrewas. In an early report by John Sparrow, published in the *Leeds Intelligencer* on 6 October 1767, it was stated that 'one lock was finished and others were in a state of great forwardness'. Four road bridges were completed and bricks and other materials were provided for many more. A bed of stone had been discovered at Armitage and this stone was intended to be used to build an aqueduct over the Trent at Alrewas. Other short sections of canal, each about half a mile long, had been made in Cheshire and Derbyshire. About six hundred men were involved in the construction of the navigation.

After this initial work, construction was principally focused on Harecastle Tunnel and the canal in Staffordshire, where it proceeded both north and south from the initial cut. The navvies gradually extended the canal north through Rugeley and the important aqueduct over the Trent north of there, whilst others worked on the line to Derwent Mouth.

The original section included a short tunnel near Armitage. Also known as Hermitage Tunnel, this was the first canal tunnel to be opened for general navigation purposes in the United Kingdom (although it had been preceded by the mine canal tunnel at Worsley, which joined the Bridgewater Canal and was used specifically for coal transport).

From Armitage the waterway was level through Kings Bromley to Woodend Lock. This was the first of nine locks on the section to the River Trent. Each lock was made to fit a narrow boat and was of a design that was common to both the Staffordshire and Worcestershire Canal and the Trent and Mersey Canals. Indeed, contractors were sometimes moved between the two construction projects. These locks included a group of five placed close together at Fradley (Shade House Lock–Hunt's Lock). Fradley also had a storage reservoir constructed later.

Land along the route of the navigation was either purchased by the company or leased. At Fradley it was leased from its owners. All the land and estates of George Adams situated at Fradley and Alrewas were leased in agreements made in 1767 for yearly rents. Subsequently, much of the canal land at Fradley had rents payable to Lord Anson.

As construction progressed, the supply of water became increasingly important for the contractors' needs. When a length of canal was finished and filled with water, that section became available for the movement of construction materials. At first it was stone and bricks, and later clay for puddling and spoil were transported by boat. Hand-made bricks were made in temporary kilns using suitable local clays where available.

Contractors had different roles. Those employed to cut the canal were paid according to the type of cutting, with the depth and the types of substance through which they were digging dictating set prices. There were the bricklayers, who made the bridges and the locks, and the stone masons, who provided coping stones for the bridges and the quoins for the gates. Then there were the carpenters, who made the gates and other timber items such as fences and even some bridges. Gardening labourers created boundary lines between

Armitage Tunnel, North End.

Bridge 53 and Woodend Lock.

Bridge 46, Gaskell's Bridge, Alrewas.

the canal towing path and the adjoining property of other landowners by planting so-called 'quick hedges', formed from a type of thorn bush that was noted for the speed at which it grew.

At Alrewas the proposed aqueduct was dispensed with in favour of joining the river for a short section to Wychnor (Wichnor). The revised route incorporated a private canal, a short waterway that had been made to supply water from the Trent to Wychnor Forge, a rolling mill and slitting mill on the river at 'Wichnor'. The partners in this scheme were John Barker, Erasmus Darwin and Samuel Garbett, an acid manufacturer of Birmingham and Prestonpans. Negotiations began in 1763 to buy the land for a canal 14 feet wide and 990 feet long, from Wichnor flour mill to the Trent. The owner of this mill was persuaded to relocate to Alrewas Mill (then disused). Making this short canal involved a bridge to carry the turnpike over it, which was agreed by the turnpike trustees in 1764. Wichnor corn mill was converted into a forge during 1765.

Samuel Garbett was a keen supporter of inland navigation and provided assistance and advice to Josiah Wedgwood, when the Trent and Mersey Canal scheme was in the process of development. He was also a shareholder of this navigation. The width of the mill waterway chosen is an indication of a use for future navigation. Wychnor lock was made north of the turnpike bridge and the length beyond enabled boats to reach the forge.

Contractors building this canal had reached Burton upon Trent by 1768, at the same time as the local landowner Lord Paget authorized the Burton Boat Company to make the Bond End Canal from the Trent. An intended junction with the Trent and Mersey Canal was prevented by the canal committee, as they were intent on moving on to Wilden and did not want to lose trade via the Upper Trent Navigation. The compromise was an interchange wharf and warehouse for the trade at Shobnall. The Burton Boat Company was then the lessee of the Upper Trent Navigation and, despite the adverse publicity that had accompanied the promotion of the Trent and Mersey Canal, were active traders along

Lock 12, Alrewas.

The River Trent section at Alrewas.

Bridge 42 at Wychnor.

the Upper Trent and the River Trent to Gainsborough, using a fleet of Trent boats.

Contractors continued working on cutting the section east of Burton, and Horninglow became the interchange point planned for barge and narrowboat traffic. This place also provided a useful interchange between the turnpike and the canal. The brewers of Burton were sending their produce by road to Horninglow Wharf. The section between Shobnall and Horninglow remained narrow, but the main breweries were then placed beside the Trent

Dove Aqueduct.

and water-based traffic favoured the Burton Boat Company trade.

One important engineering achievement was the River Dove Aqueduct, which was close to the road bridge, known as the Monks Bridge. The aqueduct carried the canal across the River Dove on a structure made principally from brick – bricklayers were recorded as working on it in 1769. This length of the canal contained a group of five aqueducts: Claymills, River Dove Floodwater, River Dove, River Dove Floodplain Second Aqueduct and the River Dove Floodplain First Aqueduct. After Bridge 26 (High Bridge), there were High Bridge Aqueduct and Eggington Brook Aqueduct. From there, the canal went on to Willington, where it was crossed by the turnpike that was used to convey goods to the Potteries from the Upper Trent Navigation. Barge-width locks (limited to barges up to 14 feet in breadth) were made at Stenson and Swarkestone.

Bridge 36, Roving Bridge at Dunstall.

A 'STANDARD FOR NARROW LOCKS'

A meeting held at the George Inn, Lichfield, on 14 December 1769, established a standard for narrow locks made on the Trent and Mersey Canal and the canals that were to be connected with it: the Birmingham, Coventry, Oxford, and Staffordshire and Worcestershire.
The report from the meeting read as follows:

It was proposed that a standing order be made at a General Assembly of all the Navigations that all the locks hereafter to be made shall be of a size not less than the dimensions following, viz, 74 feet 9 inches in length and 7 feet in width upon the sill, that the Depth of each canal in water shall not be less than 4 feet 4 inches, and that Mr. Brindley do take upon him the charge of inspecting the several locks and canals already made, to see that they in no material instance vary from such dimensions, and make his report thereof at each next succeeding General Assembly.

The aim of the standard was to ensure that craft trading along these canals would not be obstructed by locks of different dimensions and sizes.

Opening to Commercial Traffic

By 1770 the cost of making the canal had risen to such an extent that extra capital was required. The original Act of Parliament had provided for £130,000; a new Act (10 Geo III c102) authorized powers to raise another £70,000 by new shares or by mortgage. The original Act of 1766 had also approved the Trent and Mersey Canal to join the Trent at, or near, Wilden and at this time the preferred junction of river and canal was intended to be west of the ferry.

Meanwhile, the contractors proceeded with their work and followed the River Trent at various distances from its north bank. By 1770, sufficient progress had been made to allow part of the canal to open to the trade. One section was finished at the end of March 1770 and, by 24 June 1770, there were plans in place to create a navigation to join the Trent. The closest the canal came was Cliff Wood, near Weston, where a temporary interchange of canal boats and Trent boats was first intended:

The Company of proprietors of the Navigation from the *Trent to the Mersey* hereby give notice, that this Navigation will be finished and open for Commerce from the Trent at or near Wilden Ferry, in the County of Derby, to *Shutborough* in the County of *Stafford*, (where it joins the canal now making to the Severn) on the 24th Day of June next. And they are now ready to contract for the Carriage of any quantity of goods between *Shutborough* and *Wilden Ferry*, or upon the Trent between *Wilden Ferry* and *Gainsborough*, to be conveyed immediately after the 24th Day of *June*.
Application to be made to Mr Henshall at *Newchapel* in the County of *Stafford*, Clerk of Works to the said Company; or Mr Joseph Smith, Wharfinger in Gainsborough.
Newcastle-under-Lyme, 12 April 1770
                J SPARROW, Clerk to the said Company

'Shutborough', or Shugborough, was actually the intended junction with the Staffordshire and Worcestershire Canal, which was then under construction.

The committee report of 17 April 1770 noted that 42½ miles of the navigation had been cut, banked and finished. From the Trent near Wilden Ferry to Great Hayward, the canal, 33 miles in length, was almost finished and 27½ miles were navigable. One lock and two bridges were to be completed and it was hoped that the aqueducts at Brindley Bank and the Dove would be completed by 24 June 1770.

The company's plan was to open to commercial traffic on that June date and, with that in view, it had achieved the building, digging and erection of 22 locks, 68 road bridges, 24 large culverts or aqueducts and 24 smaller culverts. Contractors working on Harecastle Tunnel had vaulted and arched over 1,029 yards of the structure, whilst at Preston Brook Tunnel, 161 yards had been made. The Trent and Mersey Canal Company had fifteen boats built and other traders had seven boats for their use. Work on the canal had also continued northwards, following the route along the valley of the River Trent, and narrow locks were made at Colwich and Haywood.

ENGINEERING AND INFRASTRUCTURE

Swarkestone Lock

NAVIGATION from the *Trent* to the *Mersey*.

Notice is hereby given,

THAT this NAVIGATION is now finished and opened for Commerce, from *Great Haywood*, in the County of *Stafford*, to the River *Trent* at *Weston*, in the County of *Derby*; and in order that quick and uniform Dispatch may be given to the Conveyance of Goods upon this Navigation, Vessels will set out from *Great Haywood* on every *Monday* and *Thursday* Mornings at six o'Clock, and arrive at *Weston* on the *Tuesday* and *Friday* Nights following; and from *Weston* on every *Monday* and *Thursday* Mornings at the same Hours; and arrive at *Great Haywood* on the *Tuesday* and *Friday* Nights following.

Warehouses are erected at *Great Haywood*, *Bromley Common* and *Weston*, and Wharfingers stationed at each of those places.

J. SPARROW.

1st *September*, 1770.

The notice for the opening to Weston. Derby Mercury, *7 September 1770.*

Despite the June deadline, construction issues evidently delayed the opening to the trade and it was not until September 1770 that Weston Wharf was made available for traffic. The wharf, which enabled the transhipment of goods between narrow boats and Trent boats, was placed on a strip of land between the canal and River Trent. Company boats served the new warehouses at Great Hayward and Bromley, and the traffic in goods on this stretch represented the beginning of a trading entity that became Henshall & Co.

Proceeding Eastwards

Whilst traffic passed on to the Trent, at Weston work on building the canal proceeded eastwards to the 14-foot wide locks at Weston, Aston and Shardlow into 1771. Beyond Shardlow Lock was established the inland port of Shardlow, where a mixture of private traders and Henshall & Co. had warehouses at what became known as the Great Wharf. All were close to the turnpike to Derby, Nottingham, the North and London. This place also became the major interchange point between narrow boats and Trent boats. In August 1772, Henshall & Co. was in a position to advertise rates for the carriage of cheese from Stone, Bromley, Horninglow and Shardlow to Gainsborough. Other warehouses and wharves were created for the use of the Cavendish Boat Company, served both by the canal and the River Trent. (The Cavendish Boat Company had only a brief operating existence; when its property was advertised for sale, the warehouses were situated on the west of the road.)

Shardlow had, in the 1765 plan, been the intended junction with the Trent with the canal joining the river west of Wilden Ferry and the existing warehouse and wharves there. By 1772 that junction had been abandoned in favour of a new one at Derwent Mouth, opposite the junction of the Derwent Navigation and the Trent.

Construction works enabled the full route to Derwent Mouth to be finished in time for the completion of the Staffordshire and Worcestershire Canal to Great Haywood in May 1772. The Birmingham Canal was opened for traffic at Aldersley Junc-

Colwich Lock Cottage, bridge and outbuildings.

Stenson Lock and lock house.

tion on 21 September 1772. These developments brought traffic from the Severn, Wolverhampton and Birmingham on to the Trent and Mersey Canal and created the transport link to Gainsborough and Hull. Whilst an interchange was needed between the Trows on the Severn at Stourport and with Trent boats at Shardlow, movement of goods by water, by inland navigation, was possible between the west and east coast of England.

James Brindley died on 27 September 1772. Whilst the canal had yet to open to the Mersey, many of his objectives had been achieved by then, particularly in respect of the trading links being established between the Severn and the Trent. He had played a hugely significant role – against formidable odds – in putting in place the core of the British canal network.

Shardlow quickly attracted development and those who owned lands there were keen to exploit the business opportunities. A property sales notice for an auction on 15 March 1773 observed that, although it was in its infancy, this was a place of great trade – the reloading place for all goods navigated upon the River Trent that was coming or going to the different canals between the Rivers Trent, Mersey and the Severn.

Going Northwards

Meanwhile, other contractors were making the canal north of Great Haywood where a junction with the Staffordshire and Worcestershire Canal was to be made. Hoo Mill, Weston, Sandon and Aston locks were built as the contractors moved northwards to the outskirts of Stone, which was reached by November 1771.

Four locks were made at Stone, with Stone Bottom Lock being placed north of Stafford Road Bridge. The canal then crossed Scotch Brook by a masonry aqueduct.

The canal reached Stone in 1771, and the company decided to make this the base for their headquarters. Its General Office was built on the side of the towpath, fronting Stafford Street, and a company warehouse was also constructed for the carrying trade. The location of the committee office building has been confirmed by the 1816 survey of the canal, a copy of which is held by the Canal and River

The Canal Office, Stone (West Bridge House).
REPRODUCED FROM ORDNANCE SURVEY 1878

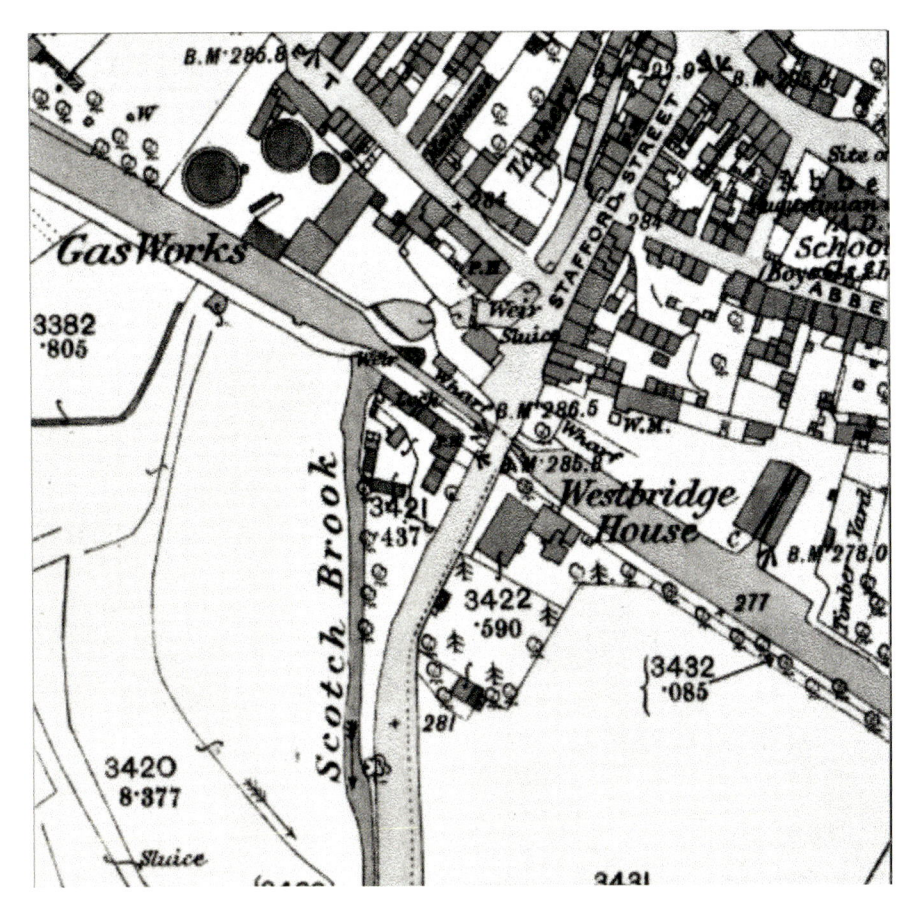

Stone boatyard.

Stone Lock 29. This lock has a separate tunnel for the towpath under the road bridge.

Trust Archive. This building remained in canal ownership until the North Staffordshire Railway Company moved all canal administration to Stoke-on-Trent, when it was sold into private ownership. It was then called Westbridge House and marked on the 25-inch Ordnance Survey for Staffordshire XXX2 1878/1879. Stone Wharf was opposite and comprised two warehouses, one of which covered a canal basin. The timber yard was also mentioned in the 1816 survey, when it was in use as a coal yard.

Working north from Stone, there was a staircase of two deep locks (a rise of 23 feet) at Meaford, followed by another lock north of there and a lock at Trentham. By September 1772, the canal workers had reached Fenton, one of a group of towns associated with the pottery trade. Work started on making a wharf (to become known as Stoke Wharf) for the carrying trade on the offside of the canal. This work was to span three years. The land on both sides of the canal at Fenton would become principal wharves for the merchandise trade up to the River Trent.

The crossing of the Trent was made by an aqueduct and north of that aqueduct the Burton Boat Company established a wharf for its business. There was a level section here that extended beyond Shelton Road Bridge. From there to Harecastle Tunnel, the builders had to overcome a rise of 50 feet to the summit level; this was achieved through the construction of six locks:

- Shelton Road Lock, with overflow weir to west with channel in tunnel under road to rejoin canal below lock
- Pentens Lock, with the overflow weir on the east side
- Twyford Lock, with overflow weir on the east side
- Etruria Double Lock, a staircase pair with a wide pound above
- Etruria Single Lock

Between Twyford Lock and the staircase was built Bells Mill Aqueduct. The summit level went on to pass by the Wedgwood Pottery through Middleport, Longport and Tunstall. As the tunnelling work at Harecastle Hill went on, two side tunnels were opened up for the supply of coal, a commodity that became known under the general title of 'Harecastle

Bridge 98 at Meaford Locks.

coals'. A further important stage in the construction work was reached with the opening of the canal through to Harecastle Tunnel and the navigation along it for a distance of 1 mile, which served the first side canal to the collieries. On 26 November 1773, the *Derby Mercury* published a 'letter from Burslem', which gave a fascinating description of the progress that had been made:

> *Extract of 'A Letter from Burslem', 1 November*
> On Wednesday last the Duke of Bridgewater, Earl Gower, Lord Trentham, The Hon Keith Stewart, with several Gentlemen of distinction attended by the Agents of the Navigation from the Trent to the Mersey, sailed upon the subterranean tunnel at Harecastle, near a measured mile, where they were highly entertained, and expressed great satisfaction at that wonderful work of Art; at night they returned in the company's boat to Trentham the seat of Earl Gower. This canal is now opened from the River Trent in Derbyshire to Harecastle, which is upwards of sixty-one miles by which means goods may be conveyed to any part of the Globe by water; the earth that is got out by making the tunnel is now brought out by boats; and we are well informed that Harecastle Tunnel will be complete in another year, the length of which is nearly three thousand yards and that the whole canal is expected to be complete

and join the Duke of Bridgewater's in about two years, which when done may with justice be said to vie with any of the canals in Holland, China, or even the famous Canal of Languedoc in France. Harecastle Tunnel cuts across upwards of 40 mines of coal, besides mines of Cannel, Iron, Stine &c. In one of the principal mines of coal, the Owners have made a collateral Tunnel out of the Grand Tunnel, navigable for boats, where coals are loaded into them out of the mines at 3s 6d per ton and will supply most of the towns and villages bordering upon the canal, as well as supplying great parts of the Pottery. Cannel will be sent as far as London by way of Hull. The owners of the said mines are now making a passage for the men to go from the surface to work in the said mines, where they may walk with an easy descent, till they meet the boats in the tunnel, which is upwards of sixty yards perpendicular from the surface, this is the only Work of the kind in the Kingdom, or perhaps the Universe.

When the tunnellers had reached the half-way mark, contractors were deployed on the next part, the canal north of Harecastle Tunnel, which involved the making of single locks from Kidsgrove. The top lock was known as Hardings Wood Lock. From the summit level the canal descended through Cheshire in a series of 25 locks to Wheelock, with the depth of each lock varying between 6 feet 9 inches and 10 feet. At Lawton there was a triple-lock staircase. Clerk of works Hugh Henshall had been asked to alter the canal route at Lawton in order to serve the salt works. Construction on this section reached Wheelock in 1775. Contractors also worked on building the canal from Preston Brook to Runcorn and from Preston Brook through the 1,239-yard long tunnel and the canal along the high ground above the River Weaver to a temporary terminus with road access to Acton Bridge. Charles Jones was the contractor for making this tunnel.

Harecastle Tunnel, Tunstall portal.

ENGINEERING AND INFRASTRUCTURE

Preston Brook Tunnel, south portal.

Preston Brook Tunnel, North End.

Lock 55, Pierpoint.

On 8 April 1774, the *Derby Mercury* published a 'letter from Manchester, dated April 5th', in which it was noted that the Duke of Bridgewater was then assisting in the 'Staffordshire Branch of the Navigation'. It reported that 'at Preston of the Hill, in the subterraneous part, 22 yards of earth lately fell upon the waters, and stopped its course; but this difficulty would soon be removed, when the remains of the Tunnel, were completed'.

Preston Brook Tunnel was 18 feet high and 13 feet wide, dimensions that excluded many Bridgewater Canal barges. Although the first boat through Preston Brook Tunnel was a barge, said to be carrying a load of 50 tons to Acton Bridge, it was narrow boats that became the most frequent users of the tunnel.

The actual boundary between the Trent and Mersey and the Bridgewater Canal was a short distance within Preston Brook Tunnel and the stop for boats was located at Dutton, where at one time the lock was covered.

Work on the canal from Kidsgrove through to Wheelock involved making single locks in a steady descent, through Lawton and Rode Heath. Two roads were crossed at Snapes and Chell Aqueduct. All these locks were later paired with another lock chamber, although Pierpoint was always two separate single locks.

The length between Kidsgrove and Wheelock comprised locks that were often spaced close together. As elsewhere on the waterway, the indi-

WHEELOCK LOCKS IN 1778

59	Stanway
60	Ellison
61	Garden
62	Mawkins Bank
63	Mawkins Bank
64	Hibberts
65	Bidners
66	Wheelock

Passing Through Middlewich to Preston Brook

Beyond Wheelock the fall continued towards Middlewich with six locks more spaced out towards Kings Lock. The canal was opened to Sandbach in April 1775 and by 26 September 1775 had reached Middlewich. There were four locks in Middlewich, three of which were combined as a staircase. These were the last locks to be completed. North of the Middlewich single lock, 14 feet wide, the canal was then level through to Preston Brook.

vidual locks, and the treble, were named. The last eight, with a rise of 73 feet 7 inches, are now known together as the Wheelock Flight.

Making the canal through Middlewich involved the alteration and straightening of the River Croco as well avoiding previous salt workings.

Kings Lock and Bridge 168.

> **NAVIGATION FROM THE TRENT TO THE MERSEY**
>
> Abstract of the Report of the Committee to the General Assembly, the 26th September 1775
> NOW finished 82 miles, navigable 77 ½ miles
> Built
> – Cart Bridges 163
> – Footbridges 11
> – Culverts or Aqueducts 155
> – Locks 72
> – Remains 3 locks which will be finished in a Month and 10 miles to complete the whole navigation.
>
> Borrowed on the credit of the Undertaking to the 2d Instant 105, 430 *l*, advanced by the *Proprietors* 130,000 *l*. Together 235, 430 *l* expended out of the above sum and the money received for freight and tonnage (including interest for the money advanced) 240, 2181 11s 1d ½ remained then in the *Treasurer* and *Clerks* hands 4250119s 2d ½
>
> Then due to the *Company* for Freight, Tonnage &c 8,247 l 11s 6d ¼, value of *Company's* stock 7,778 l 18s 8d. Boats &c employed in the trade 4,183 l 12s 9d ¾.
>
> NET Produce, from the 31st March 1770, when the first part of the *Canal* was opened, to the 2d Instant 20,532l 5s 1d ½, the last Six Months of which was 3882l 3s 0d ¼

Middlewich could also have been a junction point with the Chester Canal when contractors building the Trent and Mersey Canal reached this town. The Chester Canal's route to Middlewich was intended to serve the growing salt trade, carrying this vital commodity to the port of Chester and the River Dee. The Chester Canal Company's barge canal, with two termini at Nantwich and Middlewich, was authorized on 1 April 1772 to the plans of engineer Samuel Weston. Whilst most work was done on the canal to Nantwich there was some construction also on the line to Middlewich, which was terminated beside the turnpike to London. Weston left the service of the Chester Canal Company in 1774 and was replaced by a number of engineers, including John Moon. On 2 June 1777, a second Act of Parliament (17 Geo III c67) authorized a deviation of the Middlewich route as a narrow canal, but it also included a clause that prevented the Middlewich Branch canal from coming within 100 yards of the Trent and Mersey Canal without the permission of the committee for that canal. The Chester Canal proprietors decided not to proceed any further with construction work for the branch canal at that time.

By 1775 further capital was needed to complete the Trent and Mersey Canal. It was authorized by a third Act of Parliament and the money spent was mentioned in a published report to the shareholders in September 1775.

The last 10 miles of the Trent and Mersey lay between Middlewich and Acton Bridge. This section is level. In June 1775, advertisements were placed in local newspapers for labourers to cut the canal. They were to apply to Josiah Clowes at Middlewich or Thomas Garratt at Barnton. Plans to follow the high ground further encountered serious geological problems and led Hugh Henshall to vary the route again, to take the canal further away from the Weaver, passing through two tunnels at Saltersford and Barnton.

North of Middlewich the canal crossed the River Dane at Croxton Aqueduct, then a three-arch structure, and followed the Dane Valley to Bostock and through Broken Cross, Rudheath and Lostock Gralam, where there were aqueducts, or culverts, that crossed, first, Wade Brook and, second, Wincham Brook. Wincham Brook provided sufficient water power for water mills. The route of the waterway included several bends and later there was extensive subsidence in places. This was caused by salt workings and led to the formation of two flashes. From Lostock Gralam the canal turned west to the salt-working area at Wincham and Marston. The canal passed to the north of the navigable Witton Brook, whose navigation terminated at the

> **LOCAL TERMS**
>
> Passing through the county of Cheshire, the Trent and Mersey Canal was known locally as the Staffordshire Canal. Another local oddity was the measurement of land, where 'Cheshire acres' had different dimensions from other parts of the country.

ENGINEERING AND INFRASTRUCTURE

Barnton Tunnel.

Saltersford Tunnel, north portal.

Rumps Lock and cottage, near Middlewich.

Stud Green Bridge, 162

quay beside Witton Mill Bridge. Here on the canal there was also a culvert that spanned Forge Brook, which supplied water to Marston Forge and then Marbury Brook.

Canal contractors went on cutting the waterway through Marbury and Anderton. At Anderton the canal reached the closest point to the Weaver Navigation. From there the canal followed the side of the Weaver Valley to Barnton Tunnel. A short section of open waterway followed, leading to the tunnel at Saltersford, and then the canal followed the north side of the Weaver Valley and crossed a farm track, by an aqueduct near Little Leigh. The canal then skirted the edge of Little Leigh Pool and Oaken Clough Wood, owned by Lord Leigh, before reaching Acton Quay, where the canal company built a warehouse. This area was known as Bartington.

At Bartington the contractors met the already completed waterway that had been made from Preston Brook. There were a couple of bends in the canal as the route then passed through farming land, and a wharf made by Dutton Hall for manure traffic and farm produce.

During 1776, funds were still being spent on land purchasing and leasing, cutting, making bricks, purchasing lime and timber and contractors' wages. When it was finally completed, in 1777, the canal rose to its summit at Harecastle in Staffordshire, where it passed through a tunnel 2,888 yards long, the longest canal tunnel in the country at the time.

Engraving of Runcorn Docks and Warehouses after trade had developed.

This summit is now given as 408 feet at the ordnance datum. Heights of waterways were originally measured at the datum at Liverpool, which was 6 feet 10 inches under the sill of the old dock gates there. According to the Bradshaw's map of 1832, the summit at Harecastle was 419 feet 6 inches, which represented a difference of 11 feet 6 inches from the modern datum. The Trent and Mersey canal then had 75 locks, five tunnels and 269 smaller aqueducts and bridges. When completed, it linked a chain of waterways across the heart of industrial England, giving rise to its honorary title of the Grand Trunk, a name that is often referenced in maps and historical documents.

On to Runcorn

Although the Trent and Mersey Act provided for a canal to the Mersey, the section from Preston Brook to Runcorn, where the canal joined the River Mersey, was made for the Duke of Bridgewater, with John Gilbert in charge of the construction. This line formed a level waterway as far as Runcorn, where the canal then descended through ten locks, built as five staircase pairs, to the Mersey. These locks were completed during 1772 and opened to traffic on 1 January 1773. Barges working this part were restricted to the length at Runcorn, as work on completing the branch canal from Preston Brook was delayed until March 1776.

An extensive amount of land along most of the canal route from Preston Brook was owned by Sir Richard Brooke of Norton Priory. A clause had been included in the Act for the Bridgewater Canal to ensure that the canal did not pass within 360 yards of the Priory, and also to prohibit any piles of unsightly gravel within 500 yards of the house. Sir Richard steadfastly resisted selling, or even leasing, any land close to his property. As the canal's construction progressed, the route threatened to come closer than the 360-yard limit. In the autumn of 1775, it became clear that the issue had to be resolved, as the navigation work faced delay and there had been a legal challenge in Parliament by the Duke of Bridgewater. The canal as built involved a lengthy deviation to the south around the Priory and the whole procedure proved rather costly to the Duke of Bridgewater. With the canal completed for barge traffic, the route for trade to and from the Mersey and the whole length of the Trent and Mersey Canal became possible once that waterway was finished. A group of basins were created at Runcorn for the interchange of merchandise, timber, ironstone and raw pottery material.

CHAPTER 3

Building the Branches

It was the vision of James Brindley to have a network of canals across the Midlands. He was involved with a number of canal schemes that joined the Trent and Mersey Canal – the Staffordshire and Worcestershire (otherwise the Wolverhampton Canal), the Coventry and the Oxford Canals – as well as the Birmingham Canal Navigation, which in November 1769 was the first Midland canal to open a section to trade. That length served the coal mines at West Bromwich and brought coal to Birmingham. Once the Birmingham Canal Navigation had been completed to Aldersley Junction, a transport route for Bilston and Tipton Coals on to the Trent and Mersey Canal, by way of the Staffordshire and Worcestershire Canal, became possible. Progress with the Coventry Canal was less successful, however, and the work only reached Atherstone during this period. The Oxford Canal was similarly disadvantaged.

Brindley was also involved with the Chesterfield and Droitwich Canals. The Chesterfield joined the Trent and served an important purpose in developing the industry of that region. The Droitwich played a valuable role in bringing salt on to the Severn and improved on the existing and imperfect navigation of the Salwarp.

In addition to the main line of the Trent and Mersey Canal, various branch canals were constructed, and others were proposed. The first was the Caldon Canal, opened in 1778, followed by the Norton (1778), the Leek Branch (off the Caldon, 1801), the Burslem branch (1805), the Uttoxeter Canal (1811), the Hall Green Branch (1831), which made the link with the Macclesfield Canal, and the short Wardle branch of 1833, made as a junction with the Middlewich Branch of the Ellesmere and Chester Canal.

The Caldon Canal

The first canal branch to be made was the Caldon. James Brindley had conducted the earliest surveys of this waterway, but, after his premature death in 1772, following an illness that was the result of being caught in the rain one day, he had been replaced by Hugh Henshall as principal engineer. In planning the route, an initial course had followed the road from Leek to Ashbourne until it reached the west side of Caldon Low. A group of colliery owners near Cheadle agreed to advance £5,000 towards the cost of making the Caldon Canal, and this was influential in the change of the route towards Consall. Another factor was the purchase of Consall Forge by committee members William Bill and Thomas Griffin. Hugh Henshall surveyed the revised route, which was to be made from the summit level at Etruria through Hanley, Endon and

Cheddleton to Frog Hall, a distance of 19¼ miles, for a canal and tramway. The branch served the limestone quarries at Caldon Low, on land owned by the Earl of Shrewsbury, the Bill family and others. These quarries were worked by various people, including John Gilbert Senior, who set up a trade in the carriage of lime by canal. This John Gilbert clearly had an influence on the adoption of the particular route that the waterway would eventually follow.

There was another important reason for making the Caldon Canal and that was water supply. Any hope to bring an extensive supply of water from the mines at Harecastle, as had been the case at Worsley, were dashed when it was discovered that the water supply was insufficient and that additional sources were needed. In 1775 the water-supply problem was put to the shareholders in a printed report:

Newcastle 27th November 1775

A PLAN has long been in agitation for extending a branch of the canal from the summit at Harecastle to the inexhaustible fund of limestone near Caldon in Staffordshire. Surveys have been made of various countries and at last a very eligible one has been discovered, the length of which is 19 miles and a quarter. An accurate estimate has been made of the expence, which amounts to 23,126*l*, and which will be amply sufficient to finish the work. The committee are perfectly satisfied of the utility of this extension as well as the regard to the public, as the proprietors of the Trunk Navigation, who are in a particular manner interested in promoting it, not only on account of the advantage that may arise from it, in a commercial view, but by the plentiful supply of water it will afford to the summit at Harecastle, which the numerous Locks there stand in need of. From these (amongst others) considerations, they are induced to recommend to the proprietors at large the present design, and the plan upon which they propose shall be executed, is to divide the money necessary to be raised into shares of £200 each, which the present proprietors shall have power to subscribe and contribute amongst themselves, in such proportions as they shall think proper, so that no person do become a proprietor of more than ... shares or that they may borrow all or any part of the principal money on credit of the undertaking, and also on the credit of the Trunk Navigation, by way of collateral security, subject nevertheless to such sums as shall be due thereon, which shall always have a preference. The creditors therefore of that navigation, cannot have a possibility of objection to the proposed Undertaking, as instead of being injured, they will be benefited by it, and it is conceived it will stand equally free from difficulties on the part of the proprietors. For taking the whole of these matters into consideration, a special meeting of the proprietors is appointed to be held at the Crown in Stone in County of Stafford on Tuesday 26th Day of December next at 11 o'clock, where the favour of your attendance is desired in person or by proxy.

J Sparrow
CLERK to Company

The Caldon Canal received the approval of Parliament in 1776 and construction proceeded as work on finishing the main line from Acton to Middlewich was near to completion. The Caldon Canal was 17¼ miles in length and was made with a certain eye to economy, with lift bridges being made instead of masonry bridges in some locations. The first rise was a two-lock staircase (Bedford Street locks) that was followed by a single lock, later named Engine Lock because of the nearby Coxshead Colliery. There was a short branch towards the road at Norton Green and an aqueduct over the River Trent. From there the waterway rose to a summit level at Stockton Brook. The rise carried the canal up to the 486-foot level (ordnance datum) and then from Endon the canal descended again to the River Churnet. On the first section there were three locks on the east side of Endon, then two locks at Cheddleton. Woods Lock and Oakmeadow were the last on the canal section. After Oakmeadow Lock the canal and river shared a common course through Consall Forge to Flint Mill Lock, a distance of 6 furlongs. Here the canal followed a separate route, again passing to a terminus at Froghall. A wooden railway was used

Bedford Street Staircase, Etruria.

to convey limestone from the quarries to the first wharf at Froghall.

Feeders were also built to provide water to the summit level from Stanley and Bagnall Reservoirs and also on the west side of the summit from Knipersley Reservoir.

Construction of this waterway is said to have taken two years and the canal was opened to trade in 1778. Between 1783 and 1785, this canal was extended for a quarter of a mile through Froghall Tunnel (76 yards) to a new wharf at Froghall, where a warehouse and a group of lime kilns were subsequently built. The original, and imperfect, wooden railway was replaced by a second wooden railway from the new Froghall Wharf. Both railways were topped by iron, as reported by Peter Lead in his book *Agents of the Revolution*. John Curr, a colliery viewer at Sheffield, the person who was credited as the first to use a plate iron railway, described the Froghall Railway in his book, the *Coal Viewer*, published in 1797:

> At *Froghill*, in Staffordshire, they have a land conveyance for their limestone, which is three or four miles in length, one half of which is a flat ground, and the other half, about two and a half, or three inches descent in the yard; these roads which are upon the plan of what is called Newcastle waggon roads, are laid in a firm manner upon wood, (after having been at a great expence o stoneing about ten or twelve inches thick for a foundation) upon this wood is laid cast iron an inch and a half thick, a part of which weighs in every single yard forward one hundred and forty-one pounds, and other models weigh only eighty-one pounds: when the waggons come upon these roads, which together with the limestone weighs in the sundry kinds of these carriages, they do, and have made use of, not less than four, five, and six tons, and I believe as much as seven tons even, which burden being laid all upon four feet in length, the above roads, although enormous in the first expence, are nothing too strong. Were my roads and carriages introduced in situations similar to this, where there is nothing wanted in the road but cast iron plates half an inch thick (one yard forward of which road weighs about forty-eight pounds) and a sleeper of wood, four inches by two and a half, at every two yards asunder, and a small carriage upon the construction of our corves, by which means the draught of the horse would be dispersed upon twenty yards, instead of four feet, the savings would be very considerable indeed; not to mention, that instead of applying a friction upon the waggon wheel to hold

them down the hills, and dragging the empty ones back again by horses, they might take the opportunity of making the full carriage downhill, take back the empty one, upon the same principle as we convey our coals down the gates or ways underground at Sheffield and Attercliffe collieries.

The use of iron on wood had been adopted by the Coalbrookdale Company in 1767 and the professional associations with Shropshire of the Gilbert brothers (John and Thomas) gave them the opportunity to try this development in North Staffordshire.

The Coventry Canal Junction at Fradley

The failure of the Coventry Canal to be extended beyond Atherstone was accompanied by an inability to finish the Oxford Canal's waterway between Oxford and Banbury. Had both canal schemes been completed, there would have been canal navigation through to the River Thames and an important trading route by inland navigation to London would have been established. It was one of the cornerstones of Brindley's grand scheme and was also of great importance for trade on the Trent and Mersey, where the shortest route to London by inland navigation was through Hull and Gainsborough.

The delay was resolved in June 1782 when the Coventry, Oxford and Trent and Mersey Canal sent representatives to a meeting at Coleshill. There was also a new canal scheme present at that meeting that was become known as the Birmingham and Fazeley Canal Company. This company intended to build a new canal from Fazeley on the planned (but not yet completed) line of the Coventry Canal to Wednesbury, along the valley of the River Tame, to the region where there were extensive coal mines. The existing Birmingham Canal Navigation Company had a branch canal to West Bromwich, which was the first section completed, but the terminus was then at Goldshill, which was some distance from the lower-lying Wednesbury collieries. There was also a branch proposed to Digbeth in Birmingham, to serve the industries there.

The Birmingham Canal Navigation Company proposed an alternative means of serving these mines by a new canal branch from the existing canal near Goldshill. Following the advice of John Smeaton, they also had a plan to serve Digbeth. However, when the Birmingham and Fazeley canal received its authorization by Act of Parliament, it was decided to merge with the Birmingham Canal in 1783, creating for a time the Birmingham and Birmingham and Fazeley Navigation. Fortunately, this long-winded title was shortened in 1794 to the Birmingham Canal Navigations.

With the Coleshill Agreement came the commitment for each canal company to make, complete and maintain (at their own expense) a portion of the Coventry Canal. For the Trent and Mersey Canal Company, the distance between Fradley Heath and Fazeley was 11 miles, of which they had to make 5½ miles. A meeting was held at the George Inn, Lichfield, for the shareholders to approve. The fifteen proprietors needed for the meeting to take place were named as: Richard Bailys, Charles Bill, John Bill, William Egerton, James Falconer, John Gilbert, Thomas Gilbert, James Hollinshead, William Ings, T Mills, John Phillips, Edward Sneyd, John Sneyd, J Sparrow and Jos Wedgwood.

Authority was given under Act 25 Geo III to:

'enable the Company of Proprietors of the Navigation from The Trent to The Mersey, and the Company of Proprietors of the Navigation from Birmingham to Fazeley, to make a Navigable Canal from the said Trent and Mersey Navigation, on Fradley Heath, in the County of Stafford, to Fazeley, in the said County; and for confirming certain Articles of Agreement entered into between the said Trent and Mersey, the Oxford, and the Coventry, Canal Navigation Companies'.

The relevant clause set out the means by which the canal should be completed:

And Whereas, at a Meeting held at Coleshill in the County of Warwick, upon the Twentieth Day of June One thousand Seven hundred and Eighty-two, by certain Delegates from the said Company of Proprietors of the Navigation from The Trent to the Mersey, from the said Company of Proprietors of the Oxford Canal Navigation, and from the said Company of Proprietors of the Coventry Canal Navigation, and also from certain subscribers to a new proposed Navigation from the Collieries in the Neighbourhood of Wednesbury, to Birmingham, and from thence to join the Coventry Canal near Fazeley, it was agreed by such Delegates, on the Part of their respective Companies or constituents, that in order to effect a general Communication between the Oxford and Coventry Canals and the Canal from The Trent to The Mersey, therein called The Grand Trunk Canal, the Collieries in the Neighbourhood of Wednesbury and the Town of Birmingham, it would be necessary that the Coventry Canal should be completed between Atherstone and Fradley Heath; that the Oxford Canal should be completed from Oxford to Banbury; and that the new Subscribers should execute a Canal from such Coal Mines to Birmingham and Fazeley: And, the more easily to effect the Communication between Fazeley and Fradley Heath, it was further agreed, That the said Company of Proprietors of the Coventry Canal Navigation should, by Authority of Parliament or otherwise, relinquish to the Company of Proprietors of The Trent and Mersey Navigation, and to the Subscribers to such proposed Canal, that Part or Portion of their Undertaking which lies between Fazeley in the County of Stafford and the said Trent and Mersey Navigation on Fradley Heath in the same County; and that the same should be executed by them at their joint Expence, the Subscribers to such new Canal allowing to the Company of Proprietors of The Trent and Mersey Navigation Five hundred Pounds, as a Consideration for superintending and directing the Execution of such Branch of Canal; and it was further agreed, that the Profits arising there from should be divided in Manner following; (videlicet): The Profits arising upon the Half Part thereof from Fazeley towards Fradley Heath, amongst the Subscribers to the said new Canal, and the Profits arising from the other Half Part from Fradley Heath towards Fazeley, amongst the Proprietors of the Navigation from The Trent

Fradley Junction: 'Ivy Leigh', with attached cottages.

The dry dock at Fradley Junction.

to The Mersey; and that when the same should be completed it should be equally divided between, and each Part considered as the several and distinct Pro Agreement of Delegates of 20 June 1782 recited property of the said Parties, and be supported accordingly; and it was therein expressed to be further understood and agreed, that the Tonnage to be taken for all Coals navigated from Birmingham throughout the intended Canal to Fazeley, and upon all or any Part or Parts of the Coventry and Oxford Canals, should not exceed One Penny per Ton, per Mile; but it was therein expressed to be understood, that the Subscribers to the said intended Canal were not to be restrained from taking any additional Tonnage for all Coals passing from the Collieries, and discharged at Birmingham, or any Distance upon the intended Canal short of Fazeley.

The Trent and Mersey Canal took over the responsibility of building the Coventry Canal between Fradley and Whittington Brook, with engineer Thomas Dadford in charge of the work. The section between Whittington Brook and Fazeley was completed by John Pinkerton working for the Birmingham Canal, whilst the part from Fazeley to Atherstone was made by Thomas Sheasby for the Coventry Canal Company. When completed, the Trent and Mersey section was sold to the Coventry Canal Company, but the Birmingham Canal Company retained its section, which provided useful revenue in tolls.

Fradley became a junction with the Coventry Canal, meeting the Trent and Mersey Canal between Bridge 52 and Bridge 51. Around this junction developed a canal-side community and engineering base. There was also a graving dock at the junction.

The Junction with the Derby Canal at Swarkestone

There were opposing plans for a canal to link Derby with the navigation network, with two schemes being proposed in 1793. One was a simple link between Derby and the Trent and Mersey Canal, which was also associated with another canal scheme that promised to unite Shardlow with Nottingham (surveyed by John Rennie). The other scheme promised a link between the River Trent and Derby as part of the plan. Had the first option been made, a very different set of waterways would have existed in the East Midlands, with a particular benefit for Nottingham, as it would have avoided the

Canal toll House and stop at Lowes Lane, Swarkestone. The Derby Canal branch to the Trent was on the right of this picture.

navigation of the Trent and benefited narrow-boat transport in that region. However, it was the second option that was authorized by Parliament.

The construction of the Derby Canal provided another link with the Trent and Mersey Canal. When the Trent and Mersey was opened to Derwent Mouth, Trent boats, which served Shardlow, had the opportunity to use the River Derwent Navigation to Derby. Yet this navigation had its limitations and a better navigation to serve Derby was needed. The Derby Canal as originally built comprised a branch from the River Trent to Swarkestone, a canal from Swarkestone to Derby, a canal to join the Erewash Canal from Derby and a canal to Little Eaton. Associated with this canal was also the plateway, known as the Little Eaton Gangroad, which joined the terminus wharf at Little Eaton. There was a short section of the Trent and Mersey Canal that was used for Trent boats passing between the Trent and the Derby branch – a stop and toll house were placed on this section. Swarkestone on the Trent had a brief improved existence in the service of the carrying trade and there was a boatyard there.

River Trent Improvements

Although the projected Shardlow–Nottingham Canal was not made, the River Trent was improved, under a scheme promoted by William Jessop. By making locks and lock cuts the shallows and obstructions were avoided, and craft were able to travel to Nottingham and then along the Trent to Gainsborough. The dredging and towing path construction (1787) was followed by the building of locks at Sawley and a 2½-mile cut from Beeston to join the Nottingham Canal at Lenton. Further improvements included Cranfleet Lock (1797) and Holme Lock (1800).

The Leek Canal

During the 1790s, several schemes for branches and connecting railways were considered. A proposal for making a level branch to Leek was first put to Parliament in 1793:

> Notice is hereby given, that application is intended to be made to Parliament, in the next Session, for

a Bill, to make a navigable Canal from the Caldon Canal, within the Liberty of Endon, to or near the Town of Leek in the County of Stafford; which said Canal will pass through the several Townships or Liberties of Endon, Cheddleton, Longsdon, Lowe and Leek, and the several Parishes of Leek and Cheddleton, in the said County of Stafford
September 18th, 1793

London Gazette Notice, 21 September 1793

Such a proposal contemplated a canal about 4 miles long, but only 2 miles level. One of its benefits would be to bring cheaper coal and lime to Leek – something that was definitely needed, as one correspondent to the *Derby Mercury* on 14 November 1793 observed:

In these times of scarcity a very indifferent kind of coal is sold for 9d a hundred or 15s a ton. The poor who are only able to purchase about half a hundred at a time from the back of horses and asses often pay after the rate of 2½d for 25lbs or 20s a ton.

Following some revisions, the Leek Canal plan came to include a proposal for a feeder from a new reservoir between Horton and Rudyard. Applications were made to Parliament in both 1795 and 1796, with Hugh Henshall, James Barnitt and William Cross acting as surveyors for the plan. The applications were being made alongside other rival canal schemes. One was the Commercial Canal that promised to link the Trent at Burton with the Chester Canal. It was intended to be a modern canal and had the advantage of bypassing the restrictive Harecastle Tunnel, where movement of craft was restricted in one direction at a time. With the failure of the Commercial Canal scheme, the Trent and Mersey Canal Leek Branch bill was approved by Parliament in 1797. John Rennie (1761–1821) was appointed as the engineer for the project.

The construction of the canal involved a junction with the existing Caldon Canal at Hazelhurst and the abandonment of the three locks 10–12 at Endon. The Caldon Canal was diverted on to a new course south of the original locks maintaining the summit level through to Leek. The new, and first, Hazelhurst Junction was placed at the bend where the Leek Branch curved north and then east. A staircase of three locks was provided to take the canal down and to resume the original Caldon Canal route. John Rennie was not in favour of staircase locks as he believed they presented an obstruction to trade. Despite Hugh Henshall's determination that one should be made here, Rennie continued to campaign for the arrangement to be altered.

The Leek Canal was opened following a tour of inspection by John Rennie in March 1801. Traffic was never busy, but the branch had a key role in bringing water to the main canal.

During his inspection, John Rennie had found various faults with the construction of the works to Leek, and singled out the constructor Goldstraw for quite a lot of criticism. There were problems with the staircase of locks through Hazelhurst Wood, which, according to Rennie, was 'ill executed… [and] has given way and requires repair'. Near Endon, the canal needed to be lined and at Endon Brook Aqueduct the foundations had not been laid according to Rennie's plan. In consequence, the structure had given way and there were considerable cracks in it. Goldstraw had also left the wing walls in an unfinished state and Rennie had to order them to be completed.

Leek Tunnel, south portal.

Goldstraw's poor work did not stop there. Near Endon Brook a bridge had to be rebuilt. At Wall Grange Wood, the land was soft through the fall of springs there, but no provision had been made to take off the water. At Leek Tunnel, Rennie had recommended that a lining be placed in the bottom and sides of the arch, but this had not been done. He had to ask for a small quantity of water to be let in, rack it with fine gravel and afterwards grout and caulk the joint. On the other hand, the aqueduct over the River Churnet near Wall Grange, executed by the contractor Barnes, was much more to Rennie's satisfaction: the masonry was good and the curves well formed.

Rennie made another inspection in April 1801 when work on the Leek Canal was nearly complete. He was still more pleased with some contractors than others: the cutting and embanking had been done by the McIntosh family; Goldstraw, the mason who had made the bridges, was considered to be an unfit person for the contract; Barlow, who had built the locks at Hazelhurst Wood, was deemed to be 'not worth a shilling', and therefore not capable of carrying out the necessary reconstruction work. In the end, the rebuilding of the locks became the responsibility of the canal company.

Hanley and Shelton Canal

This proposed waterway was intended to leave the main canal north of Etruria Locks and rise 36 feet to a level that would end by Boothen Brook. From there, the intention was to make a railway to Cobridge. John Rennie suggested that four locks might be made – or a boat lift. He considered two options for the lift: one was the Weldon caisson, which was then on trial on the Somerset Coal Canal; the other was the Rowland & Pickering lift, which was on trial on the Ellesmere Canal near Ruabon. The Ellesmere Canal lift was considered the most suitable, but it would need some improvement. A fourth option would be the making of a railway from the Trent and Mersey Canal. After much discussion, the choice adopted by the Trent and Mersey Canal Committee was to build a plateway from Etruria Wharf on the Caldon Canal to Hanley, which had a rise of 115 feet. A short branch tramway was then made towards Shelton. This was one of a group of plateways that opened in 1805 for the use of the canal company, with tolls being charged on the same terms as the canal.

The Uttoxeter Canal

The first mention of the canal to Uttoxeter was made in 1796:

> Notice is hereby given, that Application is intended to be made to Parliament the next Session for Leave to bring in a Bill for making a navigable Cut or Canal from the Caldon Canal at Froghall, to or near Uttoxeter, in the County of Stafford, and which said Cut or Canal is intended to pass through the several Townships or Liberties of Foxt, Whiston, Farley, Alton, Denston, Rocester, Crakemarsh, Creighton, Strenshall and Uttoxeter, in the Parishes of Checkley, Kingsley, Alton, Rocester, and Uttoxeter, in the County of Stafford.
>
> *London Gazette*, 13 September 1796

Work started in 1805 from the Caldon Canal, where a junction was made with the Caldon Branch between Froghall Tunnel and the Basin. This canal was completed in sections, with a length being opened in 1808, which also served the Woodhead Tramway. Alton was reached in 1809 and at Crumpwood a crossing was made with the Churnet. There was a lock, which still remains. The river entered from the west and after a short length there was a weir on the east side of the canal. The towpath also changed side after the lock and there was a towpath bridge over the river as it passed over that weir.

The route into Uttoxeter was re-examined by John Rennie and a deviation was made, which led to the canal crossing of the Team by an aqueduct. Rennie considered the option of a dam with 'adequate sluices'. Rennie believed that the passage of barges on the navigation was an 'object of paramount consequence'. With the Team crossing, Rennie observed that an aqueduct, although a low

The Uttoxeter Canal crossing of the Churnet.

Coventry Canal at Fradley Heath changed the Trent and Mersey opposition to the link. The proposed navigation was suggested in bills prepared for Parliament in three concurrent years, the final being in November 1794. In answer to this scheme, the Trent and Mersey Canal proprietors finally proposed to put together a bill for a short canal at Shobnall to the Bond End Canal. This short link was duly made, together with a lock. The interchange of goods and minerals across the wharf there, which had previously been difficult, was removed and free passage on to the Trent from the Trent and Mersey Canal became possible. The improved communication would be extremely beneficial to the Burton Boat Company, which operated narrow boats along the Birmingham, Staffordshire and Worcestershire and Trent and Mersey Canals, as well as Trent boats and three boats on the Bond End Canal.

Proposals to Replace Harecastle Tunnel

The construction of the Harecastle Tunnel was begun by James Brindley and finished under the supervision of Hugh Henshall. Instead of benefiting trade, the tunnel actually proved to be a handicap to navigation, with considerable delays to boats passing through it or using the two mine tunnels that joined it. Strict regulations regarding the passage of vessels were brought in, including restrictions as to the times when boats might enter either portal.

By 1806, surveys had been made for varying the route, or for a new line through the Bath Pool Valley. An application to Parliament was prepared in June 1806 for this purpose, as well as to provide the authority for the deviation at Lawton and tramroad from the canal at Lawton Treble Locks to Trubshaw Colliery.

Whilst the bill was discussed in Parliament, at some time, either in February or March 1807, the application was altered, to enlarge powers of the company. The bill finally became an Act of Parliament on 10 May 1809. Any proposed changes to the route of Harecastle Tunnel were not made, or authorized, at that time.

structure, would be independent of floods and prevent any arguments with owners of Uttoxeter Mill caused by them being deprived of water. It was left to the committee to decide on making an aqueduct or dam. A cast-iron aqueduct was made and the canal was finished to Uttoxeter in 1811.

The Bond End Canal Link

Whilst the private Burton Boat Company canal, the Bond End Canal, terminated at Shobnall, no connection was made at first with the Trent and Mersey Canal. However, the promotion of a bill for navigation from Burton upon Trent to join the

CHAPTER 4

Development and Improvement

The policies followed by the Trent and Mersey Canal proprietors changed after the death of Hugh Henshall and John Sparrow as new people came to have influence on company affairs. By 1820, lawyer and businessman James Caldwell, in particular, was making his presence felt in the affairs of the company.

The Threat from the Railways

The early nineteenth century was a period of change, following in the wake of the Battle of Waterloo and victory over the French. There were a number of effects on trade. For the British, the trade in iron was troubled by bankruptcy and the closure of furnaces, while falling revenues affected many other industries. However, this was also a time of innovation. Developments in transport included steam locomotives being used on public roads and mechanical propulsion on canals. The turnpikes were gradually undergoing improvement, with new complete roads or straightened and widened sections of existing turnpikes being made. Such improvements benefited not only the stage-coach proprietors, but also the road hauliers who found that fly vans could compete with canals more efficiently.

It was also the era of the fledgling public railways, with their threat of taking trade away from the canals. For the new Chairman of the Trent and Mersey Canal Company, James Caldwell, these were challenging times. The opening of the Stockton and Darlington railway, in 1825, was to have a profound effect on the promotion of railway schemes across the country. (Although this railway is viewed as a pioneer in public railway development, it was in fact neither the first public railway, nor the first railway to use steam locomotive traction.) Not all the proposed schemes were successful and they often met with opposition from representatives of the canal companies in Parliament. Such opposition became costly as more schemes were put forward.

Some proposals did have positive benefits for the Trent and Mersey, such as the scheme to build a railway from Macclesfield to Red Bull in 1824. At the time, Macclesfield was served only by turnpike and previous plans to build a canal to that point had failed.

A more serious threat to the Trent and Mersey Canal trade was the Birmingham and Liverpool Railway scheme, which Caldwell was involved in opposing in 1824. The directors of that railway instigated a new survey using George Rennie and Josiah Jessop and in 1826 published a list of arguments in support of their scheme. At that time the Trent and Mersey Canal provided the only route by inland navigation between the West Midlands and the North West. It was observed that the distance in miles from Birmingham to Liverpool by canal was either 115 or 129 miles, depending on whether the route was along the Staffordshire and Worcestershire Canal or the Birmingham and Fazeley Canal. The intended railway would be 90 miles in length. The average passage of fly boats, with relays of horses by canal, was estimated at 60 hours; by railway, the journey would take just 15 hours. The rate of freight between Birmingham and Liverpool was 45s per ton; the railway hoped not to exceed 30s a ton. A load of merchandise of 16 tons (the average weight of a boat's cargo), if dispatched by railway at five in the morning, would arrive at eight o' clock that night, instead of being days and nights in the journey, and the cost of its freight would be £24 instead of £36.

At the end of February 1826, the petitions relating to the Birmingham and Liverpool Railway bill were effectively deferred, using the term 'lie on the table'. Meanwhile, the Birmingham and Liverpool Junction Canal bill progressed to gaining Royal Assent. Its engineer was Thomas Telford and, when built, it provided a second and rival canal route to Liverpool for trade from Birmingham and South Staffordshire.

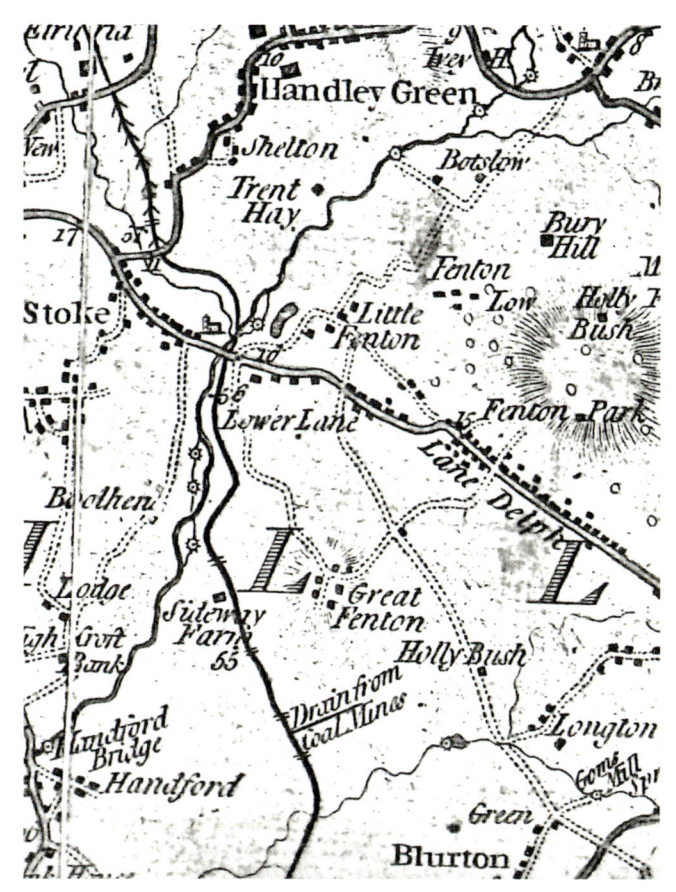

The drain from the coal mines near Great Fenton.

Water Supply

New trade was an important influence on canal improvement and also on the new schemes and routes, which came into existence between 1773 and 1840. For the Trent and Mersey Canal, another important factor was the water supply.

According to the Act of Parliament of 1766, the Trent and Mersey was empowered to supply the canal out of said brooks or streams within 500 yards of the canal and 5 miles from that lying in Harecastle vale. Provision was made to take water at the summit and elsewhere, where mill owners might not be affected. Later, by the Caldon Act, the company was empowered for water within 1,000 yards of that waterway.

The 1766 Act did specify certain exemptions. These included the brook or rivulet running from Oulton Heath through the lands of Swinsen Jarvis, and the water of the River Dane, 'on lands of James Tomkinson gentleman of Croxton Hall', with protection to the supply of Croxton Mills. No water was to be taken out of the River Trent nor the brook that flowed into the Trent between Burton and Wilden, nor could water be taken out of 'the River Weaver in Chester, the River Dane or Wincham Brook or Peover Eye or Wade Brook that communicates with the River Weaver'.

Harecastle Tunnel and the side branches to the mines also provided a share of the water, but this supply was hardly enough for the needs of the increasing trade and additional supplies had to be obtained over time. Water was taken from a brook at Lawton Treble Locks, a feeder north of the Trent Aqueduct at Stoke (Mr Broad's Gutter) and leats from other mine workings near Hem Heath. James

Brindley surveyed an underground tunnel to drain the mines of the Duke of Sutherland at Brereton near Rugeley, although there is no evidence that this supply was completed.

With the completion of the canal and the increase in trade, the supply of water remained inadequate. There was an early reservoir made at Bath Pool, which was fed by springs in the valley and the feeder from this went to the canal at Kidsgrove. There was also a storage reservoir made at Fradley.

With the building of the Caldon Canal to Frog Hall came the need to construct further reservoirs. Bagnall Reservoir and Stanley Pool drew their water from the same brook, while a third reservoir made at Knipersley (now called Knypersley) supplied water to the canal by using the Trent and the Norton Branch. The making of the short Norton Branch may have provided water from the Trent before Knipersley was constructed.

John Rennie had examined the capacity of these three reservoirs in order to investigate whether they could be enlarged. His report was presented to the Trent and Mersey Canal Committee in 1797. Stanley Brook Reservoir contained 8 statute acres penned by a head 25 feet high. Higher up the same valley was Bagnall, which was penned by a dam that was 26 feet high. Knypersley was penned by a dam 30 feet high. It was 20 acres in size and supplied by Tims Paws Brook, also known as the Scour of the Trent.

Stanley Reservoir contained about 720 locks of water and had a head capable of being raised 5 feet higher, which would create over 5 acres more of water. However, as Stanley Mill had a power of drawing down water 6 feet from that reservoir, Rennie could not see any benefit to the navigation of any enlargement. Bagnall Reservoir then contained 1,540 locks and its head might be raised 14 feet so as to contain an additional 2,686 locks; as Bagnall Mill had the power of drawing 3 feet from this head, any enlargement would be equally fruitless. Knypersley Reservoir contained 2,160 locks, but would require the head to be raised 10 feet in order to give an additional 2,900 locks. If cross embankments were to be made between this valley and Peck Mill on one side and Mill Hay on the other, a considerable expense would be incurred. There were also particular geological problems: the ground on one side was composed of a slippery kind of earth and that beside the south side of the reservoir was of a very open and porous nature. In short, Rennie's findings supported the scheme for a new reservoir in Rudyard Valley.

The three reservoirs had been made during the period when Hugh Henshall had considerable influence on canal construction. Bagnall was probably made when the Caldon Canal reached the summit, although the dam was reconstructed between 1787 and 1788 after the structure failed. Knypersley was made in 1783 and Stanley in 1786. As Henshall began to retreat to more of a 'backroom' role, other surveyors came forward to influence construction. It was William Cross who surveyed the Leek Canal, and Charles Roberts was another surveyor associated with work for the canal company at this time, but it was John Rennie who was employed to oversee the work. His recommendations formed the core argument for the establishment of the reservoir in the Rudyard Valley as he sought to find a means by which to appease the mill owners on the River Churnet. His argument was that the new reservoir would store water from the rains and that the mill owners would be supplied with the same amount of water as previously.

There were often disputes over the supply of water. Complaints were raised about the amount of water extracted at Wychnor to supply the east part of the canal through Burton to Derwent Mouth. The Earl of Moira had similar concerns with regards to the water supply to Kings Mills. In 1792 there was an agreement between the mill owner of Trentham Mill for water taken for the navigation from Burslem and Dale Hall Springs when Mr Haywood held the mill. The compensation paid in 1792 amounted to £150 and afterwards annual payments of 9 guineas were made, up to 1813. Another payment of 8 guineas for water from Foxlow Brook was made during 1813. In 1796 a bill was prepared for Parliament for the approval of a scheme that included a reservoir at the Sitch, at Burslem, which was to supply the Burslem Branch canal. In the end, this reservoir was not

Rudyard Lake.

constructed, although the Burslem branch was made with a plateway to the centre of Burslem.

At the parliamentary inquiry of 17 October 1796, the clerk Thomas Sparrow gave evidence of the need for water from a proposed reservoir 5 miles north of the Caldon Canal and 2 miles from the town of Leek. He put forward a plan on behalf of the company, which would, at its own expense, make Rudyard Reservoir and the new branch of the canal. It would not take the water from the brooks or streams in the surrounding countryside, but would be confined to using rainwater only for filling the reservoir for supply of the canals. William Cross also gave evidence, stating that he had surveyed the land to make a reservoir in Rudyard Vale and a branch of the canal, and that he was certain that it would be 'of great advantage to the town of Leek and places adjacent thereto'.

The original Rudyard Reservoir was completed in 1801 under the supervision of John Rennie; the contractors employed were Claves and Peake & Co., and Rennie wrote in support of Claves in his April 1801 report to the canal committee:

> On the work Claves has done on the waste weir at the culvert for the reservoir he has received more money than the amount of his contract, but when it is considered that neither he nor the companies agents understood the plans and that he executed a considerable amount of work that was obliged to be pulled down again – that the quarries proved to be very expensive, it is not to be wondered at his drawing out more money than the amount of his contract and there is reason to believe that he has expended several hundred pounds of his own so far as I have been able to judge, has acquitted himself honestly and with propriety and is therefore entitled to the companies indulgence.

Less than a decade later, the rainwater supply to Rudyard Reservoir was to be improved by the creation of a proper feeder. John Rennie investigated two means of improving the supply in a report dated 25 May 1810. One idea, which had been suggested at the canal committee, involved a feeder from the Dane. Rennie's recommendation was that this feeder should leave the Dane above the paper mill at Winkle and that part of it should be in a tunnel. A contemporary plan shows the feeder passing to the north of the mill and crossing the Dane on an aqueduct. Rennie also looked at an alternative source, from the Churnet, which would require a longer feeder along a crooked course. The first option was cheaper to construct and this was the one that was chosen.

The Dane Feeder, made by the Trent and Mersey Canal Company, followed a route close to and under the turnpike in order to reach the reservoir. It was not made as Rennie had suggested, as the water from the Dane was derived from a weir placed south of the paper mill. When Rennie made an inspection in 1820, he found that the feeder was unable either to receive or convey floodwater from the Dane. He recommended various alterations, to include a widening of the tunnel from the existing 3 feet diameter to the width of the feeder.

Transhipment at Anderton

Anderton proved to be a strategic location for the transfer of goods between the Trent and Mersey Canal and the River Weaver, despite there being a difference in height between the two navigations of about 50 feet. The Trustees of the River Weaver Navigation were keen to improve the means by which salt could be delivered into flats on the Weaver from the nearby canal-side salt works. A navigable link was considered, but this idea was replaced by a transhipment facility between the Weaver and the Trent and Mersey Canal. On 7 April 1791 the Weaver Trustees began negotiations to buy land at Anderton from Sir John Stanley and John Mansfield, but they were delayed until an agreement was reached with John Sparrow of the Trent and Mersey Canal, who was keen to protect his company's rights and powers. The Weaver Trustees went on to build a basin from the river. A wheeling stage and loading trough (or shoot) were constructed, where white salt was taken out of the canal boat hold into carts. The salt was then tipped from these carts into the trough for loading the flat in the basin below. This traffic began in 1795.

A second stage and trough were added during 1798, following a request from the Middlewich saltmakers. During 1796 two cranes were also erected on the river basin wharf. The beneficiaries included John Gilbert Junior, who was in partnership with Cornelius Bourne and Edward Mason. They owned boats and commenced the transhipment of salt from their Marston Works, Ollershaw Lane, during 1799. Transhipment of other materials came later and by 1802 John Gilbert Junior was acting as a merchant in pottery materials, also having clay transported in that way. From 1799 to 1800, a railway and incline were made, so that rock salt could be conveyed to the Weaver, in addition to the usual white salt.

Transport and the sale of salt had been handicapped by the Salt Tax, which provided revenue for the Government. In 1805 a new Act of Parliament imposed an additional tax on the commodity, increasing costs and resulting in a limiting of production. In 1807 the Weaver Navigation Act (47 Geo III c82) included a clause that expressly forbade the transhipment of goods between the river and canal – except salt and rock salt. With the repeal of the salt taxes and, more importantly, the withdrawal of the transhipment clause, in the Weaver Navigation Act of 1825 (6 Geo IV c29), the strategic value of the land between canal and river became increasingly important:

> Repeal of the Restrictions on the trade and navigation of the River Weaver and the Trent and Mersey Canal
>
> TO BE LET
>
> About Ten acres of LAND, communicating with the River Weaver, by a very favourable descent, and immediately adjoining the Anderton Basin and Salt Works; the River for a considerable distance flows on the one side of it, and the canal to the same extent skirts it on the other; for the construction of Wharfs and Quays, Incline planes and wheeling stages, Warehouses of any magnitude, and every accommodation required for the easy and convenient loading, unloading and transhipping of Goods, Wares and Merchandise from the River to the Canal, and vice versa, and into and from the boats, barges, Flats and other vessels navigating the same, or for any other purpose connected with the trade thereof, no ground throughout the whole line of the canal offers similar facilities.
>
> The land will be shown on application to GEORGE

BOARDMAN, farmer, Anderton, near Northwich Cheshire; and proposals may be addressed by letter (postage free) to MR WATSON, 51 Charlotte Street, Portland Place, London.

Chester Chronicle, 20 May 1825

The various decisions opened up what was to become a busy trading route for the salt trade and for the trade of other merchandise. At the same time, the link enabled the establishment of a new company by Alexander Reid, a Liverpool salt merchant, which became known as the Anderton Carrying Company from 1836.

Reid consistently pursued the concept of improved connections between the canal and the Anderton Basin at the lower level. He established wharves and warehouses at Anderton and arranged for better transhipment facilities there. The land belonged at the time to the Earl of Mansfield and was placed on the downstream side of Anderton Basin, as it then was. The land occupied by the new Anderton Carrying Company extended from the Weaver to the Trent and Mersey towpath. On the upstream side of Anderton Basin were the salt works of Abram & Co. and Broughton, Sutton & Co. The latter also extended from the Weaver to the Trent and Mersey Canal and there was a basin made, spanned by the towpath side bridge, for traffic to and from their salt works on the canal.

An alternative to transhipment at Anderton was considered for a link from the canal near Little Leigh, across lands owned by Lord Leigh, to the Weaver south of Pickerings Lock. Land was purchased during 1832, but the connection was never made.

Removing, Replacing and Updating Staircase Locks

Lawton Staircase Locks

James Brindley had chosen to build staircase locks in four locations: Middlewich, Lawton, Etruria and Meaford. On the Caldon, another staircase pair of locks was made at Etruria when that canal was opened, and a three-rise staircase was later built at Hazelhurst, to accommodate a new junction with the Leek Branch.

Lawton was the first set of locks to be removed following a recommendation from John Rennie. At the request of secretary William Robinson, Rennie looked at the canal from the north end of Harecastle to the bottom of Lawton Treble Locks, and reported to the committee in April 1801. John Rennie noted the 'great detention and inconvenience to the boats' in passing through the treble locks and the two single locks lying near the church. Such a delay in the 'present and increasing trade of the Grand Trunk Canal', he considered to be a very serious matter; he was also concerned about the 'immense waste of water which took place'. In his view, 'these issues, together with the many sharp turns, which were found in different parts of the canal, demand the serious consideration of the committee, and their attention ought to be particularly directed to these matters, whenever the repairs of locks, bridges and other things require the canal to be emptied of water.'

Rennie went on to observe the following:

> Whoever travels along the canal would see, that in consequence of the difficulty of navigating the boats round the sharp turnings, the towpath in many places has been cut away to the width of 2 or 3 feet, and shoals in consequence have been found in the canal, in so much for want of a proper depth of water the boats were never able to carry a full load. There was a need of cutting off these turns, and of widening and deepening the canal wherever it could be done. Especially if accomplished without stopping the trade. In this manner the canal would be gradually improving to the great convenience of the traders, and benefit of the company, without any heavy expense.

Two lines of variation were suggested, one on the east side of the canal and the other on the west side. The one on the east side would be the cheapest, because it would join the old works at the south end of the valley, and therefore save the expense of embanking. However, a considerable part of this

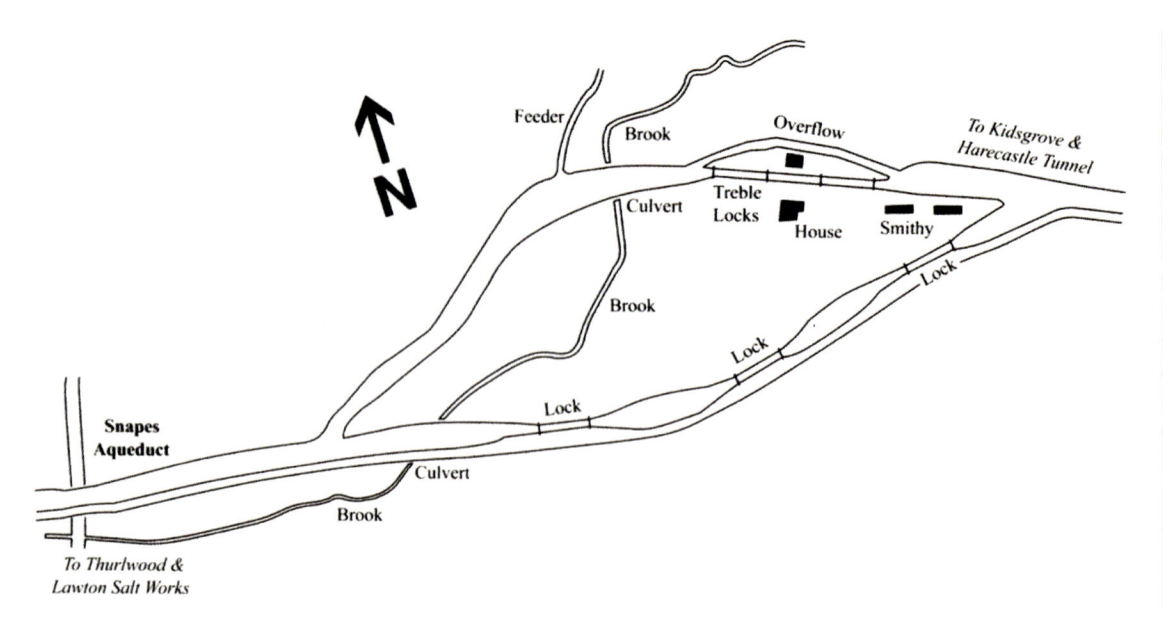

Sketch map of Lawton Locks, Cheshire.

line would run along the top of a steep bank, and therefore might have been liable to accident. The existing canal also ran for some distance along a steep slippery bank, which had not only been expensive to maintain, but was also still in danger of failure.

The other line of variation would avoid the difficult ground and allow the locks to be renewed where necessary, and to be placed at a convenient distance from each other. It would shorten the canal and provide a convenient opportunity to improve the part near Lawton church. The whole length to be cut and embanked was about a quarter of a mile; where the fall was regular, the expense of cutting would be small.

John Rennie also suggested that the cut should include not only the treble locks, but also the two locks above, which would enable them to be spaced more evenly. Double and treble locks should be done away with whenever the opportunity occurred, both to save water and to limit the time taken to navigate boats through them.

Following the lock reconstruction, a lock house and a stable were built at the second lock, with a blacksmith shop opposite. The smithy was retained as a workshop, whilst much of the land was used by James Faram as a farm. Mr Faram lived at the former Treble Lock House.

The Faram family had a long association with the Trent and Mersey Canal. The most notable family member was William Faram, who worked his way up in the company from a carpenter to the more senior positions of agent and surveyor and had regular meetings with James Caldwell regarding canal infrastructure.

Middlewich Staircase Lock

During July 1815 William Faram met James Caldwell at the reconstructed Lawton Treble Locks, to discuss land disposal issues and the replacement of the Middlewich Staircase. It was Hugh Henshall who had advocated making a treble staircase lock at Middlewich, but now it was argued that water could be saved by replacing the staircase with three single locks.

This work was duly carried out, with three new locks being made to the east of the original locks. Two circular weirs were provided to aid the overflow of water between the two intermediate pounds.

Etruria Staircase Water Supply

James Caldwell was evidently concerned about the

Sketch plan of the locks at Middlewich.

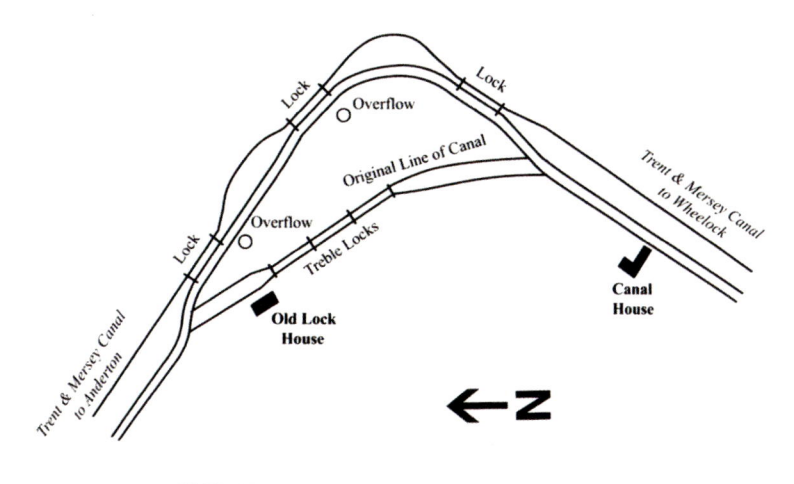

Circular weir at Middlewich.

Middlewich Locks as reconstructed: three single locks replaced the original staircase locks at Middlewich.

DEVELOPMENT AND IMPROVEMENT

> **CANAL SIDE PUMPING**
>
> The provision of pumping engines by the Trent & Mersey Canal Company to pump water into their network to assist water supply included steam engines, as mentioned, at Coxshead, Etruria and Kidsgrove. They also had an engine for sale at Lawton, in 1816. At Coxshead, Boulton & Watt had supplied a beam engine, which was described as double-acting engine, with 48½ inch cylinder, 8 foot stroke, parallel motion, unequal beam, separate air pump beam.

loss of water at Etruria Staircase Locks. This issue was discussed in November and December 1823 and in December James Potter suggested a means of pumping water by a steam engine out of the Stoke Pound into the Caldon Canal, complete with a new culvert. The work seems to have been started by February 1824. Caldwell's diary entry for 6 February 1824 records that he 'met Mr. Potter & Mr. Vaughan at Etruria Locks receiving the Locks & the Attention as now commenced'. During April 1824, George and John Cope offered to supply a steam engine.

The Issue of the Poor Rates

The canal when built towards Shardlow crossed Findern Common, near Derby. In making the canal across this land, there was a matter of compensation that needed to be resolved:

> Trent and Mersey Canal Navigation
> We whose names are hereto subscribed being commissioners named and appointed by Act of Parliament passed in the sixth year of the reign of his present majesty intituled 'An Act for making a navigable cut or canal from the River Trent at or near Wilden Ferry in the County of Derby to the River Mersey at, or near Runcorn Gap' and acting for the county of Derby, do hereby, in pursuance of an application made to us in that behalf by BENJAMIN WARD OF Willington, in county of Derby esq, JOHN COOKE in Findern in said county of Derby, Gent, and the reverend JOHN ORRELL of Findern, aforesaid, Clerk on behalf of themselves and the rest of the freeholders at Findern aforesaid, appoint a general meeting of commissioners, in and by the said act named and authorised to be holden at the George Inn in Derby

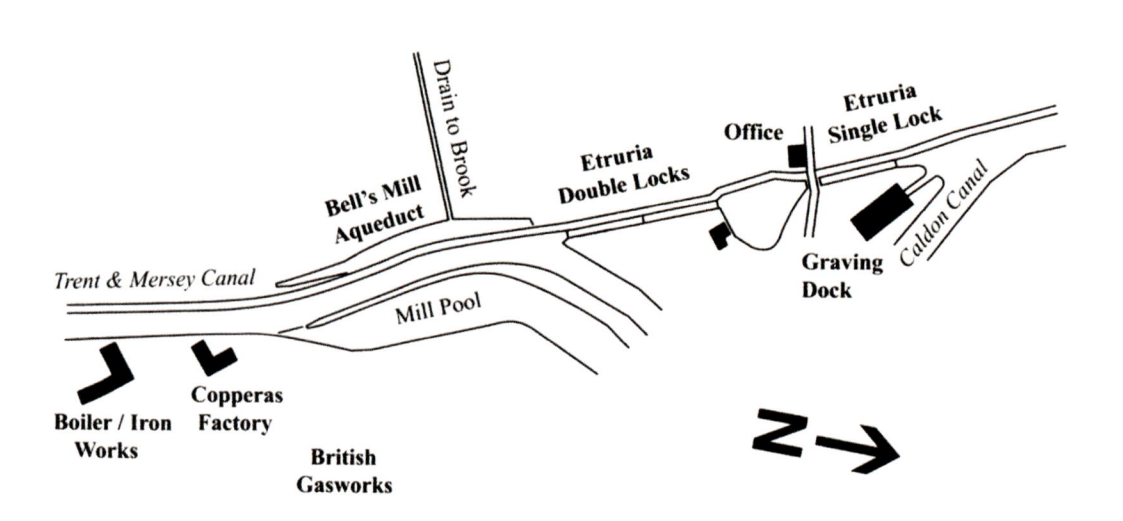

Sketch of Etruria Locks prior to reconstruction.

on Saturday the Seventeenth day of December next by ten o'clock in the forenoon on the same day, to settle, determine and adjust or by a jury to be then returned for that purpose to enquire of assess and ascertain the recompense to be made to the said freeholders, for the damages by them sustained, in and by the company of the proprietors of the said navigation, their agents, workmen or servants, by taking away and converting to the use of the said proprietors of the said company of proprietors, several acres of land, parts of a certain common or waste called Findern Common, lying within the liberty of Findern aforesaid for the purpose of making the said navigable cut or canal; and for digging and taking clay and making bricks and getting turf on said common; And also to expedite, transact and do all other articles, matters and things necessary or authorised to be done by said commissioners, or and seven or more of them, in, about or concerning the premises by virtue and authority of the Act of Parliament aforementioned, given under our hands this seventeenth day of October, One Thousand, Seven Hundred and Seventy Four.

Samuel Crompton, George Mellor, Francis Ashby. Gilbert Fox, John Heath, Joseph Greaves, Leonard Fosbrooke, Alph.Burgin

London Gazette notice, November 1774

Although that particular issue of compensation was resolved, the passage of the canal through Findern Common was nonetheless involved in a government prosecution against the Trent and Mersey Canal in 1823. James Caldwell spent time in preparing the company appeal.

'The King vs Trent and Mersey Canal' was the first case since the establishment of canals to rate the waterways themselves, as land covered by water, rather than the buildings that stood on the land. The piece of land occupied by the Trent and Mersey Canal at Findern was 1 mile and 52 yards long. The company had no lands, warehouses or other property except the canal and the towing path, and therefore no tolls, rates or other revenue were received from the town of Findern. Across the country the Poor Rates – the taxes levied on all property in a particular parish to provide for the poor of that parish – were to affect all navigation companies. The Trent and Mersey Canal Company launched an appeal against the tax, arguing that it was neither the occupier of any ground, nor the owner of any rateable property in Findern. By an assessment made on October 1818 for the relief of the poor of Findern, a rate of 4s 11½d was set. The Court of Quarter Sessions confirmed this rate and the Kings Bench decided that the company was in fact liable for the tax as the occupier of land in Findern. Not only had the Trent and Mersey Canal Company lost its legal case, a precedent had also been set, to which reference would subsequently be made in published accounts of British law.

The Second Harecastle Tunnel

At the General Assembly held on 17 October 1820 it was reported that the mortgage debt for the canal had been paid off. In general, the waterway was in good order, but now there were funds available for some improvements to be made.

James Brindley's Harecastle Tunnel had serious limitations. Built at a level of 197 feet from the highest summit on the hill above it, it would permit the passage only of a narrow boat with moderate loading, and even then it required leggers to be employed to propel it. It took around two hours to pass through the tunnel and movement in either direction was restricted to specific times.

John Rennie arrived at Red Bull in August 1820 and stayed at the inn. He conducted various surveys for the Trent and Mersey Canal Company, including one of the original Harecastle Tunnel, and made several suggestions for improvements to the route through Harecastle. These included incline planes and tramways over the hill and a canal with 16 locks through the Bath Pool Valley. However, his principal aim was a second canal tunnel. James Potter drew a map of the new tunnel and James Caldwell set about preparing material for the bill to be presented before Parliament. John Rennie died in October 1821, before his idea could be put into practice, and the Trent and Mersey Canal Committee turned to Thomas Telford for a new survey for the tunnel. James Caldwell, chairman of the company, was then the principal person in charge of the navigation and James Potter was the resident engineer. In March 1822, Caldwell recalled in his diary one of his early meetings with Telford about the plan:

> **Tuesday 5th March 1822**– Mr. Telford & Mr. Potter breakfasted at Linley Wood after which explaining to Mr. T the principal objects in view. Long conversation with them on the intended Tunnel & other works & then accompanied them to the Tunnel, on the survey of which Mr. Telford commenced– Called upon Mr. Johnson as my custom who expressed himself much satisfied with Mr. Telford– Gave up going to Betley Hall where we managed to drive in order that I might see Mr. Telford again & communicated more fully with him. Met him again at the Red Bull where I dined with him & Mr. Potter & had another long & satisfactory conversation with him & particularly so far as related to the present Tunnel.

Work on the tunnel began in 1824, and the first sod for the open part of the cutting was turned on 30 March. The contractors were William Hoof and Daniel Pritchard. They were engaged first at the Tunstall end, where local Tunstall brick-makers secured the bulk of the work. (Interestingly, one such brick-maker was William Smith, whose son George, born in 1831, became a reformer for living conditions on canal boats.)

In comparison with the length of time it had taken to build the Brindley tunnel – some 11 years – the slightly longer Telford tunnel was completed relatively quickly, in just two and a half years. With the initial task of sinking shafts and making the tunnel came the need for bricklayers to line the tunnel. On 3 September 1825, Daniel Pritchard placed an advertisement in the *Staffordshire Advertiser*, seeking the right kind of workers:

> WANTED immediately twenty to thirty bricklayers; those who are accustomed to work under ground would be preferred; good and steady workmen will meet with immediate employment by applying

HARECASTLE CANAL SIDE TUNNELS

The original Brindley Canal is known to have had two side tunnels for bringing coal directly from the workings onto the canal. A 1795 distance table records the branches as 'Turnrail Coal' and 'Birchenwood Coal'. Turnrail was nearer Tunstall, about 800 yards from that portal on the west side of the tunnel. The longer Birchenwood Tunnel was about a mile from Tunstall and was on both sides of the main tunnel. The west tunnel was short, and the east tunnel (or boat level) travelled to underground workings at Goldenhill.

COSTS OF MAKING THE SECOND HARECASTLE TUNNEL

Details	Cost (£)
Sinking 15 shafts, 9ft in diameter	1,610
Driving heading through the hill	7,057
Driving cross-heading to carry off water	470
Driving headings in coal measures to drain sand at north end	540
Excavating body of tunnel, turning brickwork, including timber, length 2,926½ yards	43,435
Expense of towing path	9,600
Expense of railway, 6½ miles	7,000
Expense of providing bricks, mortar and centering	22,750
Labour upon mortar and centering	1,537
Carriage of materials	4,060
Expense of open cutting, entrances and turnover bridges at each end, workshops. mills, engines, pumps, damages of land fences &c	14,622
TOTAL	**112,681**

Harecastle Tunnel in 1827.

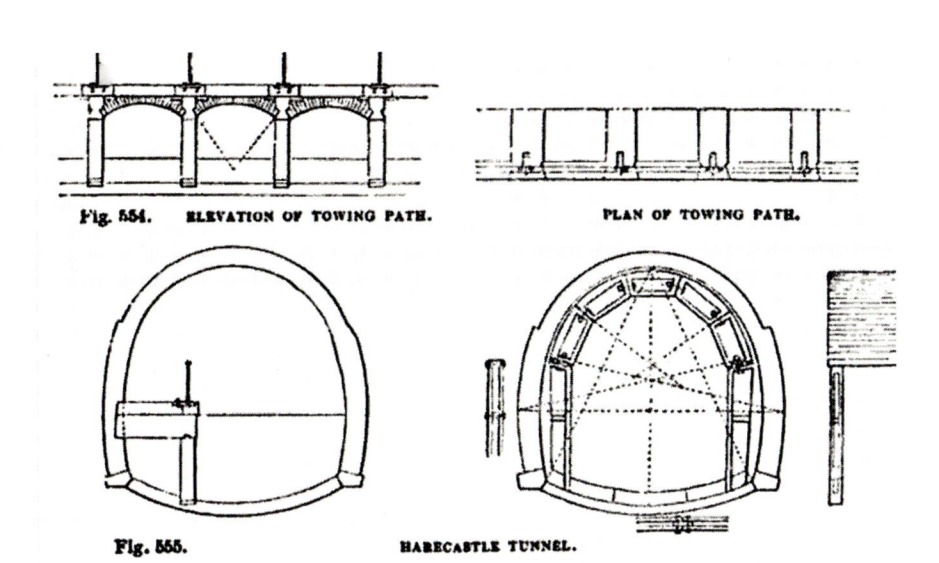

Harecastle Tunnel portals at Kidsgrove.

Turnover Bridge, Harecastle Tunnel, Kidsgrove.

to Daniel Pritchard, the contractor, at Harecastle Tunnel near Newcastle-under-Lyme.

The first brick was laid on 21 February 1825 and the last was secured in place in the top of the arch by James Caldwell on 25 November 1826. The tunnel was opened in 1827. Fifteen construction shafts had been sunk, and a total of 8,814,000 bricks had been used for the tunnel lining, shafts and culverts. A railway had been laid to assist with the construction of the tunnel – Thomas Telford often used railways in his construction projects, and temporary lines had been made during work on the Birmingham Canal, the Birmingham and Liverpool Junction and the Forth and Clyde canals. There had also been a construction tramroad laid over the hill, which James Caldwell travelled on once.

The contractors' plant was auctioned on 14 November 1827, and included two steam engines, a 14hp engine built by Boulton & Watt and a 6hp engine supplied by the Eagle Foundry in Birmingham (by partners Francis Smith and William Brunton). There were also two mills for grinding mortar and rollers and machinery for crushing marl and tempering clay for making bricks.

The ceremony marking the laying of the last brick of the second Harecastle Tunnel, held on 25 November 1826, was attended by James Potter with James Caldwell, along with two of the Pritchard family and Mr Hough, the head bricklayer. The finished tunnel was 2,926 yards in length, 14 feet wide and 16 feet in height. It was the last tunnel made for the Trent and Mersey Canal Company, bringing to eight the number along the length of the main canal and branches.

The Telford tunnel incorporated a towing path 4 feet 9 inches wide, supported by pillars, enabling the passage of horse-towed boats. The original Brindley tunnel did not have a towing path, and the boat horses would use the path over the tunnel that linked both of its portals. A set of steps were provided at the Kidsgrove end to access the offside side of the canal. For the new Telford tunnel there was a roving bridge made for the boat horses to cross over the canal at Kidsgrove to reach the towpath.

CANAL TUNNELS ON THE TRENT AND MERSEY CANAL

Armitage	130 yards, towing path
Barnton	572 yards, no towing path
Froghall	76 yards, no towing path
New Harecastle	2,926 yards, towing path
Old Harecastle	2,888 yards, no towing path
Preston Brook	1,239 yards, no towing path
Saltersford	424 yards, no towing path

Hall End Branch

The making of the Hall End Branch canal was rendered necessary by the creation of a canal to Macclesfield. This was a canal of the later era, made in the time of early railway plans and schemes. The Macclesfield Canal, as built, formed an end-on junction with the Hall End Branch, which in turn joined the main line of the Trent and Mersey Canal above the top lock at Kidsgrove. The junction, like the top lock, was called Hardings Wood. The work at the junction involved the making of a 'winding hole' opposite the junction and a roving bridge over the entrance to the branch for the towpath.

Pool Aqueduct.

Hall End stop lock in 2010.

The Hall End Branch was made under the direction of Thomas Telford, by the contractors William Hoof and Daniel Pritchard, with the bond agreed and signed in October 1827. Cutting starting after the contract was signed. This short branch was only 1½ miles in length, but required several important engineering features as part of the work. From a right-angle junction with the summit level of the canal at Hardings Wood, the canal turned north and then curved to cross over the Trent and Mersey Canal main line at Pool Lock Aqueduct. This aqueduct crossed over the canal between Pool Lock and Red Bull Lock and then the turnpike at Red Bull Aqueduct. It was also necessary to build an embankment at the level of both aqueducts. Making such works required time for the ground to settle.

The Wardle Branch

The plaque on the entrance to the Wardle Branch bears the date 1829, but the Middlewich Branch to which it was joined did not open until 1833. Authority for the Wardle Branch (along with the Hall End Branch) had been given by an Act of Parliament passed in 1827, but this short branch of 4 chains and 54 links (about 100 yards) relied on the completion of the Ellesmere and Chester Canal Middlewich Branch, which had encountered serious engineering problems.

The Middlewich Branch of the Chester Canal had been a cornerstone of that original canal scheme, providing access to the salt works at Middlewich. James Brindley was paid to survey the route as first suggested, in 1768, with a canal that was to unite Chester with Middlewich. That scheme did not proceed, but in 1772 the Chester Canal Company did obtain an act for a canal to Middlewich. The Trent and Mersey Canal Committee consistently enforced the 100-yard distance clause of the 1777 act, with the result that the Chester Canal Company never completed its branch to Middlewich. Later, with Thomas Telford as engineer, the making of a new Middlewich Branch did finally begin, following a similar route to that of 1777.

Telford surveyed the complete Middlewich Branch from the Ellesmere and Chester Canal to the Trent and Mersey in 1825. He was at that time engaged as engineer for a number of canal companies. The 9¾-mile long Middlewich Branch was made across land where deposits in the earth known as Cheshire marl made embankment construction difficult. The marl could become liquid, and this delayed the settling of the embankment across the Weaver, which in turn delayed the opening of the branch until 1833.

Wardle Lock, Middlewich.

Wardle Branch Junction, Middlewich.

The short Wardle Branch had one lock and also had the financial advantage of controlling tolls on all craft passing through it on to the Trent and Mersey Canal. Although the fees charged on both the Hall End Branch and the Wardle Branch contributed to the income of the Trent and Mersey revenue, they were of much concern to canal carriers. There were regular complaints about them from traders conveying pottery goods and raw material this way to the potteries at Stoke.

Dane Feeder Improvements

Following a recommendation from John Rennie, new work was carried out on the feeder from Wincle, including improved embankments and a widened tunnel.

Modifications to the feeder continued after Rennie's death. Following a resolution of the General Assembly on 25 April 1821, an application to Parliament was prepared for improvement of the Dane Feeder, or a feeder from the Churnet to capture the floodwater. The Dane feeder was improved by canal workmen under the supervision of James Potter.

A New Reservoir at Knypersley

A new reservoir was made at Knypersley to improve the supply for the second Harecastle Tunnel and the double locks on the Cheshire side of Harecastle

Tunnel. John Rennie had been cautious about improvement at Knypersley, but Thomas Telford took on the engineering challenge to construct the new reservoir with a plan to make a dam across the valley of the Trent. The length of the dam needed would prove to be a challenge to both the engineers and contractors.

Improvements to the water supply were first considered in May 1820, with the investigation of such ideas as the raising of the existing dam or the creation of a new reservoir. Present at the meeting were William Vaughan, principal agent, John Trubshaw and James Caldwell; Trubshaw was delegated to examine water supplies and soon expressed his concerns about the length of dam that would be necessary. The site was visited by John Rennie, when he surveyed Harecastle, and a subsequent conversation with James Caldwell suggested that the new reservoir was feasible and could hold 3,000 locks of water. Once the project had been sanctioned by Act of Parliament in 1823, Telford was able to get on and pursue it.

Telford had recommended that the dam be made to a height of about 60 feet. Construction of the reservoir was conducted under the supervision of resident engineer James Potter, and the contractors were Buckley and Dutton. Telford was not confirmed as engineer to the Trent and Mersey Canal Company until 18 March 1825. In the meantime, Joseph Potter, then chief engineer to the company, used the design of the dam built at Rudyard Lake, to the plan of John Rennie, as a model for the Knypersley Dam.

There were serious constraints on the making of the reservoir imposed by the landowner William Bateman, who insisted on having the old watermill taken down and a new mill built downstream. Before the main work could start, the company needed to secure possession of the land. Although James Potter had commenced a puddle trench foundation during January 1825, the rest of the year was taken up with various negotiations and a draft agreement was not drawn up until December 1825. It was a difficult excavation and work went on until June 1825 before a solid foundation was reached. A steam engine was needed to drain the trench and it was not until August 1825 that the puddle-clay base was at ground level.

The drainpipes for the reservoir should then have been put down, but William Bateman's new mill remained unfinished and James Potter was not permitted to lay the discharge pipes until March 1827. In January 1827 Bateman refused to permit the filling of the new reservoir until he got his deeds and had resolved all the remaining issues regarding the land exchange.

Bateman also insisted on a provision that the fish in the mill pond should not be harmed through the draining of the pond. This restriction meant that the pipes had to be positioned higher than planned. Work on the dam had continued through 1826, leaving a gap for the pipes, but 36 feet of this gap had to be filled in with the pipes placed on top. After this, a period of time should have been allowed for the dam to settle before filling with water; however, the urgency of having the reservoir completed seems to have overridden the need for settlement. The upstream face of the dam was paved with stone, and a puddle gutter was made to the sluice. By December 1827 the dam had been finished and permission had been granted to fill the reservoir with water.

The assembly of the sliding valve, the sluice and the casing associated with releasing the water from the reservoir was soon damaged. The cause was believed to be the failure to allow the dam structure to settle. The problem was first noticed in April 1828, and it proved to be serious and significant, as it meant that water could not be delivered to the canal. Various engineers, including Thomas Telford, James Potter, Joseph Potter, John Trubshaw and William Faram, all made visits to the reservoir, in an attempt to resolve the matter. James Potter, in particular, spent many hours there.

Thomas Telford inspected the reservoir site in December 1828. He recommended to James Potter to take up the masonry that covered the valve assembly and then rebuild the structure. He also suggested that puddle clay be made up to 2 feet above the top water level.

Fearing resentment from the canal committee, James Potter confided in James Caldwell that he would resign once the reservoir had been repaired. However, in January 1829, the committee was already pressing for Potter's resignation. Meanwhile, the Trubshaw family carried on looking for a way to render the reservoir complete. James Trubshaw recommended that improvements be made to the draw-bar collars and, following that work in May 1829, it was suggested that the reservoir be refilled.

Despite the remedial action carried out by both James Potter and James Trubshaw, the dam still leaked. William Vaughan wrote to Telford in September 1829, noting that the new reservoir was still imperfect. Water escaped through masonry at the discharging pipes and the culverts were not watertight. It was a problem that would not be resolved until 1868, when the North Staffordshire Railway constructed a wet well to assist water delivery from the reservoir.

Water supply continued to be a matter of concern for the canal company, particularly at times of drought, which occurred sometimes. In 1831, John Trubshaw and William Faram investigated the supply of water from Coxshead Engine to the Caldon Canal. The Coxshead pumping engine, which had been leased to the canal from 1815, had provided a supply for a number of years – possibly from the mid-1790s, when Sparrow, Hales and Co. operated this colliery. The discontinuation of the use of this engine was regularly discussed by the select committee, yet the lease was extended again for three years in 1827. The Coxshead Engine lease became more of a matter of contention in 1831, when John Trubshaw presented a report to James Caldwell on alternative sources of water from the brooks, mines and reservoirs. Water was also pumped from Hardings Wood stream into the summit level.

Duplication of Cheshire Locks

Following the completion of the New Harecastle Tunnel, the locks between Kidsgrove and Wheelock had an additional lock built alongside them. This work has been attributed to Thomas Telford and the work was done during the time when Telford was associated with the Trent and Mersey Canal, but the engineer responsible for making the additional locks was probably William Faram. Such work aided the movement of salt and pottery goods to the Bridgewater Canal and the improved interchange point at Anderton.

Work on these new locks was begun by 1828. In August 1828, 'Mr Pickford from the canal carrying

Lower Thurlwood, Lock 54, on the Cheshire double lock section.

Snapes Aqueduct, at Lawton.

firm had expressed his satisfaction on travelling through the double locks when a model of the new set-up was shown to the select committee.

At the time, the Trent and Mersey Canal had a dedicated team of staff, who could not only maintain the waterway but also make improvements. At the heart of this team was the Faram family, William, James and Samuel. William Faram, of Lawton was particularly engaged in surveying and construction works on the Trent and Mersey, having frequent discussions with James Caldwell, the company chairman, on the various projects being undertaken. These included plans for new works on the Trent and Mersey, as well as other waterways. Faram was instrumental in explaining to the select committee the advantages of the double locks – traffic would speed up and boats travelling along this length of canal would save time – and his evidence seems to have convinced the committee to continue with the lock duplication. William Faram's contribution to canal improvement was certainly significant and deserves as much recognition as possible.

Whilst information on the Cheshire Locks duplication is difficult to find, the advertisement for the sale of bricks by Samuel Faram of Thurlwood in May 1833 is a useful clue. This sale comprised a large amount – 150,000 bricks in lots of 10,000. There were also several lots of pieces of bricks,

Top Lock gates, Malkins Bank, Betchton.

Examples of Bridges

Bridge 97 Turnover Bridge and lock 32.

Turnover Bridge 68, Bellamour.

Towpath Bridge, Hardings Wood Junction.

about 20,000 red and blue draining shells, and a quantity of timber. This may well be a reference to the disposal of bricks that were not needed for the Cheshire Locks, reflecting a decision to cease further work. Four of the locks were left unduplicated; those that had the additional lock comprised the section from Kents Lock to Wheelock Bottom Lock (21 locks).

A large workforce was needed at this time for brick-making, bricklaying, cutting and masonry, and these men were conveniently on hand to assist with an accident on the turnpike on Friday 11 September 1829. The Birmingham to Liverpool down mail coach reached Pointon Mill Bridge, near Lawton, at 2am that morning. The river there was in flood and, as the coach crossed over, the bridge collapsed, throwing the coach and horses into the torrent. The coach driver, guard and one passenger escaped, but two other passengers within the coach were drowned, as was one of the four horses. By the time James Caldwell arrived at the site of the accident, between 8 and 9 in the morning, James Faram and his men were actively engaged in trying to get the coach out of the river. They managed to get it done between 11am and 12 noon, recovering one of the bodies. The body of the other unfortunate passenger was found much later.

The Steam Boat Experiment

Whilst the carrier Henshall & Co. had restricted its operations to the pottery trade, there was a need for improved carriage facilities. In December 1820 the use of 'an invention for passing boats upon the canal', presented by Mr Rangeley of Stone, was considered by the canal committee. Further interest had been provided by the trial of Mr Gordon's Steam Boat at Red Bull Lock on 18 September 1828. These developments inspired James Caldwell and the Trent and Mersey Canal with the Faram family to carry out experiments and trials with such a boat between 1829 and 1831. Despite initial reservations, the idea of building a steam boat for themselves seems to have been instigated by a general desire to reintroduce long-distance canal carrying.

It is through the diary of James Caldwell that the experiments and trials are revealed. Power from the engine was transferred through a chain, suggesting that a form of paddle had been adopted, as had been the case with Gordon's craft. William Faram was also closely involved with the project, in consultation with Braithwaite & Erickson, who had been responsible for the Novelty, a steam locomotive that took part in the Rainhill Trials. The result was the building and trialling of a stern wheel chain-driven paddle boat.

An important trial was conducted on 25 Friday 1830. John Faram recorded the results and passed them on to James Caldwell:

> 1 Boat weighed 10 Tons, Cargo 17 Tons, total 27 Tons. Speed 4.02 Miles an hour
> 2 Boats weighed 20 Tons, Cargo 34 Tons, total 54 Tons. Speed 3.75 Miles per hour
> 3 Boats weighed 30 Tons, Cargo 51 Tons, total 81 Tons. Speed 2.89 Miles per hour
> 4 Boats weighed 40 Tons, Cargo 68 Tons, total 108 Tons. Speed 2.35 Miles per hour

At a further trial on 1 July 1830 at the 'Aqueduct', the engine drew four boats, total weight 108 tons, 220 yards in 2 minutes and 40 seconds, travelling at very nearly 3 miles an hour. The results led Caldwell to conclude that the average speed with a cargo of goods of 15 or 16 tons would be about 4½ miles an hour, and that this could be achieved without injury to the sides of the canal. The engine would consume about 200lb of steam in 10 hours. It appeared that goods from Manchester might be delivered in London in time for the markets on the third day after departure. A visit was then arranged to Liverpool to inspect the locomotives of the Liverpool and Manchester Railway. Mr Lock accompanied Caldwell and his team to show them the locomotives of the railway.

A new engine for the Trent and Mersey boat was arranged to be built by Mr Kirk of Etruria at a cost of £205. It was funded personally by Caldwell, who was determined to give the project a fair chance, and the engine was to be ready in October 1830. Trials were made with the new engine in June 1831 and the experiment seems to have ended at about the time when the Grand Junction Railway was created. Later, canal carriers Robins & Co. had a trial boat that travelled through to Manchester, using a form of screw propeller.

Replacement of Etruria and Meaford Staircase Locks

The replacement of the staircases at Etruria and Meaford appears to have been done during the early 1830s, following the making of the additional locks in Cheshire, the Hall End and Wardle Branches.

At Etruria the new line of locks was made on the east side of the existing locks. Two locks, each of 10 feet rise, replaced the original three. The staircase pair had a rise of 12 feet 8 inches, and the single top lock was 6 feet 4 inches. The canal was built up to the east of the former Bells Mill Aqueduct

The alterations may be dated to some extent by looking at the Ordnance Survey maps, which may be found at the Staffordshire Records Office. For Meaford, the fact that the routes of both new and old courses are shown on map 72 of the early Ordnance Survey would suggest that the alterations were carried out in the 1830s. With Etruria, there are maps for the 1830s that show the before and after arrangement of the locks. The earlier maps show the canal from Fenton through to Hardings Wood, and include the junction with the Hall End Branch. The other, later, maps show the Caldon Canal through to Stockton Brook. At Meaford, the canal was diverted on to a straighter course with three new locks and the complete abandonment of the former route.

New Locks at Hazelhurst

John Rennie had pressed for the replacement of the Hazelhurst staircase locks by conventional locks, and this work was eventually carried out when

The revised line of locks at Etruria.

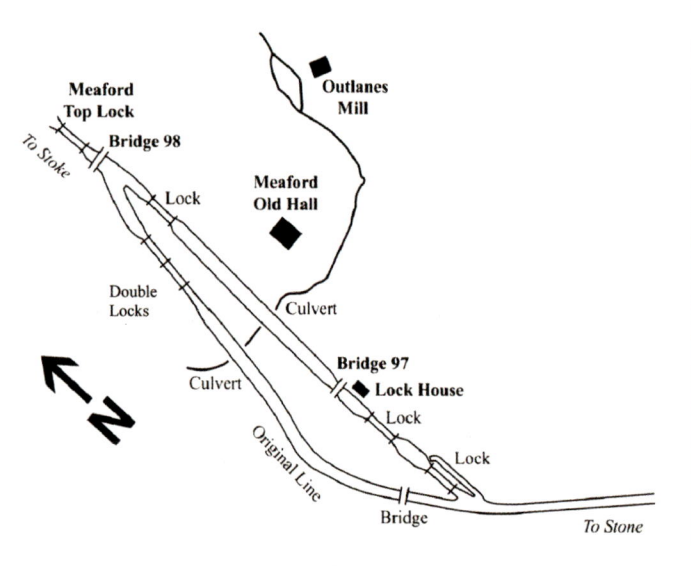

Sketch map of Meaford Locks.

Hazelhurst Aqueduct.

Lock 10, Caldon Canal.

the diversion followed part of the original Caldon Canal route. A new junction was made with the Leek Canal, and a lock house and roving bridge were constructed at the new Lock 10. Three locks were made, along with an aqueduct, at Hazelhurst, to carry the Leek Branch over the diversion. The staircase locks were abandoned, but their empty chambers remain.

The aqueduct bears the date 1841 and the roving bridge has the date 1842. The aqueduct, made of brick with stone dressing, has a single round arch that spans the waterway and the towpath. Construction of the aqueduct was carried out when James Trubshaw was employed as engineer to the Trent and Mersey Canal.

The Spiritual Needs of the Boating Community

During the 1820s, missions to look after the spiritual needs of the boating community started to appear along the canal side in London and elsewhere. From 1840, the need for missions became more urgent, following a well-publicized incident on the Trent and Mersey Canal near Rugeley. A woman named Christina Collins was travelling from Liverpool to London as a passenger on a Pickford fly boat, when she was assaulted and killed by boatmen working on the service. Although the perpetrators were apprehended on the Birmingham Canal Navigations at Pickford's warehouse at Fazeley, the event led to much discussion among the public and politicians. Questions were asked about the general moral character of the boating population. There was a strong feeling that 'the numerous classes of boatmen and their families employed on the Trent and Mersey Canal and other canals passing through this county' needed to be raised 'from the state of spiritual destitution and consequent moral degradation to which they have been unhappily left'.

With the creation of a Boatmen's Pastoral Instruction Society, in August 1840 a meeting was held at the home of R. F. Kitchin at Stone. The Reverend Gibson Lucas was chairman. The meeting discussed among other issues a resolution that had been raised in Parliament by Lord Sandon regarding the cessation of Sunday trading on canals and railways. This was viewed as an important step in saving the bargemen and boatmen from their 'moral degradation'.

The provision of places for boatmen to attend for religious purposes was another important factor. A new church for boatmen was erected at Butt Lane, in the parish of Audley, close to the turnpike and a few yards from Red Bull Wharf. This project was originated by C. P. Wilbraham, vicar of Audley, and was built by James Booth of Lawton. The church was completed in March 1847. A boatman's mission was also established at Stoke Wharf, alongside the warehouses on the towpath side of the canal.

The proprietors of the Trent and Mersey Canal declared their intention to stop, as far as they were able, Sunday traffic on their canal. This decision was made by the General Assembly and their ruling was published by Henry Moore, Principal Agent, in April 1840:

Resolved
(1)   That no wharfinger, or other person in the employ of this company do transact any business at their respective wharfs, warehouses, offices or elsewhere or allow the company's cranes to be used on

The original dam of Bagnall Reservoir, 2011. DAVID HENTHORN BROWN

the Lord's Day except to cases of the most urgent necessity

(2) That all wharfingers and others in the employ of the company be, and they hereby required to resort some place of public worship on the Lord's Day

(3) That all persons employed on this line of Navigation do vigilantly watch the conduct of persons navigating boats on the canal, and of their steerers, drivers and attendants; and that every do report to the chief clerk, in Stone, any irregularity or impropriety of conduct which he may observe, especially on the Lord's Day

Circulars were sent to all traders to inform them that such regulations would come into force from 1 June 1840 (some notices stated 17 June) and that the company wharves would not be open for the receipt or delivery of goods on Sundays.

Bagnall Reservoir

Bagnall Reservoir was also known as Stanley Pool. This title became more relevant after the dam at Stanley was raised in 1840 and the original Stanley Reservoir effectively merged with Bagnall Reservoir. James Trubshaw was involved with the dam reconstruction and the resulting increase in capacity.

Dutton Stop Lock

The stop lock at Dutton, at the south end of Preston Brook Tunnel, is unique. It is not shown on early maps of the canal, or on the Cheshire Tithe map, so it must have been made after 1840. There were stop gates provided from the time the canal was made, but when the stop lock was made the structure resembled Etruria – that lock once had a roof over

Red Bull Aqueduct: Stone date plaques were fitted to both aqueducts and the junction roving bridge.

it and boat gauging (or checking) was conducted there. The company lock house at Dutton had previously been in private hands; the Cheshire Tithe refers to Edward Reeves as the occupier and Sir Arthur Ingram as the owner. The land thereabouts was owned by the Ingram family and the Trent and Mersey Canal Company leased the bed of the canal from them.

Consall Forge New Lock

Consall Forge Old Lock, on the Caldon Canal, experienced difficulty with subsidence and a new chamber was reconstructed on land between the existing chamber and Consall Flint Mill. The date of reconstruction has yet to be determined.

CHAPTER 5

Railways and Railway Ownership

Railways already had a long pedigree as a form of transport, even as the first canals were being proposed. Waggonways had been used to transport minerals such as coal for many years. Originally laid on wooden sleepers, they were gradually replaced over time by ways made of metal. During the 1790s the use of cast-iron, plate or edge rails laid on stone blocks became more common, and stone block railways became the preferred choice of canal companies as a means of reaching places adjoining their network.

> **PLATEWAYS**
>
> A plateway comprised flat iron plates with a raised edge, often laid on stone blocks. Plateways were used to convey minerals to the canal where the terrain was not suited for canal construction. Later, edge rails came to be used, to allow for an increase in the weight carried in wagons.

Canal Company Tramways

From 1778 the Trent and Mersey Canal owned a tramway from Froghall to the Caldon Low Limestone Quarries, constructed of wood topped with iron. This was replaced in 1783–1785 by another, also made of wood rails topped with iron, but this time starting at the new canal terminus. A third tramway was constructed between 1803 and 1804, to the design of John Rennie. It had three self-acting inclines, with horse haulage in the level sections, and was made up of an iron plateway laid on stone blocks.

In a report to the canal committee in September 1801, John Rennie had put forward two alternative proposals for tramways, 'F' and 'G':

F has three planes – First Railway 1958 yards long; a plane of 264 yards; second railway 2244 yards long; a plane 132 yards; third railway 1364 yards and a plane of 308 yards.

G has 4 planes – First Railway 1958 yards; a plane of 198 yards; second railway of 1573 yards; a plane of 33 yards; a third railway of 847 yards; a plane of 121 yards; a fourth railway of 1364 yards and a plane of 308 yards.

Whilst a Mr Holmes estimated that the three-plane line would cost more than the four-plane version, it was more favourable to be worked by horses and as such it was preferred by John Rennie.

A fourth line, made to the design of James Trubshaw, was built between 1842 and 1847. This last

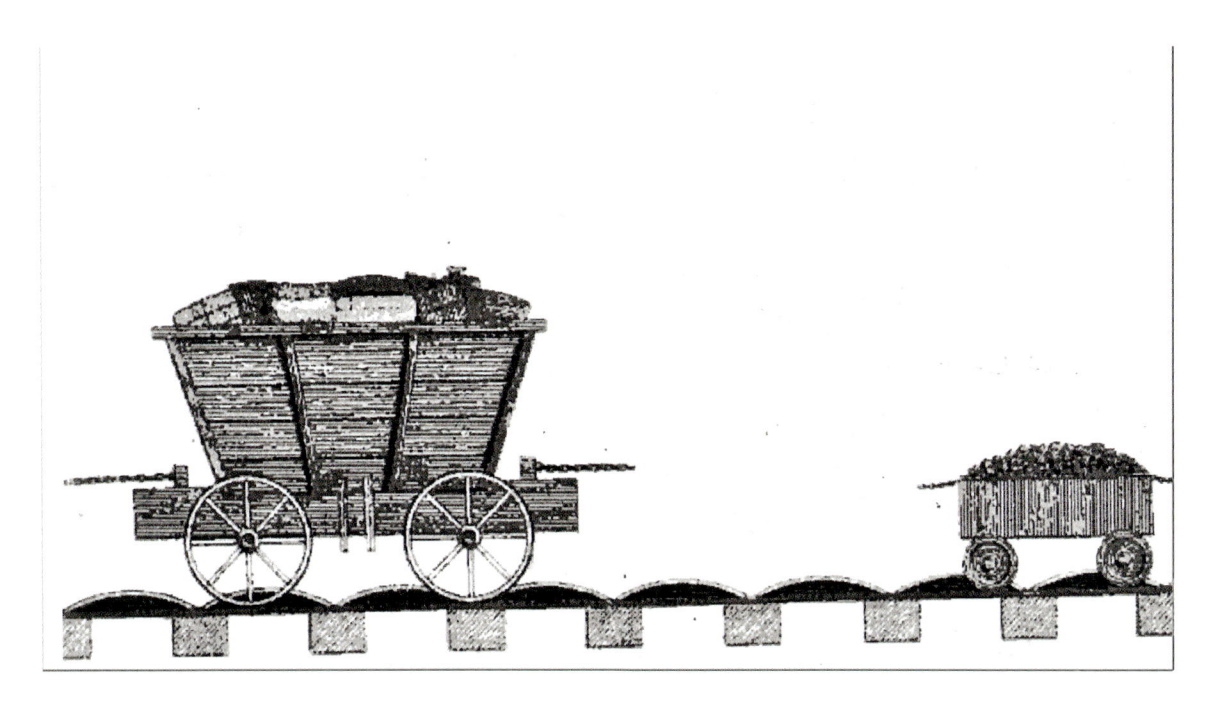

The arrangement of plate rails laid on stone sleepers and examples of wagons conveyed.

line was made as single-track edge-rail railway, with gravity-worked inclines and passing places. It was built for the Trent and Mersey Canal Company without parliamentary powers but with the consent of local landowners. The gauge was 3 feet 6 inches, and from 1849 it also had a connection with the Churnet Valley Railway, opened in 1849. There was a tunnel near Caldon Low and the gradient was a clear improvement on the line engineered by John Rennie. This line closed on 25 March 1920.

In the Potteries, the changing level of ground limited canal construction in certain areas and tramways were chosen as a means of transport to the canal banks. Instead of using edge rails, the canal company chose to use plate railways made to the gauge of 3 feet 8 inches for three tramways. John Rennie carried out a survey for a canal at Burslem, and suggested a waterway with two locks. What was built was a short canal on the level with a plateway up to Burslem. A second plateway from Etruria Wharf was built to Hanley, whilst the third and longest plateway was made from Stoke Wharf to Lane End. There had been a suggestion that a canal should be made to Lane End in 1796, but this was replaced by the plateway, even though this was not completed as far as the destination on the parliamentary plan. The Lane End Plateway served potteries, collieries and ironstone mines. A separate, and private, tramway, which for a time connected with it, was made to the Fenton Park Collieries and then Fenton Park ironworks, which were developed in the 1830s.

A short canal-owned tramway was also used for stone transport between Hoo Mill and the canal at Hoo Mill Lock.

Private Tramways and Railway Links

Several private tramways were connected to the Trent and Mersey Canal in different locations. Near Shardlow there was a tramway that brought alabaster to the canal from quarries at Aston. At Rugeley, there was a long 'railroad' that linked Hayes Colliery (owned by the Marquis of Anglesey) with the canal. There was also a separate tramway from the adjacent Brereton pits (owned by the Earl of Shrewsbury) to the turnpike, which may have been on the route as suggested by James Brindley when a sough was surveyed by him:

The sough to be begun 45ft 9in above the canal from which place to the pool in the Hayes is 57ft 3in and from the pool to the Kennel Pits is 157ft

The sough proposed is to be about 1 yard high and 30 inches wide

The course of it from Brereton Hill to the Hayes about 840 yards

It is apprehended that the greatest part of the way will go through free stone

The expense per yard if through stone about 12 to 15s per yard and if through earth about 8s per yard

A great advantage in point of expedition will arise from the erecting of an engine about the middle of the work to be worked by the old sough water which will by means of a pump take off the water and three sets of men may work at the same time– supposing the sough to lay the coal dry then the coal will be raised out of the pits by a horse gin and a railway must be made about 4ft and a half wide to carry the coals to the road– and if necessary the canal and if the quantity got be great then there should be another railway to take back the empty wagons– the expense of these railways are about 4s per yard 5 sets of men may be set on and if so it is supposed if nothing unforeseen happens to impede the work the whole may be completed in the year, if three sets one year and a half.

The whole expense of the sough computed if stone is about, including accidents and other incidental expenses   £800

Froghall basin and incline.

> The Horse gin and engine to draw water during the time of working at about £100
> The Railway at about £180
> Another Railway £180
> The whole expense to set the works a going so as to deliver coal at the Road on Brereton Hill
> £1260

Later, the Brereton Colliery tramway was extended to the canal after crossing the road. That crossing was reconstructed as an under bridge following an accident.

In the Harecastle area, there were tramways that linked the Golden Hill Collieries and ironworks with the canal near Tunstall (also known as the Holly Wall). North of Harecastle Tunnel, there were a group of separate lines that served Clough Hall and White Hill Collieries, Clough Hall Ironworks and Collieries, Trubshaw and Stonetrough Collieries and Woodshutts Colliery. Most were believed to have been plateways, whilst the later Clough Hall Ironworks, which included the Dragon Tunnel line to the canal, seems to have been edge rail.

Within the county of Cheshire there was a narrow-gauge tramway that linked salt works belonging to Charles Newman with Witton Brook navigation north of Witton Quay. This line came to serve the rock salt works at Platshill, British and the white salt works, called Imperial, beside the Trent and Mersey Canal. There were also the incline railways at Anderton owned by the River Weaver Trustees.

The Caldon Canal had various tramway links. At Norton-in-the-Moors there were three short tramways to the Caldon Canal. The North Stafford Railway, also called the Consall Plateway, was owned by Lee & Bowyers and laid to a gauge of about 3 feet 6 inches. This line was built between 1815 and 1819 and served Cellar Head and Chase Colliery. There was also a short tramway to the Cupola Flint Mill at Froghall.

Connecting with the Uttoxeter Canal there was the Woodhead Tramway, which was opened in about 1808 and served the Royal George and Woodhead Collieries. The section to the canal wharf was closed in about 1847, but the track associated with the colliery and a landsale wharf was retained.

New Railway Schemes

At this time, the Trent and Mersey Canal Committee was engaged in an ongoing battle with railway promoters, and was having to bear the costs of opposing various schemes in Parliament. One project that presented a serious threat to the canal company was the Birmingham and Liverpool Railway scheme, which was first proposed in 1824 and then again in 1828. The opening of the Liverpool and Manchester Railway in 1830 led to new plans for railways and a third application to unite Liverpool with Birmingham was made in that year, when a junction with the Warrington to Newton Railway was suggested. The Warrington and Newton Railway was approved in Parliament, but the Liverpool scheme failed again, for the last time. A railway link between the West Midlands and the North West was not abandoned completely, however. During 1832, the Grand Junction Railway came into being. This railway, which linked Warrington with Birmingham, was granted approval by Act of Parliament on 6 May 1833. The London and Birmingham Railway received its parliamentary go-ahead on the same day.

These two lines, together with the Warrington and Newton Railway, formed a complete railway route that linked London, through the West Midlands, with the North West. It was an impressive alternative to the Trent and Mersey Canal. On 30 June 1836, the Birmingham and Derby Junction Railway was also granted permission by Act of Parliament, creating another option for the carriage of goods travelling to the East Midlands.

The Grand Junction Railway was completed, from the temporary terminus at Vauxhall, Birmingham, on 4 July 1837. It would provide serious competition in terms of the carriage of goods on both the Trent and Mersey and the Birmingham and Liverpool Junction Canal.

Whitmore provided the means of carriage by rail and road to the Potteries. Contractors had used the stone found in Whitmore Cutting for bridge building and ballast and at Whitmore a station was made where the Newcastle to Market Drayton Turnpike crossed. This station was 7 miles from Stone and 7½

NORTH STAFFORDSHIRE RAILWAY CONSTITUENT COMPANIES

Railway Company	Engineer	Capital (£)	Date
Staffordshire Potteries		1,200,000	3/1845
Churnet Valley	George Watson Buck	1,000,000	6/1844
Derby and Crewe Junction	Joseph Locke	750,000*	5/1845

*increased to £950,000

miles from Burslem, but improved roads had made transit easier. The next station was Madeley, which also provided carriage by road and railway. There was also the private railway to Leycett Colliery and Ironworks, owned by the ironmaster Thomas Firmstone.

After Madeley Station the Grand Junction Railway crossed into Cheshire and was served by Basford Station and then Crewe, which subsequently became a major railway centre. At this time, it had the benefit of the turnpike road from Sandbach to Nantwich as well as access to the salt works at Wheelock. At Winsford station the turnpike was a link with Middlewich and at Acton Station there was access to the extensive salt works at Marston. From Acton the railway continued to the cutting at Preston Brook. Here, the proximity of the line to the Trent and Mersey Canal had caused concern to James Caldwell, during his time in charge of the select committee.

Other railway schemes that came into being included the Preston Brook and Runcorn Railway and the rival Preston Brook and Chester Railway (surveyed by Henry Robertson), both put forward in bills of 1844. Both schemes failed. Another was the Manchester and Birmingham Railway; the original route was to pass through the Potteries to join the Grand Junction Railway, threatening to take more traffic away from the Trent and Mersey Canal, but an alteration to a junction north of Crewe temporarily gave some respite. New railway schemes suggested in 1844 and 1845 included one that became the North Staffordshire Railway. This last scheme promised a new future for that canal!

Such was the mood for railway investment and speculation at this time that a host of new schemes were proposed. Parliament was overworked, dealing with a flood of applications and having to weed out those bills that lacked merit or were unworkable. Some promoters viewed the issue of shares as a way to accrue cash, rather than being committed to building a railway. However, some had a genuine interest in improving transport links, including the businessman and politician John Lewis Ricardo (1812–1862), MP for Stoke and lifelong chairman of the North Staffordshire Railway.

The origins of the North Staffordshire Railway lie in three different schemes. The Churnet Valley bill was submitted to Parliament in 1844 and was dealt with by Committee O, but serious objections led to it being left for resubmission at the next term. In May 1845 the provisional committee of the Staffordshire Potteries Railway, whose shareholders included several local industrialists, concluded an agreement with the Churnet Valley and Trent Valley Railway Companies. Under the terms of this agreement, the Staffordshire Potteries Railway would become incorporated within the larger undertaking of the North Staffordshire, or Churnet, Potteries and Trent Junction Railway.

Another railway that passed close to the Trent and Mersey Canal was the Trent Valley. This line and the Churnet Valley Railway had a brief alliance, which ended during 1845. The Trent Valley went on to have its bill authorized by Parliament in July 1845. As construction began, the Trent Valley company was purchased jointly by the London and Birmingham, Grand Junction and Manchester Railways in 1846 and formed part of the London and North Western Railway network, when those three railway undertakings merged in 1847.

The lengthy title of the railway (North Staffordshire, or Churnet, Potteries and Trent Junction Railway) was shortened to become the North Staffordshire Railway during 1845, and separate bills were submitted to Parliament in the same year. The North Staffordshire (Churnet Valley Line) Bill proposed the making of a railway from the Manchester and Birmingham Railway at Macclesfield to join the Birmingham and Derby Line of the Midland Railway with a branch to Stoke-on-Trent. Powers were sought to discontinue the Caldon Canal as a canal, and to amalgamate with the Potteries Railway, if sanctioned by Parliament. The capital was £1,200,000, with powers to borrow an additional £400,000. The North Staffordshire (Harecastle and Sandbach) Bill had a capital of £200,000 (and powers to raise an additional £65,000), and proposed the making of a railway from Harecastle to join the Manchester and Birmingham Railway at Sandbach, with powers to purchase the Trent and Mersey Canal and also to amalgamate with the Potteries Railway, if sanctioned by Parliament. Finally, the North Staffordshire (Pottery Line) Bill had a capital of £1,500,000, with powers to borrow an additional sum of £500,000. If this bill passed this session of Parliament, the Trent and Mersey Canal was to be amalgamated with the railway.

Rival schemes included the Tean and Dove Railway, which promised a better route between London and Manchester; this bill was withdrawn in the February 1846 session of Parliament. There was also 'The Staffordshire Potteries and Liverpool and Manchester Direct Railway', provisionally registered in July 1845. Although this particular scheme failed, railway speculation remained fertile ground and a number of other proposals came and went.

The Derby and Crewe Junction Railway, which, like the Churnet Valley Railway, promised a route through Uttoxeter and a junction with the Birmingham and Derby Junction Railway, had a bill before Parliament at the same time. The capital was set at £950,000, with powers requested to raise another £300,000. There was to be a branch to Burton upon Trent and a commitment to lease or sell to the Grand Junction Railway.

Union of the North Staffordshire Railway and the Trent and Mersey Canal

In November 1845 the North Staffordshire Railway bills had been made ready for Parliament, seeking to authorize the union with the Trent and Mersey Canal Company. By December 1845 arrangements had been entered into with the Trent and Mersey Canal Company with regards to laying out their line, which, without impeding navigation, would reduce the cost of construction of the railway. The Derby and Crewe Junction Railway had also been incorporated into the North Staffordshire Railway Company. At the same time, the original bill for a railway to Liverpool was altered to seek authorization for one that terminated at Crewe.

The relevant bills were supported by John Lewis Ricardo, Liberal MP for Stoke-on-Trent, who had begun his railway involvement with the Potteries Railway. Success was achieved in 1846, after a long process through to the committee stage, when a decision was made for progress. Committee 27 dealt with the three bills, which were returned and passed by the House of Commons, then taken on to the House of Lords by Ricardo and from there went on to receive Royal Assent.

Purchase of the Canal

A key part of the act was the purchase of the Trent and Mersey Canal and a commitment to continue to work the canal. The only part proposed to be closed was the unprofitable Uttoxeter Branch. The three acts were authorized by Parliament in 1846:

> North Staffordshire Railway (Harecastle and Sandbach) Act, Vic 9 and 10, 26 June 1846, c84
> North Staffordshire Railway (Pottery Line), Act Vic 9 and 10, 26 June 1846, c85
> North Staffordshire Railway (Churnet Valley), Act Vic 9 and 10, 26 June 1846, c85

Another Act of 1847 was needed to consolidate these three (Vic 10 and 11, c108, 2 July 1847). G. P. Bidder became principal engineer for the railway and it was decided that the main line would run from Macclesfield, through Stoke-on-Trent to Colwich, where the Trent Valley would be joined.

Arrangements for a lease of the Trent and Mersey Canal had been announced at the General Assembly of 1845, under the chairmanship of Francis Twemlow. The chairman of the select committee for the Trent and Mersey Canal and the chairman of the provisional committee of the North Staffordshire Railway had discussed a lease of the canal in perpetuity on payment of £30 per annum per share, until the opening of the whole railway.

The Trent and Mersey Canal General Committee met at Stone on 8 July and agreed the following:

> In the opinion of this committee, it is desirable for this company to come to an arrangement for the immediate alliance, and ultimate connection with the North Staffordshire Railway Company, on terms by which the management and profits shall be reserved to the Proprietors until the railway comes into complete operation; and after that period the same to be ceded to the railway company, on stipulation of a fixed guarantee of interest up to a certain amount, and a contingent interest beyond, dependent on the profits of the joint concern.

This resolution was considered at the General Assembly on 14 July 1846, under the chairmanship of Viscount Sandon. The terms of purchase were revised and included the appointment of three directors of the canal company to the North Staffordshire Railway board. Wilbraham Egerton proposed the motion on the sale, and it was agreed by the assembly. During September 1846, the arrangement between the Trent and Mersey Navigation Company and the North Staffordshire Railway, as agreed by Francis Twemlow and John Lewis Ricardo, was subject to the approval of the Trent and Mersey Canal shareholders. With the takeover, a new set of staff came in to replace the former Trent and Mersey team, with H. B. Farnall becoming manager, based at Stone. It was a positive move for the canal company, with the new partnership between canal and railway being created to mutual benefit, and canal shareholders being guaranteed revenue on their shares. A similar arrangement was established between the Birmingham Canal Navigations and the London and Birmingham Railway, and their successors the London and North Western Railway.

The Canal Carriers Act

Henshall & Co. had continued to be a carrier of pottery goods to the canal company wharves and depots from 1812. This decision had opened the way for other carriers to have control of the trade that came on to and through the Trent and Mersey Canal. Some businessmen observed that the independent carriers often set their rates in collaboration with each other and for that reason there were those who desired the return of Henshall & Co.

Canal companies were not allowed to carry goods themselves, for fear that they might vary tolls preferentially to their own advantage. The Trent and Mersey Canal Company had avoided the parliamentary ruling by having Henshall & Co. as a nominal independent carrier, even if it was not, strictly speaking. The same applied on the Bridgewater Canal, where the firm of Worthington & Gilbert operated on other waterways, but had a close connection to the Duke of Bridgewater and, later, the Bridgewater Trustees. The Canal Carriers Act of 1845 permitted canal companies to become carriers in their own right and several chose to do this. The North Staffordshire Railway acted early to set up again as a long-distance carrier when they took over the former Shiptons business in July 1847 and appointed George Skey as their agent at Albion Wharf, Wolverhampton. Shiptons briefly retained a trade to London thereafter.

The Canal Carriers Act allowed the North Staffordshire Railway to bring in some additional revenue at a time when they were actively building a railway network. Once that had been achieved, the canal-carrying business became a partnership between the North Staffordshire Railway and the Duke of Bridgewater's Trustees, with the Bridgewater Trustees having access to North Staffordshire Railway wharves and other depots. For a number of years, boats owned by the North Staffordshire Railway, Shiptons and the Anderton Carrying Company became part of a combined fleet. The arrangement continued in different forms until 1894, when the North Staffordshire Railway decided not to continue with the expense of being a canal carrier.

Building the Railway Lines

The essential core of railway lines was constructed between 1847 and 1849, when the headquarters had been established at Stoke-on-Trent. The main station was built close to the canal and it was there that new offices were made and it was also there that the canal company offices were transferred from Stone. The railway offices were located in the right wing of the station façade, whilst the canal offices occupied the left wing.

Closures, Alterations and Improvements to the Canal

Uttoxeter Canal

The Uttoxeter Canal was replaced by the North Staffordshire Railway line from Uttoxeter to North Rode Junction. The canal was finally closed on 15 January 1848, which meant that it was in railway ownership for a year.

The route of the railway varied in places from that of the canal, leaving isolated pockets of the waterway. A long section remained near Oakamoor towards the copper works, where the railway line passed through a tunnel. At Uttoxeter the deviation to cross the River Tean was avoided by a railway line to the east. The canal to the aqueduct became disused although the aqueduct structure was retained as a footbridge for a time. The Churnet Valley was a railway that included tunnels and had, as built, two timber viaducts over the River Churnet. The route followed the east bank of Rudyard Reservoir to North Road Junction and on the section between Froghall and Cheddleton required realignment of the Caldon Canal and the Churnet in places. Rocester Canal warehouse is said to have been re-used as a railway goods shed.

Proposed Middlewich Canal Alterations

Benefiting significantly from the salt trade, the town of Middlewich became a popular place for projected canal routes to pass through. W. A. Provis was the surveyor for the Manchester and Birmingham Junction Canal scheme of 1837 and 1838, which promised to link Altrincham with the Ellesmere and Chester Canal. The scheme failed, probably a victim of the momentum gathering behind railway promotion.

The bar toll at Wardle Lock was a reason why new canal schemes sought to avoid the short Wardle Branch. In 1851 Edward Hines surveyed a new line of waterway from the Middlewich Branch of the Shropshire Union Railway and Canal Company at Rushall Bridge through Newton to join the Trent and Mersey Canal south, or above, Kings Lock. This scheme was unsuccessful and the bar tolls remained for goods passing to and from the Shropshire Union Canal. Such tolls were of particular concern to the North Staffordshire ironmasters, whose association would appeal for reductions from time to time. In 1867 the Shropshire Union made an attempt to claim back tolls in the Court of Common Pleas. The failure of this claim led to a new canal proposal, with a bill being presented to Parliament in November 1867. It included a canal from the Middlewich Branch at Clive to join the Trent and Mersey Canal above Rumps Lock at Tetton, and incorporated a large turning basin at Tetton that would be 100 feet wide and 500 feet long. It also included a clause to alter tolls levied by the North Staffordshire Railway.

An unexpected challenge to this proposal for a new canal came from the Conservators of the River Dee and the riparian owners of the mills on the Dee, led by mill owner Mr Hardcastle. It was felt that the making of such a canal would cause an increase in water loss from the Dee. There had been ill feeling in this matter since the 1827 Act for the Ellesmere and Chester Canal, when there had been a promise to return water lost back to the Dee. However, as there was no monitoring of the situation, the mill owners believed that the canal company was not fulfilling its obligations. In order to placate the mill owners, the Shropshire Union withdrew the canal from the bill, although they did press ahead with requesting parliamentary approval to have the tolls altered.

The loss of water remained a matter of concern for the Dee mill owners, despite a canal plan that would avoid two locks and the water loss sustained there. At a hearing held at the House of Lords on 16 May 1868, Mr Gregory, acting for the riparian mill owners, argued that water loss would increase because of the higher number of boats passing through the four locks of the Middlewich Branch once the tolls were eased. Despite the fact that the Lords decided that no case had been proven, their committee chose to reject the bill, in spite of the eloquence of the promoters' counsel Mr Dennison QC, Mr Davidson QC and Mr Salisbury. The key point was that the original Act that sanctioned the making of the canal junction had specified the toll rates. The bar toll was to remain a handicap to trade along the Middlewich Branch until canal and railway rates were altered following Acts of Parliament made in 1888 and 1894.

Canal Maintenance and Improvements

When John Forsyth was engineer to the canal there was a marked transition in its operation, as new railway schemes crossed over it and it became necessary to divert or change the waterway in places. At Colwich, for example, the making of the Trent Valley Railway led to the straightening of two bends in the canal. Later, in 1863, the canal was altered at Etruria. The North Staffordshire Railway Branches Act (Vic 27 and 28, 29 July 1864, c309) sanctioned the diversion of the canal through the high ground to the east. This was made because the North Staffordshire Railway wanted to run passenger trains on the freight-only Hanley Branch, as part of the loop line construction. The existing Hanley Branch railway had been made with a swing bridge over the canal. The Board of Trade inspector was adamant that passenger trains should not run across it, so the canal was diverted, to allow the railway to rise to an embankment and cross the diverted canal by a bridge. The original canal route became two long basins. The southern part served Josiah Wedgwood's pottery, whilst the northern part served the Shelton Bar ironworks and the Etruria furnaces.

The 1864 Act also sanctioned the use of steam tugs at Preston Brook, Barnton and Saltersford Tunnels, and trials were done during that year to see whether it was feasible for a tug to work through the tunnels. James Forbes, the resident engineer, was present at tests conducted through Preston Brook Tunnel in the autumn, and the results led the company to place an order for three such boats from Edward Hayes of Stoney Stratford. All of these started work during January 1865. Preston Brook Tunnel, which was longer than the others, needed more ventilation shafts to be made, to assist with clearing the smoke more effectively. In February 1865, after an engine driver and stoker had been overcome by fumes, Forbes ordered the construction of two new shafts – subsequent maps show that, in the end, there were five in total. While the work was being carried out, under the direction of James Billington, the tugs were allowed to remain in operation. Sadly, one of the North Staffordshire Railway workers, Peter Cawley, became a victim of this oversight. On 23 May 1865, he and another bricklayer were working from an ice boat. Badly affected by the smoke in the tunnel, Cawley fell into the water and was drowned. The verdict at the inquest was accidental death, but as a result of the tragic incident, the working of the steam tugs through Preston Brook Tunnel ceased until the shafts had been completed.

Later tugs included one that was constructed at the Stoke Engine Works of the North Staffordshire Railway, during 1870, under the direction of John William Hartley (1845–1942), while other tugs were made by Richard Smith & Son of Preston in 1877 and 1879. Their successors, the Lytham Ship Building & Engineering Company, are believed to have supplied another in 1905.

The nuisance of smoke continued to be an issue for discussion. The surveyor of the Northwich Rural Sanitary Committee, a Mr Bennett, raised the matter at a meeting held in 1889:

> The surveyor read a letter from the Trent and Mersey Navigation Co, dated 25th October. 'With

Entrance basin to the Anderton Lift.

reference to the conversation I had with you since about the Barnton Tunnels. I have asked our locomotive superintendents to go into the question of using better fuel, and also to see that the drivers of the tugs do not fire up in the tunnels. He has promised to make a visit to Barnton with a view to improve matters.' Continuing, Mr Bennett said that since the receipt of that letter he had noticed that a better class of fuel had been used.

Northwich Guardian, 13 November 1889

Another part of the 1864 Act authorized a widening of the section between Preston Brook and Sandbach. It is unlikely that much work was done at that time, but the provision of ventilation shafts in Preston Brook tunnel might be considered as part of that authority.

One significant improvement to the canal was the completion in 1875 of the Anderton Boat Lift, to the design of Edwin Clark (1814–94), which enabled the movement of boats between the River Weaver and the Trent and Mersey Canal. Whilst the lift was made across the Weaver basin, there was a wrought-iron viaduct from a basin that linked with the Trent and Mersey Canal.

Traffic to and from the Weaver benefited from favourable tolls, unlike those carriers at Wardle and Hall End for the Manchester, Sheffield and Lincolnshire Railway.

Railway Improvements

The North Staffordshire Railway embarked on a gradual period of expansion, which included new branches to the various industries and towns in the region. The core network was completed in 1849, with a number of branches built thereafter. Some branches served as only mineral lines. The land beside the canal at Stoke was also enlarged for sidings and a goods depot. The crossing of the

Fradley Workshops, 1996.

canal at Cockshotts was improved by a widened skew iron bridge.

Extensive goods sidings were constructed on the land between the canal and railway, including a goods shed that was adjacent to the canal, although there is no evidence of any transhipment there, as there was elsewhere on the canal.

The North Staffordshire Railway also became associated with the movement of goods between a select number of interchange basins. There were three depots, at Cockshott (Cockshute), Ettiley Heath and Newcastle-under-Lyme. Later there was also an interchange siding beside the Caldon Canal at Endon.

From time to time, alterations and improvements were made by the North Staffordshire Railway to their maintenance facilities along the canal. At Fradley, where there were carpenters' shops and timber storage for the lock gate, a new workshop block was made in 1865.

Waterways at Newcastle-under-Lyme

Although a canal to the important town of Newcastle-under-Lyme had been part of the original waterways plan devised by James Brindley, that branch was not made by the Trent and Mersey Canal Company. Newcastle-under-Lyme, where the law firm of John and Thomas Sparrow was located, had to rely on three other schemes for communication by water.

The first was a form of tub-boat canal, Sir Nigel Gresley's, which was made from Newcastle-under-Lyme northwards to the Apedale Ironworks and neighbouring iron and coal mines. Authorized by Act of Parliament in 1775, this 3-mile canal was completed in about a year and remained a private waterway, which brought coal to a wharf at the north of the town. It became the property of R. E. Heathcote following the death of Nigel Bowyer Gresley.

The second was the Newcastle-under-Lyme Canal, which united with the Trent and Mersey

Canal and followed a course first south to Trent Vale and then north to the terminus at Pool Dam. The engineer was Josiah Clowes and the route lacked a single lock. There was no communication with Sir Nigel Gresley's Canal, chiefly because of a difference in height. Another factor that contributed to the lack of a junction was the ill-fated Commercial Canal, in which the Gresley family were involved. Robert Whitworth had surveyed a route for a barge canal that would connect the River Dee and the Port of Chester with the Trent and Mersey Canal near Horninglow, the Bond End Canal and the Ashby Canal. Although the Commercial Canal bill did not progress, the construction of the Newcastle-under-Lyme Canal was sanctioned in 1795. A committee was formed to operate the canal, but it held few meetings once construction was completed in 1797.

A third canal, the Newcastle-under-Lyme Junction Canal, was authorized by Parliament in 1798, but failed to live up to its name. This short waterway was built to unite Sir Nigel Gresley's Canal with the Newcastle-under-Lyme Canal, following the failure of the Commercial Canal bill. Alongside its authorization, permission had been granted to build tramways from Sir Nigel Gresley's Canal north to the ironstone mines. There was to be an incline plane to link the Junction Canal at, or near, Stubbs Walk to the Newcastle-under-Lyme Canal. Historical accounts have been steadfast in recording that no incline plane was ever made, even though several attempts were made for that link. However, it is a published fact that some form of tramway link existed, albeit briefly. This information relates to sales particulars that were produced for the Apedale ironworks, which were put up for sale more than once. One agent assured prospective purchasers that a link to the Trent and Mersey was to be made, while another, following the death of Nigel Bowyer Gresley, stated that a 200-yard link was already in place. This could only have been the one from Stubbs Walk. Such a link was not shown on Chapmans Map of 1832, however, indicating that it was there only temporarily.

Part of the Newcastle Junction Canal was purchased in 1851 by the North Staffordshire Railway to make a branch railway to Newcastle-under-Lyme. The North Staffordshire Railway leased the Newcastle-under-Lyme Canal from 1863.

Between 1849 and 1850 a mineral railway was made from Silverdale Ironworks and collieries to the Newcastle canal. It was constructed by Francis Stanier and Ralph Sneyd, the ironmaster partnership at Silverdale, to carry coal and iron to Pool Dam about half a mile from the terminus of the Newcastle-under-Lyme Canal. In 1853 the Newcastle-under-Lyme Canal Company had tried to fight off railway competition by building the Newcastle-under-Lyme Canal Extension Railway from their basin to Pool Dam and Sneyd's line. This short line of half a mile was said at first to be horse-drawn, although Silverdale did have a couple of stream locomotives for the standard-gauge railway and these locomotives also seem to have worked to the canal wharf later. In 1859 Ralph Sneyd was authorized to operate his line as a public railway and obtained the permission of the Newcastle-under-Lyme Canal to use their Extension Railway – at the rate of 2d per ton. This line created a railway and canal interchange wharf at the Pool Dam terminus of the canal.

The North Staffordshire Railway took over the Newcastle under-Lyme and Silverdale Railway from 1860, and gained control of the Canal Extension Railway with the lease of the canal in 1863. Pool Dam canal wharf was used by Silverdale Ironworks locomotives for railway and canal interchange.

Foxley Canal

The private Foxley Canal was made from the Caldon Canal near Milton to serve an ironworks and furnace complex at Ford Green, worked by Robert Heath. This branch had a towpath and included a lock, and was constructed at about the same time as the ironworks (in the 1860s). A short basin and wharf had existed at Milton previously. With the closure of the ironworks in September 1928 (including the steelworks built in 1924), the branch was retained to serve an interchange wharf for the private railway, which served Norton Colliery.

Closure of the Bond End Canal

The River Trent was reached by the Bond End Canal after passing through locks at Shobnall and Bond End and continued to be used by fly boats and other craft until the 1860s. The canal route was used to build the Midland Railway Shobnall and Bond End Branches (1873–1875), with the work authorized by an Act of Parliament in 1874. Some work was done prior to the passing of the act, including the filling in of the canal at Shobnall. The lock and the link with the Trent and Mersey Canal were retained as an interchange wharf with the Midland Railway branch, as well as the subsequent railway links built as the London and North Western Railway Dallows Lane Branch.

Canal Improvements in Cheshire

Edward B. Smith, engineer for the North Staffordshire Railway, put forward plans for improvements to the canal in 1890. Larger locks were proposed and the canal would be deepened to a uniform depth of 6 feet. A shaft was to be made in Harecastle Tunnel and the waterway width increased to 14 feet, to allow barges to reach the Potteries. An application to abandon the Lane End Plateway was also made. The scheme had been devised following the proposal for a Birmingham and Liverpool Ship Canal.

New locks at Church Lawton were intended to replace Kents, Townfield, Churchfield, Halls and Lawton Locks. At Astbury a lock would be made instead of Thurlwood No 1 and No 2 locks, and Hassall Green, Ellisons, Garde, Hibbards, Malkins Top and Bottom Lock, Bidners and Wheelock Locks would also be replaced. At Middlewich the 'New Locks' (which were three in number) and Big Lock would be replaced, too. The total number of locks would be reduced by fourteen, allowing for a shorter passage between Kidsgrove and Runcorn. Whilst the promise of barges of 60 or 70 tons passing through to the Potteries generated business interest, there were those at the local Chamber of Commerce who believed that this scheme should offer even more. The potteries and other business on the Caldon Canal needed transhipment at Etruria, should this improvement be made. There were those who wanted even more extensive improvement, to reach other parts of the canal and to accommodate boats of a larger capacity of up to 100 tons.

Some at the Chamber of Commerce preferred the ship canal option, a scheme that was essentially the vision of one man, based on his theories for water supply. Actively promoted by Beriah Shepherd, the secretary and a mining engineer, the Birmingham and Liverpool Ship Canal was one of a group of schemes that were planned to serve West Midlands industry. This waterway was to be 64 miles in length and would pass through Oldbury, Wolverhampton, Stafford, Stone, Trentham, Burslem, Tunstall, Kidsgrove, Wheelock and Winsford, where it would join the Weaver Navigation. It would be 72 feet wide at the top, 52 feet wide at the bottom and 11 feet deep, and it would be lined with concrete. Unlike other proposals, such as the improvement of the River Trent, it was a scheme that was driven forward with much publicity, but, with a lack of serious investment or the attention of a credible engineer, it enjoyed little progress.

The widening scheme proposed by the North Staffordshire Railway, authorized by Act of Parliament in 1891, involved twenty-one new barge locks replacing the existing thirty-five to Preston Brook and the removal of the horse towing path in the Telford Tunnel. However, it failed to be implemented, although work did proceed on the aqueduct over the Dane at Croxton, and the more modest task of widening just a part of the canal was adopted. Powers granted in 1891 led to the improvement between Anderton and Middlewich between 1891 and 1893, a distance of about 11 miles of waterway. The canal was widened and deepened to permit the passage of larger barges, of 40 to 60 tons. Middlewich Lock (75) was widened to 16 feet 6 inches and the section beyond the area known as Middlewich Pool was widened from 16 feet to 50 feet, with the provision of a concrete wall separating the canal from the river. At Middlewich Pool steam cranes were to be erected to serve the needs of the Salt Union and Cheshire Alkali Company, but there is little proof that these cranes were actually constructed.

Middlewich Big Lock.

Bridge 183, Broken Cross.

Wincham Brook Aqueduct, 2010.

A solid masonry wall had been built alongside the towpath to a depth of 4 feet 6 inches. By May 1893, 4 miles had been done and another 2 miles remained to be done. It was constructed from stone quarried at the Company quarries, at Consall, and also the Runcorn and Helsby Sandstone Quarry Company.

A steam dredger of the Priestman type, capable of raising 800 tons per week, and twelve spoon boats, worked by manual labour and capable of raising 80 tons a week, were used to widen and deepen the canal. On the length of canal near Marbury, a light railway was laid and narrow-gauge tip wagons were used to transport spoil. The contractors employed lived on gang boats, specially fitted for their use. Between 80,000 and 100,000 tons of spoil and mud were removed over a fifteen-month period. Eighteen bridges were reconstructed and widened. The former brick arch was removed and replaced in each case by an iron girder – Pearson & Knowles Iron Company of Warrington supplied wrought-iron girders and Hamer & Son of Northwich provided cast-iron girders. The whole section was widened to the design of Edward Smith, whilst the brickwork for the bridges and the masonry walling was done by F. Barke of Stoke. W Scott, assistant to Edward Smith, took charge of this project with H. A. Smith as clerk of works.

In addition to Croxton, other culverts and aqueducts were widened, or reconstructed, and faced with new bricks.

Subsidence at Marbury

During the summer of 1907, North Staffordshire Canal workers had been engaged in building a retaining wall along the canal section at Marbury. On Sunday 21 July 1907 the workings of Marston Hall Rock Salt Mine collapsed, resulting in the canal water flowing into the mine and draining the canal at a broken culvert. This culvert conveyed Marbury Brook under the canal and the breach came to be 76 feet by 60 feet at the canal surface and 30 feet deep.

The stop gates at Marbury and Marston Bridges had only partly stemmed the flow of water and makeshift dams had to be made to seal off the canal. Canal workmen set about repairing the damage, under the supervision of district inspector William Jones. Even though they worked by day and night (by torchlight), the task of filling the breach went on to occupy weeks rather than days. Clay for the repair was brought by boat from Anderton up to the Marbury dam, and each load had to be barrowed to the site.

The Royal Commission on Canals

During 1906, a Royal Commission was appointed to inquire into and report on the canals and on inland navigations of the United Kingdom. Other commissions followed until 1911, but the First World War put paid to any immediate improvements, until a time when transport itself had changed. The evidence given to the commission by William Douglas Phillipps helps to understand the times when the Trent and Mersey Canal was part of the North Staffordshire Railway.

There were four reports conducted between 1906 and 1911 into the British waterway system, which investigated the history, development and disadvantages of the existing network and looked at means of improvement. The investigation of 1908 produced the most significant recommendations, published in a report in 1909. These included the establishment of a new waterways board and waterways financed by the government. Such waterways would carry vessels 'from 100 tons up to 750 tons burthen'. For the route between Birmingham, Wolverhampton and the Mersey, 100-ton craft were the preferred choice and incline planes of the type employed at Foxton provided for level change instead of locks.

Phillipps observed that £311,400 had been spent carrying out various improvements since 1846. During the previous 20 years (1886–1906), over 1,100,000 cubic yards of earth had been dredged up, and the width and depth of the canal between the Potteries and Runcorn had been increased so that barges could carry 28 tons between those two points.

There had been a good trade from the iron-making districts in the Potteries to Hull for export to Germany and elsewhere on the Continent, but competition from the Midland Railway had led to that trade practically dying out. Improvements by the Trent Navigation Company to the River Trent had met with 'very indifferent success', with seemingly little opportunity to raise income. The Trent Navigation Company was still pressing on with improvement schemes and the North Staffordshire Railway intended to get two directors on to the Trent Navigation Board. Yet Phillipps admitted that there was a desire to wind up the Trent Navigation Company and replace it with an improved navigation between the Potteries and Hull. It was the object of the North Staffordshire Railway to improve through traffic via a joint operation.

The Royal Commission decided that the best means of improvement for the Trent and Mersey route was a new route that would be fit to take barges that had a 100-ton capacity.

Harecastle Tunnel Tugs

A steam tug was considered in 1890, but the actual provision of such a craft came later, during the time when Harry Curbishley was engineer. The use of tugs was enabled by the novel design of a battery-powered version.

Traffic congestion at Harecastle Tunnel had been discussed by the North Staffordshire Chamber of Commerce at a meeting in 1911, but by February 1913 the issue was so serious that a special meeting had to be called to discuss it. The custom had been to work traffic going north through one tunnel and traffic going south through the other. Under the original Act of Parliament, passed in 1766, some 40 yards of minerals were to be left to either side to preserve the original tunnel. Whilst the close minerals did remain unworked, the pull of other workings had nonetheless affected the structure of the tunnel. The Brindley Tunnel had been closed for about fifteen months some seven years previously and about 200 yards had been rebuilt. All traffic passed through the Telford 'horse tunnel', but that one, too, had deteriorated and required repairs. Further complications were caused by the side tunnels that brought coal to loading wharves in the main tunnels.

At this time there was a considerable trade on the canals in potter's material that was brought by narrow boat originating at Ellesmere Port, Weston Point and Runcorn. The three routes comprised the following:

1. The Shropshire Union Railway and Canal Co. line from Ellesmere Port and the Middlewich Branch to join the Trent and Mersey Canal at Middlewich.
2. The Weaver Navigation line from Weston Point through to the Anderton Lift, where boats were transferred between the Weaver and the Trent and Mersey Canal.
3. The Bridgewater Canal line from Runcorn Docks to Preston Brook and from there to Stoke along the Trent and Mersey Canal.

In 1911 213,000 tons of potter's material was brought by canal to the Potteries, compared with 37,000 tons transported by rail. Siding accommodation was at the time considered to be insufficient for any increase in rail traffic. During 1911 Harry Curbishley had proposed a scheme for a diversion canal that would involve only a short tunnel. The 1913 joint reports were prepared by J. A. Saner, who was engineer to the Weaver Navigation; Curbishley looked at canal improvements, whilst G. R. Jebb, engineer to the Birmingham Canal Navigations, was asked to report on the mining subsidence aspect.

Canal improvement proposals comprised two schemes, with the aim to 'enable boats of 100 tons burthen to ply to the Potteries'. The first, as suggested by Curbishley, was to deepen the Trent and Mersey Canal to 7 feet and permit boats between 70 tons and 100 tons to travel to Northwich and the River Weaver. The second scheme, as suggested by Saner, comprised the building of a new and larger waterway from the Potteries through Harecastle, Alsager and Crewe. This second scheme was to carry the waterway westward of Harecastle Crag and would avoid the necessity of enlarging Harecastle Tunnel. The Crewe Construction Syndicate had already prepared a scheme to construct a canal from Crewe to the Rookery, but it was willing to abandon this scheme if a canal was made from Winsford to Crewe.

The concept of diverting the canal at Harecastle had been proposed by the prominent civil engineer Sir John Wolfe-Barry (1836–1918) in a report to the Royal Commission. It was to be 2 miles 5 chains long, extending from Chatterley to Harecastle, and would be made to the west of the existing tunnels and in open cutting, except for a short length of tunnel of 370 yards. It was part of a larger scheme under which the existing forty-three locks required between Weston Point and Stoke would be reduced to twelve, at a cost of roughly £1,143,000. J. A Saner continued to promote the tunnel diversion and revised lock scheme through to 1914, which also included a new canal section through the flashes at Winsford across to Middlewich.

Despite these various proposals, nothing was done to improve the waterways at Harecastle and the authorities also failed to follow up on their intention to close the canal for repair and enlargement. With the onset of the First World War, the canals and railways came under government control. Their response to the shortcomings, it appears, was to implement improved railway links to the Potteries. Labour troubles at Runcorn also contributed to the decline in the quantity of goods being shipped by waterway to the Potteries. In 1913 some 81 per cent of traffic from Runcorn to Stoke had come by water; by 1920 this figure had been reduced to 26 per cent.

A 1904 Act of Parliament had granted powers to the North Staffordshire Railway Company to use tugs worked by electricity or mechanical power other than steam, but such a system was not brought in until 1914. The *Staffordshire Advertiser* mentions that the tugs were operating from August 1914.

Subsidence in the old Brindley Tunnel had eventually forced the hand of the North Staffordshire Railway to use a tug in the Telford Tunnel, which possessed a horse towing path. The decision to use a combination of electric traction and cable haulage had been determined by the fact that the company did not want to use overhead wires in the tunnel, and, whilst this opinion was subsequently changed,

An electric tug at Kidsgrove.

the design and installation of cable haulage went ahead during December 1913.

A motor tug for the task was to be capable of pulling a train of up to 17 barges through the Telford Tunnel. Boats waiting to pass through were to be marshalled at either end. The steel haulage barge was built by Mr Bullivant of Millwall. A fixed steel cable was laid on the bed of the canal and two drums activated by 15hp electric haulage motors were fitted to the haulage barge. With one drum winding the cable in from one end, whilst the other paid it out at the other, the tug pulled the train of barges along the tunnel. In each case the haulage cable entered and left the haulage barge at the boat bottom.

To avoid any problems with the supply of electricity, it was decided to use accumulators carried in a boat immediately behind the haulage barge. Two accumulator boats would be provided, each containing 115 cells capable of discharging 150 amps for about 7 hours. The boats would be 72 feet long by 7 feet and 4 feet and the accumulators in each would weigh about 18 tons. The power house for charging the accumulators was located on the land between the two tunnels at the Chatterley end, along with buildings for storing coal. The plant there comprised two sets of Campbell producers and two 77hp Campbell gas engines and two 45kW dynamos from the GEC at Witton. The power house at the Tunstall end of the tunnel sat on the island between the old and new lines of the canal.

The work was directed by Mr A. F. Rock, chief electrical engineer to the North Staffordshire Railway, assisted by Mr H. A. Lewis and H. Leason. Generally, the scheme was deemed to be successful, although W. H. Boddington of the Anderton Carrying Co. did complain that considerable delay was experienced at either end of the tunnel where the boats were marshalled. He requested that the canal might be straightened to enable craft to be drawn straight out and the haulage boat to return immediately. The North Staffordshire Railway considered this option, but difficulty in obtaining the land at a cost-effective price meant that it was not pursued.

The accumulator boats were discarded in 1931 and replaced by two tugs that collected power from an overhead cable. This system was operated until about 1950, when the tugs were laid up following declining traffic.

The generating house at Tunstall.

The electric haulage, it would appear, was a compromise using the existing Telford Tunnel for moving traffic as quickly as was practical. Yet with a closed Brindley Tunnel (some sources state 1914, others 1918), it was, perhaps, the best solution in order to maintain traffic through the remaining tunnel. Following the takeover at grouping of the North Staffordshire Railway by the LMS, any assistance for canal improvement became less likely.

Further Developments on the Canal

Duplication of Locks at Kidsgrove

Despite the decision not to proceed with the enlargement of the locks on the Cheshire side of the canal, there were four – Yew Tree, Red Bull, Pool and Hardings Wood – that had not been duplicated. The North Staffordshire Railway decided that these should be done under the powers of the 1891 act, although the work was not all carried out at the same time. The top lock had been duplicated by the time of the second Ordnance Survey (1896), while the other three double locks are shown on the third Ordnance Survey, so this duplication was carried out at the end of the nineteenth century.

Pool Lock was originally named Furnace Pool Lock, but its name was subsequently shortened, and the aqueduct that crossed near the tail of the lock became known as Pool Lock Aqueduct. More recently, the Canal and River Trust have chosen to rename Pool Lock as Limekiln Lock and Hardings Wood as Plants Lock.

Pool locks, Kidsgrove.

Increasing the Capacity of Rudyard Reservoir

The 1904 Act of Parliament that authorized electric traction through Harecastle Tunnel also sanctioned the raising of the dam walls at Rudyard Reservoir, or Rudyard Lake. Whilst the railways had had a negative impact on the carrying operations on canals in recent years, there was still a demand for water, which could be scarce in summer months. The company canal engineer Edward Blakeway Smith was instructed by the directors to increase the capacity of the reservoir. Work began in August 1904, under the supervision of assistant engineer Harry Curbishley, and with as many as 150 men employed. As originally built and later improved to the specification of John Rennie, the reservoir was 2¼ miles in length and three-quarters of a mile wide at its widest part. It had been estimated to hold 770 million gallons of water; after the work, this figure was believed to have increased to about 850 million gallons.

Under the parliamentary powers obtained in 1904, the North Staffordshire Railway were able to proceed with raising the level of the reservoir by 2 feet. To achieve this, a concrete wall was put across the weir at that height. At the southern end a very substantial stone and rubble wall was erected to a height of between 4 and 6 feet. This held the walls up at that end and a puddle gutter was also built, between 6 and 7 feet in depth and between 4 and 5 feet in width, the whole length of the existing dam. The stone wall was made with coping stones set in cement. On the western side of the reservoir a dry rubble wall was built to prevent the water damaging the property of adjoining landowners. At the northern end another wall was built to a depth of between 4 to 5 feet, and earth embankments were raised for the purpose of protecting the land.

As a large amount of water came along the feeder from the Dane, that feeder had been deepened, widened and embanked, and strengthened along the full length to Wincle Weir, a distance of 3½ miles. The paddles of the Dane Feeder had been renewed and re-laid. Full advantage was to be taken of the water that flowed over the weir at Wincle. As the principal source of water for the canals in Staffordshire, where the supply also comprised Knypersley and Stanley Reservoirs, the enlargement at Rudyard was vitally important.

There was also an intention to develop Rudyard Lake as a leisure resort, although a decision to purchase motor boats in the summer of 1905 was deferred. Rowing boats could still be hired, however, and the boat houses had been elevated to allow for the rise in the water. With the purchase of the Cliff Park Estate, walks were established from Cliff Park Cottages through Cliff Park and Barnes Lee Estates. A new station named Rudyard Lake was also opened on the Churnet Valley Railway, to give access to the estate.

Planet Lock, Hanley (1909)

Mining subsidence had caused such serious damage to the Caldon Canal at Hanley, that the Hanley Corporation had taken legal proceedings against the North Staffordshire Railway Company. Subsidence had also resulted in a need to raise the bridges at Cauldon Street, Russell Street and Bedford Street. An ingenious solution to the problem was devised by engineer Harry Curbishley, with a plan to build a new lock 30 yards east of Cauldon Place, Hanley. This lock was constructed to one side of the waterway, to allow normal traffic to pass by while the work proceeded. It was perhaps unique in the history of canal navigation in that it allowed the canal to be reduced in stages between it and the double lock at Bedford Street, in steps of 1 foot 6 inches to a depth of 6 feet, if necessary. The lock was 77 feet long and 10 feet deep and 8 feet 3 inches wide and was constructed on concrete foundations with common bricks, with a facing of best blue bricks. An overflow weir supplied the canal below.

The tubes for filling the lock were also embedded in concrete and at the head of the lock a combined weir and a sluice with an earthenware pipe track 2 feet 9 inches in diameter was installed. Adjacent to the lock a berth or lay-by for two boats was constructed, in keeping with the lock. The contractor for the brickwork and masonry was Thomas Godwin of Hanley. The lock gates and sills, which

Planet Lock, 2020.

were of English oak, had been made by canal company workmen in the charge of an inspector named Shaw. A coffer dam assisted with the work when stoppage was needed. The whole task was supervised by company engineer Harry Curbishley, according to his own plans and specifications.

A formal opening ceremony was arranged, with the *Planet*, one of the latest Anderton Carrying Company boats, made to carry 29 tons, being placed in the lock. Mr O. W. Boddington and Mr Smith represented the Anderton Company, whilst Mr Tonman Moseley, chairman of North Staffordshire Railway Company, general manager W. D. Phillipps, engineer G. J. Crosbie Dawson and Harry Curbishley were among others who attended.

Endon Railway Interchange Basin

The lengthy journey for boats along the Caldon Canal to collect limestone delivered by tramway from the Caldon Quarries was effectively rendered impossible following a landslip near the terminus in 1920. Limestone traffic to that point then ceased. In 1904 the North Staffordshire Railway had built a railway to Waterhouses to serve new limestone quarries east of their existing Caldon Quarries. A new interchange basin 200 yards long was made at Endon, beside that branch railway, during 1917, for the interchange of limestone traffic.

A metal tip for railway wagons, constructed at Stoke works to the design of Thomas Francis Coleman (1885–1958) and erected at Endon basin in 1917, allowed limestone to be dropped into the boats. A qualified mechanical engineer, Tom Coleman had come up with an innovative design, which included a mechanism in the structure by which wagons could be tipped to the side and the limestone would fall down a shoot into the canal boat below. Coleman later became a chief draughtsman for the London, Midland and Scottish Railway and worked on significant locomotive design work at Horwich and Crewe works.

Government Control and Railway Grouping

With the outbreak of the First World War, railways came under government control, but independent canals were not included. For canals owned by railway companies, the arrangements were more complex although there was some control under the Army Council Instructions from 1916. Full government control for all inland waterways came in on 1 March 1917, with the creation of the Canal Control Committee and the establishment of three regions. The Trent and Mersey Canal was designated as part of the Midland Committee, which continued for about two years after the ending of hostilities.

The North Staffordshire Railway had survived many merger proposals, which not only would have ended its separate existence but also possibly threatened the existence of the canal. When the period of government control ended, proposals for change in the British railways system led to a different type of merger. Railway companies would be combined under the Railways Act of August 1921 through a process that occupied a period of fifteen months to accomplish.

From 1 January 1923 a new age dawned, as the London, Midland and Scottish Railway absorbed the North Staffordshire Railway, and also acquired a number of canals in the process. The Trent and Mersey Canal now had a common ownership with the Shropshire Union, which owned the junction at Middlewich and had at first charged suitable tolls for traffic to pass. Private canal ownership was retained at Great Hayward for the Staffordshire and Worcester Canal, at Preston Brook for the Bridgewater Canal, then owned by the Manchester Ship Canal, and also for the River Trent at Shardlow, which was the responsibility of the Trent Navigation Company. At Hall Green the junction with the Macclesfield was a junction with a canal now owned by the London and North Eastern Railway, who also owned the Ashton and Peak Forest Canals, having acquired them from the Great Central Railway on grouping.

For the Trent and Mersey Canal this was another period of challenge, as the London, Midland and Scottish decreased investment in the canal network. Repair and maintenance facilities were gradually adversely affected.

In 1927, heavy rainfall led Stanley Reservoir to over-top, causing scour damage to part of the dam and a consequent lowering of the water levels in the reservoirs owned by the London, Midland and Scottish. There was an inevitable effect on water supply, which was always vulnerable. In July 1934 abnormally low rainfall in the feeding grounds of the canal led to a prolonged water shortage and low water levels in the canal. A small colony of boats had to remain tied to the bank at Harecastle Tunnel, waiting for a flow that would enable them to resume their journey or start on a new one. The company's decision to close part of the canal was announced in the Staffordshire Sentinel on 7 July 1934:

TRENT AND MERSEY NAVIGATION

The LMS RAILWAY COMPANY HEREBY GIVES NOTICE that owing to the SHORTAGE OF WATER through continued drought, they are UNABLE TO MAINTAIN THE SUPPLY OF WATER and therefore on and from MIDNIGHT TUESDAY 10th JULY 1934, the TRENT AND MERSEY CANAL and its BRANCHES WILL BE CLOSED FOR NAVIGATION between the following points :-

MIDDLEWICH (Kings Lock) and FRADLEY JUNCTION including Branches until further notice
For the present the waterway will remain open for navigation in the two separate sections viz, between Preston Brook and Middlewich (Kings Lock) in the North and between Derwentmouth and Fradley Junction in the South
W. Bingham
District Goods and Passenger Manager, LMS Railway Stoke-on-Trent

The closure of the central section of the canal so that water might be reserved for the other two sections had a dramatic effect on trade, forcing traders' boats to use the Shropshire Union route for transport between the Midlands and the North West. This

Bagnall dam and spillway in 2005. DAVID HENTHORN BROWN

COMPANY BOATYARDS AND MAINTENANCE BOATS

Whilst the principal boatyard was at Stone, there were also depots at Middlewich, Lawton and Fradley. Until 1894 the boats comprised the company carrying fleet and craft for maintenance. The Canal Company, North Staffordshire Railway and London, Midland and Scottish all had requirements for maintenance craft and ice boats of wood and iron and brought in new craft as needed. The original independent company also had an inspection boat that toured the network, and the North Staffordshire Railway had a steam-powered inspection launch named *Dolly Varden*. In London, Midland and Scottish times there was a specification for a motorized tug and ice breaker, which was built with a diesel engine by Yarwoods, who made a wooden-hulled tug named *Roamer* in 1938. There were also mud boats, a bricklayer's boat and timber trading boats in the fleet at that time.

WORK ON THE CANAL

John Hollinshead, a Middlewich boatman, recalled the difficulties of his working life in an interview for the *Staffordshire Sentinel* published on 6 September 1934. Although he had never experienced a shortness of water in his fifty years on the canal, there had been times when he had been frozen in for short spells. Fog was also an issue. He was one of the few boatmen who could remember the hardship of 'legging' through the old Harecastle Tunnel:

> *It was really hard work, lying with our backs on the load and our feet on the roof and pushing the boat through…To get through the tunnel in two hours was exceptionally good. Sometimes we have been five or six hours in getting from the locks to the other side of the tunnel. Some of the younger men do not know they are born now the tug takes them through in 40 minutes…There were always men waiting at both ends of the tunnel who never did anything else but helped to leg the boats, all they wanted was bite of food and a bob.*

John Hollinshead recalled a time when both the Brindley and the Telford tunnels were in use. Even then, when the towing path enabled the horses to continue their hauling and it was no longer necessary to leg everything, it was not always plain sailing. Some of the horses resolutely refused to enter the tunnel, whilst others whilst inside became panicky: 'Often I have known horses slip or kick themselves into the water, and as it was nearly impossible to get them out in the tunnel, they had to be secured and dragged along to one end or the other before they could be pulled out.' He normally worked fourteen hours a day!

trade had already been eroded through increased competition. It was increasingly clear that canal haulage had its limitations, and that the alternatives that were being developed might be preferable.

After the closure in July 1934, normal traffic did not recommence until mid-October. Levels in the reservoirs had increased, but there was still a restriction on what could be carried. A normal load of 25 tons on the main waterway was limited to 20 tons, whilst on the Caldon Canal the same load was limited further to 15 tons. The pairing of boats

The Newcastle-under-Lyme Canal, Stoke-on-Trent.

through the Cheshire locks was also recommended. Prosecution of boatmen who were deemed to be wasting water had occurred before the stoppage and continued afterwards – lock-keepers tended to be vigilant in this regard. Some used the excuse that they were trying to get to Kidsgrove for the tug. On each occasion, a fine of £1 was levied, with 10 shillings costs.

Whilst water supply was a perennial issue, there was also the continued threat of floods. The London, Midland and Scottish did make some alterations to the canal reservoirs in an attempt to prevent this. During 1927 the work included improvements at the Dane Feeder. The top stone blocks at Knypersley New Reservoir spill weir were replaced with concrete in 1932 and the road across the dam was raised in 1935, with a new bridge over the spill weir. During 1936, the company built a new face to the downstream side of Stanley (Bagnall) Reservoir Dam with concrete blocks and concrete wing walls.

Closure of the Newcastle-under-Lyme Canal

Much of the traffic to the terminus of the Newcastle-under-Lyme Canal had ceased by 1910. The section from Pool Dam to Trent Vale was abandoned by the North Staffordshire Railway in 1921, although clauses in earlier bills before Parliament had pressed for partial closure of this waterway. There was still trade to Trent Vale Tileries and there were also working potteries remaining in this section.

The London, Midland and Scottish applied for the transfer of another part of the Newcastle-under-Lyme canal from Trent Vale to Church Street, Stoke-on-Trent, in the 1934–1935 session of Parliament, which effectively closed that canal to navigation to the terminus at Pool Dam. Only the short part of the canal remained open from the junction, which was more a long basin than a canal.

CHAPTER 6

Facets of Trade

The Canal and British Trade

When the plans for the Trent and Mersey Canal were first being formulated, those who were promoting it were keen to emphasize the potential benefit to British trade. In making their case to parliament and the public, they were able to give assurance that there would be significant savings in transport costs. The new waterway would enable landowners, manufacturers and merchants to convey many articles to markets where previously the expense of land carriage would have been prohibitive. It would also bring into use many natural resources, such as coals, stone of various kinds, timber, iron ore, alabaster, and so on, which were found in unfavourable situations and could not have been exploited otherwise. The proposers of the canal mentioned three matters that they considered to be important:

> The natural production of the counties that lie near the canal.
> Cultivated commodities and manufactures.
> Imported raw materials, and general commerce.

The planning for the building of the Trent and Mersey Canal came at a time when Britain's domestic industry was developing through mechanization. The short peace following the Seven Years War (1756–1763), in which England and Prussia had fought side by side against the rest of Europe, and in particular France, gave the country an opportunity to focus on increasing its national trade. With the completion of the canal, freight rates were immediately reduced to a fraction of what they had been. Many of the transport limitations that had been faced by the potters, in particular, were overcome.

The canal systems would continue to hold sway until the establishment of the public railway network. With the creation of the Railway Clearing House in 1842, the accountancy of goods between separate railway companies enhanced freight transport across an expanding railway system. There were some bitter fights and controversies between the interests of the canal, turnpike and coaching companies and the railway promoters, but progress could not be halted. Ultimately, the rail system would supersede water transportation. The variations in canal tolls had always been a burden on canal conveyance and, although toll reductions on canals such as the Trent and Mersey did aid carriers, it did not prevent the decline in traffic.

Whilst canal trade was seriously affected by competition from the railways, there were some waterways where traffic using boats remained a key element. This was the case with the potteries, the industry that had, in part, led to the canal being made and would help to keep it open in later years with its traffic.

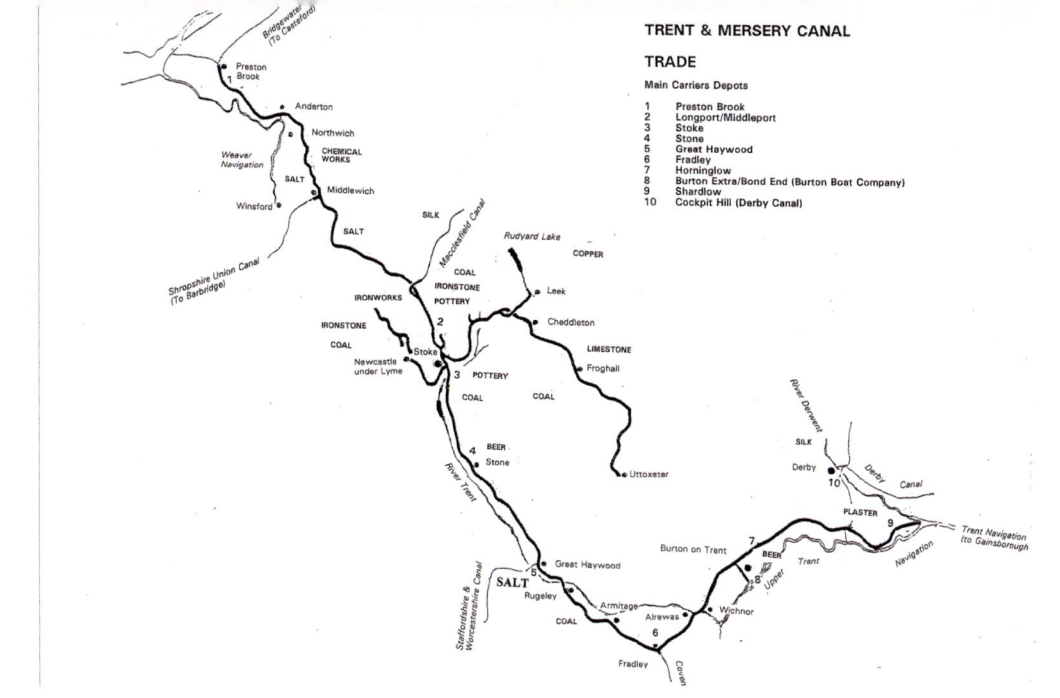

ABOVE: *Trent & Mersey trade.*

BELOW: *Trade map of 1765.*

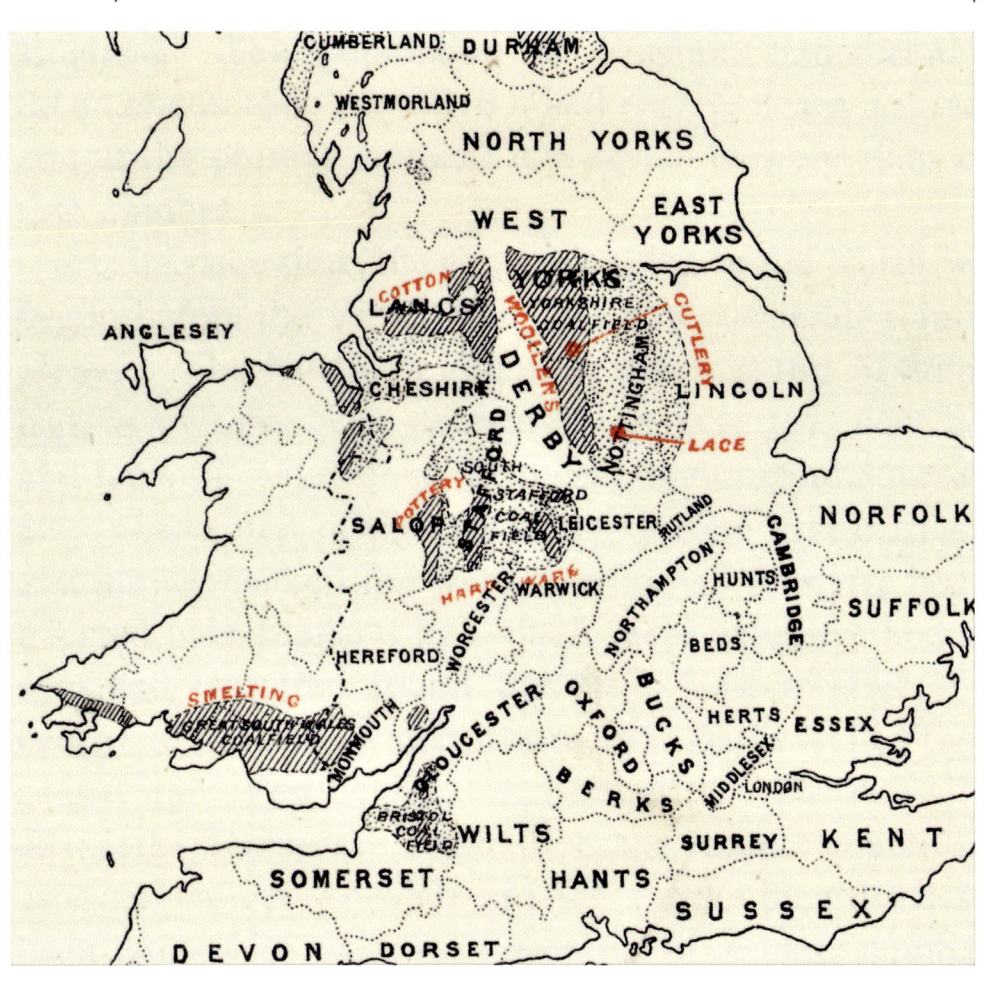

Pottery

Between Lawton and Newcastle lay Burslem, the chief manufactory for flint ware, a delicate white earthenware that had become popular before the making of the canal. It was a rival for imported porcelain and was of such a high quality that the export market in 1765 amounted to £100,000. The principal potters encouraged the making of turnpike roads, so that their wares could be more conveniently transported. The first potteries were established along a line from Hanley to Longton, with Burslem having a high concentration of works in this new pottery district.

A new navigation was viewed as an opportunity not only for the potteries to ship their wares to the European markets, but also for coal that was to be found in abundance within 2 miles of Burslem to be transported across the nation. These coals were deemed to be 'equally good with those which the metropolis is generally supplied with' and there was a belief that there was 'hardly any circumstance that contributes more to the flourishing state of a manufacturing country, than plenty and cheapness of fuel'.

The ready supply of coal and of clay for making pots led to the rapid establishment of the earthenware and stoneware trades in this region. Among other companies that benefited from the improved transport links were carriers of various complementary materials – flints used for grinding up the pottery mix in local mills, animal bones for crushing, and the components for the pottery glazes. Later, from 1740, white china clay became available, shipped by way of the River Teign and relying on coastal, river and road transport to reach Burslem.

Burslem was home to several generations of the Wedgwood family. The pioneer potter Josiah was born at a house next to the Churchyard Pottery in the town in July 1730, the youngest child of Thomas and Mary Wedgwood. He grew up to follow the family trade, becoming associated with several local potteries and entering into a number of partnerships in the pottery trade over the years.

This was a time of innovation and experimentation in the industry. Production had been limited to certain types of earthenware and trials with new glazes and colours would give a firm a temporary advantage in the market. Traditionally, there were two essential types of pottery: items for everyday use and the artistic or ornamental pieces, which commanded a higher price and were sought after by those who had the funds for purchase.

Once the canal had been made, there was a strong incentive to build new potteries alongside the waterway. Josiah Wedgwood was ahead of the game. He had been in regular contact with James Brindley, ensuring that he was privy to the plans showing the exact route of the canal as it would cut through the Potteries. In July 1766 Wedgwood completed his purchase of the Ridge House Estate – right on the projected line of the canal – which would become the site for his new factory, Etruria.

The new factory was designed by Joseph Pickford, the architect from Derby, in consultation with Wedgwood and his partner Thomas Bentley. The site had been chosen for its location directly alongside the Trent and Mersey Canal, but Wedgwood also wanted the building to have architectural merit. The front of the works faced the canal. It was a symmetrical building, with a three-storey central range surmounted by a cupola containing a bell, and two lower wings on either side. There was a roundhouse at each end of the main façade. The factory behind the front ranges was divided into the Useful and Ornamental Works, each laid out around its own square.

Towering over the front range of the building was a windmill, designed by Erasmus Darwin, for grinding colours. Between 1782 and 1784, this was superseded by a Boulton & Watt steam engine that had been installed for the purpose of driving the clay, flint and colour mills. According to Boulton & Watt records, the engine supplied to the order of January 1793 was of the 'Sun & Planet' type (10hp). In 1807 Boulton & Watt also provided boilers and heating apparatus for a drying house.

Etruria opened in 1769, but construction on the site continued for many years afterwards. Once the locks and the summit level to Harecastle Tunnel had been finished, the canal was capable of serv-

Enoch Wood's pottery at Burslem.

Royal Staffordshire Pottery, Burslem, 1980.

Pottery ovens at Burslem.

The Kilns, where the Ware is fired.

Pottery kilns.

ing the pottery. At about the same time, Wedgwood had built up sufficient finances to construct a new family home, Etruria Hall, which was also designed by Pickford and was built within view of the factory.

Despite his close relationship with James Brindley, Josiah Wedgwood's wishes regarding the canal were not always automatically granted. In a letter to Thomas Bentley in 1767, he recalled a contretemps with Hugh Henshall, the clerk of works for the canal committee. Brindley had given instructions that the canal was to go 'the nearest, & best way', which meant that it would follow a straight-line route through Wedgwood's Etruria estate, despite his protestations: 'I could not prevail on the inflexible vandal to give me one line of grace.' It would seem, however, that Wedgwood got his way in the end, as a number of late eighteenth-century maps show a distinct curve to the canal just west of the factory, as well as an island arboretum in a direct line of vision between the factory and Etruria Hall.

Although Wedgwood's pottery was the first to be built along the side of the new canal, the waterway did go near other existing establishments as it passed through Stoke. Once the canal had reached Longport, three new potteries were built in, or shortly after, the year 1773. The first Longport Pottery was established by John Brindley, brother of the late James Brindley. Edward Bourne had a second pottery built and a third was erected for Robert Williamson, who went on to marry Anne Brindley, the widow of James Brindley.

John Brindley's pottery was taken over in 1793 by John Davenport. For a time, litharge and white lead for potters' use were made there, followed by glass-making from 1801. Subsequently, Williamson's pottery was purchased by Henry Davenport and incorporated in the Davenport Pottery.

Originally, the Davenport Works, like all others, produced earthenware, but later they also made china. The production of china, or porcelain, was an established trade in China and Japan and later in parts of Europe. It relied on a supply of kaolin, china stone and alabaster, so it was only feasible for potteries that were located relatively near to a port. Factories at Bristol, Chelsea and Bow all had the benefit of being near a shipping route. Derby and Worcester made a bone china that included bone dust in the pottery mix and both relied heavily on river transport – for Derby, it was the Trent and Derwent, and for Worcester it was the River Severn. White clay was also carried from Bridgnorth to Burslem by road and then canal. The discovery of kaolin in Cornwall, in 1768, proved to be a milestone in the production of porcelain in Britain.

The first pottery on the Trent and Mersey Canal to manufacture china was the Newhall Works. Richard Champion, of the Bristol Pottery, had purchased the patent right of William Cookworthy of Plymouth, the person who developed a process using Cornish clays. In 1781 he sold on these rights to the Newhall Works, a company that comprised six people at the time: Samuel Hollins of Shelton, Anthony Keeling of Tunstall, John Turner of Lane End, Jacob Warburton of Hot Lane, William Clowes of Port Hill and Charles Bagnall of Shelton. The clay and china stone were brought by coastal vessels from ports such as Fowey, following the difficult passage around the tip of Cornwall, through the Bristol Channel and along the Welsh Coast to Liverpool. From there, the clay and stone were taken by barge to Preston Brook and finally by narrow boat to the Potteries. Some clay and stone also travelled to Stourport and along the Staffordshire and Worcestershire Canal to the Trent and Mersey. One of the principal carriers on the Liverpool route was Henshall & Co., the company carrier.

In 1796 Thomas Minton established a pottery at Stoke, and began to arrange for making porcelain there. Between 1798 and 1799, Minton was instrumental in setting up the Hendra Company, leasing land and establishing clay mines at Trevalour Common. The Hendra Company continued to operate for about twenty years, with Minton entering into a partnership with a number of potters: John Wedgwood, Josiah Wedgwood, Samuel Hollins, Peter Warburton, William Clowes, John Daniel, Anthony Keeling, Enoch Keeling and William Pownall.

The trade in clay was not a profitable venture in the long term. Acquiring and transporting the material was fraught with difficulties of all kinds. Sometimes, watercourses were obstructed, and there were robberies and the demands of the lords of the manor to satisfy. Bad roads, imperfect machinery and the complications of extracting the minerals were other factors that increased the cost. The Hendra property was within 3 miles of St Austell, but Charlestown became the port of shipment, and the cost of transit in wagons to Charlestown, over poor roads, was 8s per ton. The cost of raising, working and casking was £1 15s 0d and other expenses increased the cost to £4 15s 0d per ton. Freight from Charlestown to Liverpool was 12s, port dues were 2s 6d and canal freight to the Potteries was 11s 6d. Taking all these expenses into account, as well as an allowance for capital invested, the clay could not be delivered for less than £6 15s 0d per ton.

Another key figure in the pottery trade was Josiah Spode, whose manufactory was located at Stoke-on-Trent and was already established when the Newcastle-under-Lyme Canal was made beside it.

Canal-side potteries.

The canal became a vital transport route for coal, raw pottery materials and finished pottery. Spode began making porcelain at his pottery in 1800 and was the first to use feldspar in the production process. In 1805 Spode began marketing opaque china, otherwise called ironstone china. Originally, flint had been ground for Spode by a watermill, but by 1804 Boulton & Watt had supplied a 6hp crank engine to drive a flint mill at Stoke-on-Trent. Between 1810 and 1811 a larger, 36hp crank engine was made by Boulton & Watt for Spode for the flint-grinding process. Boilers were also provided for heating the slip-drying house. There was a regular demand for coal and slack to be brought by canal for various purposes at the potteries, including heating for drying houses, and fuelling the steam engines and kilns.

With time, many potteries and related industries grew up alongside the canal from Tunstall through to Stoke. There were also a group along the Caldon Canal and the three canal plateways to Burslem, Hanley and Lane End also served a number of firms.

As well as the raw materials, clay, flints, chert, feldspar, alabaster and the components for colours and glazes, the canal was also used to transport the timber and wood needed for making the packing cases for the pottery items. The huge variety of materials and equipment required for making pottery is illustrated by a sale at the manufactory of Poole & Shrigley, Burslem, in November 1798:

Shropshire Union Wharf Building at Burslem.

> materials used in the manufacture of earthenware and stock of earthenware – plain, painted, enamelled and black ware of various kinds. Utensils common and engine lathes, stove pots, pipes and a large assortment of block and working moulds, squeezing boxes, boards, saggars, drums and shords, glaze tubs, sieves, lawns, drying and beating flags, throwing wheels, copper plates, ovens and a crane.

Among the raw materials were 'colours for different kinds of enamelling and under the glaze, Liver and crude Antimony, distilled verdigrease, red lead, litharge, crocus martis, terra de sienna, china clay, venice turpentine, and 50 tons of good block clay'.

The production of earthenware began with the mixing of clay with water to create 'slip'. The slip house was just one of the structures at a pottery, or potworks, along with the throwing and turning house, mixing house, drying house, saggar-making house, and packing house. Also on site were the distinctively shaped biscuit and glazing ovens, which were such a feature of this area. All the special structures began to decline in numbers as the years went on. The extensive use of coal in pottery manufacture diminished during the twentieth century, as gas-fired ovens became common in the industry. In the 1950s and 1960s, the West Midlands Gas Board, at Etruria, was active in promoting the use of town gas.

Salt

Of the two most important facets of the Trent and Mersey Canal trades, one was pottery and the other was salt. Whilst the movement of raw materials and finished pottery wares was essential to keeping the Trent and Mersey Canal open, salt was also an important cargo, along with coal for heating the salt pans. Yet, as this industry along the canal banks became localized to an area between Anderton and Middlewich, one of its major legacies was the adverse effect of subsidence, with the consequent and increasing cost of maintenance.

From Northwich to Lawton there was a vast bed of rock salt, about 40 yards thick, which was suitable for purification for home consumption and exportation. The presence of salt was first discovered in the year 1670, while boring for coals, in the lands belonging to William Marbory, Esquire. It was located about 34 yards below the surface. The salt industry developed in Cheshire – where the works were originally called 'wiches' – and manufactured salt was carried on horseback to Derbyshire, Leicestershire, Lincolnshire, Nottinghamshire, Staffordshire and Yorkshire. When the Trent and Mersey Canal was first proposed, those who were trading in salt were able to contemplate a cheaper and more convenient means of transport to these counties. By this time the major salt works were placed beside, or close to, the Weaver at Northwich and Winsford. Northwich was also the place where the headquarters of the Weaver Navigation Trustees was based. Home consumption of salt was so significant that a duty of £67,000 was paid into the Exchequer for 1765 from the salt works of Northwich alone. At the Northwich and Winsford works, about 24,000 tons of salt were being produced annually, yet the river navigation was a long time from being improved and there was no towpath until 1792.

There were essentially two types of salt that were conveyed by the canal: rock salt and white salt. The white salt was grouped into four main grades: fine, basket, export and manure, although the terms 'fine' and 'coarse' came to be used more commonly to differentiate between the better and cheaper white salts. Among the other terms that were used were 'agricultural', 'bay' and 'cheese'. The methods of production were completely different for the two principal types. The extraction of the rock salt left vast caverns underground, whilst surface works were limited. In contrast, most white-salt works occupied a space of a few acres on the surface. Within these works were the brine pits from which the brine was pumped from underground to cisterns and from there to the pans. An extensive industry was built up for the supply of plate iron for the pans and iron for the associated pipe works. The brine was heated by burning coals in furnaces built below the pans, which were sheltered from wind and rain by various sheds and buildings. The demand from the salt works for coal and slack gave employment to boatmen whose narrow boats brought coal from Staffordshire.

After the brine had been heated, workers used rakes to skim the salt crystals to the side of the pans, then collected the salt in wicker baskets or, later, wooden moulds. The baskets or moulds went to a hot house to complete the drying process, in a process called stoving, and the blocks of salt were then kept in adjacent store houses ready for transport by water. In later times, fine salt was produced by grinding the blocks by machinery.

Transporting salt by sailing flats on the River Weaver was the preferred route to Liverpool, although there was also the option of transport by canal to Manchester, London or the East Midlands. In the early days, many of the flats were owned by various salt works, often through the medium of shares, which could be transferred with changing fortunes or on the death of a shareholder. The shareholder might also own a stake in the salt works.

When completed, the Trent and Mersey Canal offered a transport route for salt destinations along the navigation network, as it grew. The number of works refining salt was limited to a few on the Staffordshire and Chester, located on the side of the canal at Marston, Wincham, Middlewich, Wheelock, Roughwood and Lawton in Cheshire.

In the Marston district there was a group of rock-salt works that extended westwards to Witton Bridge. The earliest canal-side works had been oper-

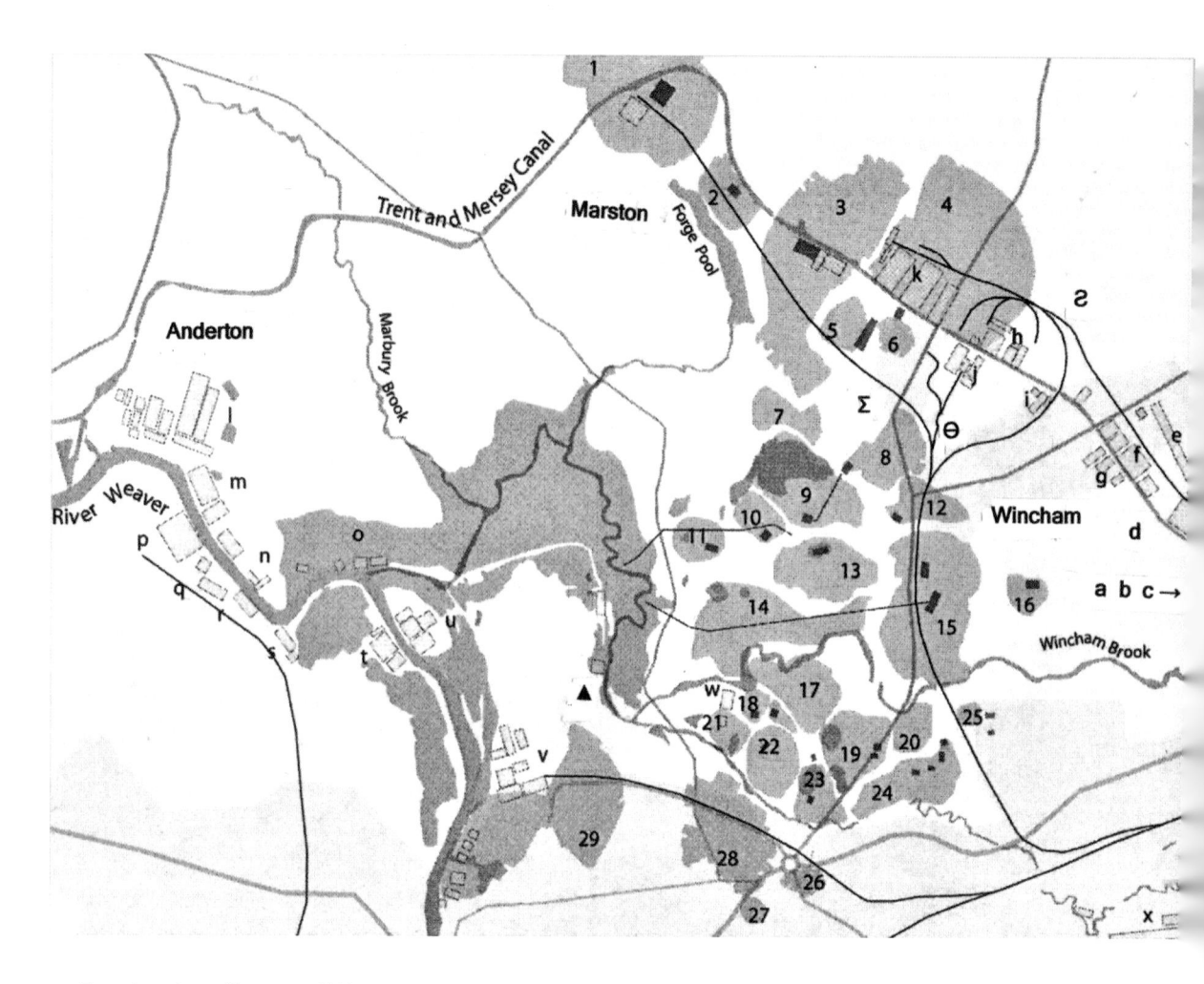

The salt works at Marston and Wincham: Rock-salt mines: 1 Marston Hall; 2 Pool; 3 Marston Old; 4 Adelaide; 5 New Zealand (Gregory's); 6 Fletcher's (Crystal); 7 Blackburn's New; 8 Ollershaw Lane; 9 Blackburn's Old; 10 Thomas Chantler's; 11 Littlers; 12 Gibson's; 13 Broady & Hadfield (Townshend); 14 Platt's Hill; 15 British; 16 Williamson's; 17 Kent & Naylor's; 18 Tomkinson's; 19 Barton's; 20 Thompson's; 21 Ashton's Old; 22 Ashton's New; 23 Marshall's No 1; 24 Worthington, Firth & Co; 25 Worthington's; 26 Penny's Lane; 27 Neuman's; 28 Witton Hall; 29 Baron Quay. White 'open-pan' salt works: a Woodside; b Sunbeam; c Wincham Hall; d Bridgefield & Victoria; e Wincham; f Wincham Patent Machinery; g Imperial; h Ollershaw Lane; I Royal Oak; j Alliance; k Adelaide, l British Company; m Blackburn's; Spearman's; o Littler's; p Caldwell's; q Marshall's; r Handell's; s Byflat; t Okel's; u Island; v Witton; w Dunkirk; x Bowman, Thompson & Co. Other features: ∆ End of Navigation Witton Brook; Ø Nelson Pumping Station; ≤ Alexander Pumping Station; Σ Albert Pumping Station

ated by Gilbert & Co., and by 1829 comprised seven works, for rock salt and white salt. This number increased after 1863 following the making of the branch railway from Northwich. These included the Bridgefield & Victoria Works, which were operated by a limited company registered in 1873. The Thompson family had started the Alliance Works in 1856 and they sold it to the Salt Union in October 1888. (A cartel of almost all the salt producers in the area, the Salt Union had been set up in 1888 to control the price of this important commodity.) The Union also acquired Adelaide, Marston Hall, Marston Old Works, Victoria and Wincham salt works. The Thompson family then founded another

Ingram, Thompsons, Lion Salt Works.

site producing white salt there, naming it the Lion Salt Works.

More works were subsequently built, as new brine streams were discovered at Wincham. These three works – the Wincham Hall, Sunbeam and Woodside Works – relied on canal transport and had no rail access. The Lion Salt Works did benefit from a rail siding from the Northwich Salt Branch. Coal and slack were transported by both canal boat and railway wagon, whilst salt could also be sent by rail or water. In the days of Ingram, Thompson & Co., there was a keen desire to reach to the Anderton Boat Lift before their competitors, Seddon's.

Taking brine from underground affected a large area of land and, whilst the white-salt works were concentrated together for the purposes of transport, the impact of subsidence extended much further. After Wincham the next group of canal-side salt works were to be found at Middlewich, where there were five establishments in existence at the time when the canal was made around the town. Indeed, salt-working had been conducted there for centuries. The remains of Roman roads in the area are an indication of the routes by which salt was transported in those times. The Newton Salt Works, in Wych House Lane, was located below the Treble Locks. The records show that, in 1815, George Chesworth of Newton lost a boat load of salt at Meaford.

In 1829 there were three salt-makers listed at Middlewich: John Thomas Braband, Samuel Berereton and William Henshall. Henshall, who was based at Pepper Street, was also a boat-builder and, from 1826, a canal carrier based at Bridge Wharf. The canal side from the bottom of the Treble Locks to the Big Lock had works placed near by, with six or seven operating along that section at one time. Joules took over Henshall's works and produced various salts, including cheese salt. King Street had a canal-side works called Kinderton. The Newton Works was owned by Joseph Verdin & Sons, while Richard Yeoman owned the Middlewich or Dairy Salt Works in Wych House Lane.

The working conditions at the salt works were hot and uncomfortable, and Seddon's works at Middlewich was no exception. The pans were heated by coal brought from collieries in the Stoke-on-Trent area. After the heating process was completed, 'lumpers' would perform the physically hard work of skimming the salt from the brine to put it into wooden moulds. The men who then knocked the blocks of salt from the moulds were known as 'lofters'. They would carry the blocks of salt into the flue house, or hot house, to dry – between sixty and eighty blocks would be equal to a ton in weight.

More brine springs were discovered at Middlewich in the 1880s and 1890s. Henry Seddon first built a salt works here in 1888, which formed the basis of an extensive salt empire. By 1892 he had acquired the cheese-salt works that had belonged to Joules. He then dispensed with any commercial carrying services and had invested in his own boats by 1898. He built a new works in Pepper Street, took over Aman's Works in Brook House Lane, and then, in 1904, acquired the two works of the Dairy & Domestic Salt Company. Their extensive boat fleet passed to Seddon, whose company became Henry Seddon & Sons Ltd from 1907. He maintained a canal and river craft until 1960. Cerebos, which operated the Booths Lane works in Middlewich, took over Seddon's works in 1959. In 1960 the canal traffic in salt was diverted to road transport.

In 1889 George Murgatroyd, a Manchester-based engineer, discovered another source of salt to the east of Brook House Lane. Henry Seddon became the first manager there, until he decided to set up in business himself. These works were essentially served by the London and North Western Railway, which passed through Middlewich. The largest fleet of boats was owned by the Salt Union, which had narrow boats and steam vessels for the Weaver.

At Wheelock, there were two works, one placed west of Wheelock Wharf, and the other near Wheelock Bottom Lock. The original Wheelock salt works was leased by September 1798 to a partnership comprising 'John Twiss, the younger, of Odd Rode, ironmaster; John Morris of Lawton, carrier; John Hodgkinson of Odd Rode, gentleman; James Colclough of Sandbach, gentleman; and George Shaw of Odd Rode, yeoman', to 'manufacture, vend and sell salt at Wheelock Salt Works for the term of twenty-one years'. James Colclough operated the Old Wheelock Salt Works for a period. He lost three boats loaded with salt on the Trent and Mersey Canal, where salt duty was reclaimed in 1808, 1812 and 1813.

Further east, at Malkins Bank, John Morris, of Lawton, was a partner in a business producing salt and carrying goods by canal to Manchester and London (Paddington) with William Carter, of Wavertree in Liverpool. In July 1811 Thomas Hall of Spitalfields, in London, purchased a quarter of the shares held by Morris and the fourteen boats used in the canal trade. Hall quickly left the partnership the next year, but continued to be the agent in London. William Carter ceased to be a partner in October 1823, leaving the business to Morris, who advertised the works and boats for sale in 1824. The firm of Barker, Carter & Allen took over the salt trade and also became general merchandise carriers between Liverpool and Manchester from 1826 until 1830, when Tildasly & Sturland purchased their boats. Francis and James Mills later occupied these salt works and the canal basin.

At Hassall Green, John Stringer operated a salt works. West of lock 57 and east of Thurlwood Locks was the Lawton Salt Works, which had a long existence under different proprietors. Shortly after the canal was completed to Lawton, Richard Morris leased the salt works from Robert Lawton on 28 October 1776. In 1800, when the works were operated by the firm of Broughton, Sutton & Co. (a partnership between Sir Thomas Broughton of Broughton Hall in Staffordshire and James Sutton of Shardlow), a boat load of salt was lost when it became iced up at Trentham. During 1807, the same firm lost a boat load of salt on the canal between Fradley and Fazeley. This partnership later comprised Henry Delves Broughton and James Sutton and lasted until February 1829, at which time they ran three Cheshire salt works, at Lawton, Roughwood and Wheelock, as well as operating lime kilns. Sutton & Co. also owned the salt warehouse at Shardlow.

There were two works in Staffordshire. Brine deposits at Weston-on-Trent had first been exploited in the late seventeenth century, when the earliest works were known as Shirleywich. The Trent and Mersey Canal reached Weston in September 1770. These works were later connected to the main line

Salt Union narrow boats, Anderton Boat Lift.

by a short branch canal. Narrow boats owned by the Moore family carried Staffordshire salt on to the Oxford Canal (for the River Thames) and also later along the Grand Junction. There is evidence that flints were carried on the return journeys.

William Moore subsequently entered into a partnership with James Sutton of Shardlow, a Mr Broughton and William Furnival (who had salt interests in Cheshire and Droitwich), established to exploit a patent for reducing fuel costs. A few months later Moore was bought out and the British Patent and Rock Salt Company was formed to control the Staffordshire and Cheshire works. This company's control ended in 1859, Shirleywich being leased by James Sutton. In 1869 the lessee was G. Allport.

In 1821 Earl Talbot had a brine shaft sunk on the west side of the Trent. The brine was piped to a new works on the east bank of the canal, south of Weston village and half a mile north of Shirleywich.

The Weston Salt Works was managed by Jeremiah Ginders, agent to Earl Talbot, and there were warehouses in London by 1823, Birmingham by 1827 and Wolverhampton from 1830. Coal for the works came by canal from the Brereton Collieries, also part of the Talbot estate. Salt from Weston was despatched in both small consignments and by the boat load. The extent to which canal carriers were involved in the salt trade is exemplified by records showing substantial purchases by Jos. Smith & Sons (Horninglow), Henry Ward (Oxford) and Nathaniel Wheatcroft (Cromford), Thomas Best, Thos Ebbern, Sutton & Co., R. Heath & Co., Flower & Son, Soresby & Flack and Pickford's. The Weston Company also had their own boats.

The Weston Salt Works traded in other commodities as well. From 1831 records show that flints were transported via London and Gainsborough, and Cornwall stone (china stone) via the Severn and via Liverpool. Chalk, plaster and oil cake are also mentioned. Some of the flints came up the Trent; there is a payment to Soresby & Flack, carriers of Shardlow, for these materials and the freight on them on 21 November 1832, and another to Jos. Smith & Sons (Horninglow) soon after. Most appear to have come via the Weston Company's wharf at 28 City Road Basin. The types of flint dealt with were 'Newhaven Boulders', sold by them at 22s to 23s per ton and 'Best Gravesend' at 26s to 27s per ton. The quantities were quite substantial – one payment was made to Messrs Axley & Taylor for the carriage of 222.5 tons at 10s 9d per ton, less wharfage at No 28 City Road Basin, and a similar payment to Robins, Mills & Co. on the same day. The company's usual lighterage contractor in London was J. Golden, to whom they were paying 2s 3d per ton in 1832. In 1834, the Weston Company had contracts with Hugh Henshall Williamson to take 300 tons of flints delivered to Alexander Reid's wharf at Brownhills (Tunstall) and quoted flint and Cornish stone prices for Messrs Finlow, Colton Mill, to be delivered at Brindley's Bank, near Rugeley. In 1835, there were more contracts with Williamson and one with Stubbs & Taylor of Coxshutt Mills.

The flint trade from London by canal, being in competition with the Trent route, was toll sensitive. As best Gravesend flints could be sold to the flint mills at 26s to 27s per ton, the Weston Company could expect to make a profit of 4s 9d to 5s 9d per ton. In the same year, the Weston Company was able to quote 37s per ton to Colton Mill, cheaper than the Stoke via Liverpool rate for a longer distance, which indicates the possible use of the Severn route. Trading in other commodities provided back loads for the Weston Company's salt boats. Plaster and whiting were brought back from Barrow upon Soar by the Leicester and Melton boats, with some being sold to William Wayte, the wharfinger at Stoke Wharf, and flints were sent by the Gainsborough route, providing return loads for salt boats trading to Shardlow for Lincolnshire and Hull.

After 1854, the Weston Salt Works concentrated on coarse salt and supplied only local customers. In 1888, Weston was taken over by the Salt Union, which temporarily revived the trade. Neither Weston nor Shirleywich was in regular operation after 1893 and both closed in 1901. The end of salt production at Weston may have been hastened by the development of brine deposits at Stafford, which were first discovered in 1877. Part of the Weston works was occupied by Alabaster Industries Ltd between 1919 and 1963.

Most salt works had separate ownerships, but by May 1826 the British Rock & Patent Salt Works managed works at Anderton, Lawton, Roughwood, Wheelock and Shirleywich and had depots at Liverpool, Bristol and London. Their principal agent was Alexander Reid, whilst J. Young & Son also served their interest at Bristol and W. W. Greenhill acted for them at 59 Lower Thames Street and No 14 wharf, Paddington.

Salt transport changed with the coming of the railways. Whilst the boat traffic continued into the twentieth century, there was a general decline in the amount of salt sent along the Weaver Navigation. This was due in part to the diversion of salt carriage to railway wagons, but also to the building of a brine pipe-line to Runcorn, whereby the need to transfer salt between narrow boat, flat and ship was avoided. The firm behind this innovation was the Mersey Salt and Brine Company Ltd, formed in 1881. They sank a new brine pit on the land of A. Smith Barry at Marbury and by 1883 had constructed the pipe-line to Runcorn. There was a set of James Watt pumping engines at the brine pit and another pair of Watt engines at the forcing station near the towpath of the canal at Marbury Bridge. Brine was pumped from there over the canal in 15-inch diameter iron pipes supplied by the Stanton Iron Company of Ilkeston. The brine was sent to a new works at Weston Point.

Whilst coal for the boilers at the pumping and forcing stations needed to be transported to the works, the salt was extracted at Runcorn near the docks of the Weaver Trustees and beside the Runcorn and Weston Canal. These works were taken over by the Salt Union, which was responsible for the making of other pumping plants at Marston and Wincham. Considerable concern was felt for jobs in the Northwich area as the volume of salt sent by pipe-line increased during the first decade of the twentieth century.

The use of steam in making salt came about in the 1860s when multi-effect vacuum evaporation was introduced to the industry. This involved a series of closed units, where steam under pressure was used to heat brine and, using the effect of a partial vacuum caused by the condensing steam, the boiling of the brine was continued despite the lower temperature. This continuous process produced over 1,000 tons of salt per day. It was a vast improvement on the open-pan method, saving on both labour and fuel, with a long-term reduction in the amount of coal needed at the salt works.

Another factor affecting trade was the subsidence issue. This, exemplified by the collapse of the culvert near Marbury, in July 1907, had a serious long-term effect on trade through the Anderton Lift. Both the pottery and the salt trade were affected. While the canal was closed, temporary arrangements had to be made, including the transport of pottery goods by road between Marston and the Weaver Navigation at 'Top of the Brook'. Otherwise, potters' clay and finished pottery faced the long diversion from Weston Point Docks via the Runcorn and Weston Canal, the Bridgewater Canal, Rochdale Canal, Ashton Canal and Macclesfield Canal to reach the Hall Green Branch of the Trent and

Mersey Canal Company. It made the journey to the Potteries at Stoke 81 miles instead of 44 miles. It was suggested that salt could be conveyed via railway to the Weaver at Winnington. Piling at Barons Quay was done so that a railway siding could be put down, which would link with the Cheshire Lines near Northwich.

Alkali and Soda Ash

Salt brought by boat from Droitwich and Stoke Works to South Staffordshire had provided the basis for alkali and chemical manufacture at Oldbury and Wednesbury, where it was combined with sulphur, obtained at first from local supplies of pyrites. In Cheshire, this industry was a later development. Works were constructed for making alkali from local brine supplies, including the firm of Brunner and Mond. Whilst some plants such as the Lockstock Works had canal frontages, the principal mode of transport used was railway.

Chemical manufacturing processes also took limestone and there was traffic between Caldon Low Quarries and the Brunner Mond works at Sandbach using canal boats. Brunner Mond owned a large fleet of narrow boats for this traffic, firstly to and from Froghall and then on to Endon Basin to their works. The Sandbach works were located at Malkins Bank and had been set up by Richard, Kearns and Gaskell to make soda ash. When Brunner Mond took over the plant, they carried out extensive enlargements to it between 1883 and 1892. Further improvements were made during the First World War and after then production also included the manufacture of sodium carbonate. This traffic ceased with the closure of the Sandbach works, following the takeover of Brunner Mond by ICI. The works were closed in January 1932, and demolition began just a couple of months later.

The Mid-Cheshire Alkali Works at Middlewich was served by a long basin that terminated to the rear of Kings Lock. These works were subsequently owned by Brunner Mond and were accessible to both canal and railway traffic. Soda was carried by canal boat as far as Birmingham by the Midland & Coast Carrying Company. Brunner Mond also operated the Lostock Works.

Chemicals

Used in the cleaning of metals such as copper and brass, acid was produced at a works owned by John Singleton, located beside the Trent and Mersey Canal at Rugeley. The works included three lead vats, coppers and stills, and made sulphuric acid (oil of vitriol) and sugar of lead. Singleton's bankruptcy in 1831 led to him transferring trade to an acid works near the terminus of the Uttoxeter Canal, where the scale of production was smaller than at Rugeley. It had just a brief existence.

There was a lead works, which produced the material for pottery glazes, beside the Newcastle-under-Lyme Canal, with a short tramway to the canal. The premises closed in 1830.

A chemical works at Tunstall, owned by Child & Co. in 1835, produced borax, Paris white, rock crystal and silex. Tunstall was also the location for the refining of gas by-products. By 1862, Samuel Bray and Richard Thompson at the Heyford Alum Works were making alum from colliery shale. The process involved boiling ammonium sulphate with the calcined shale in lead vats before transferring it to cisterns where the alum was allowed to crystallize. Ammonium sulphate was made at the works through heating 'Spanish ore' and spent oxide from local gasworks in furnaces. The sulphur content was used to make sulphuric acid and then that acid was mixed with ammonical liquor from the gasworks. The spent ore was sent on to the copper-makers in the Churnet Valley to be smelted.

Bray and Thompson were made bankrupt in April 1876. Josiah Hardman subsequently became associated with the Tunstall works, which developed into an extensive rail-served chemical factory operated under the name of the Stafford Chemical Company. Hardman's principal venture was the chemical works beside the Caldon Branch at Milton. These works, where tar was distilled, received gas tar, gas liquor and spent oxide and had access to both canal and railway transport. Josiah Hardman was at first in a partnership of seven people, which was reduced to three (Josiah Hardman, Charles Sherratt, and Ralph Steele) in 1873. Hardman was also a partner in other chemical works in Manchester.

The tar distillery business led to a patent for the production of anthracene. Its works, built on the offside of the canal near the junction with the private Foxley Branch Canal, produced the following:

> Anthracene, Benzol, Naptha, Carbolic Acid, Creosote Oil, Pitch and Black Varnish, Sulphate of ammonia, Sulphuric acid (rectified and brown) made from brimstone only, paraffin oil, paraffin wax, torch oil, waggon oil, rope oil and all kinds of oils and greases used about collieries, ironworks and brick works.

The acid plant was alongside the Foxley Branch and there was also a brick works where red bricks were made. Josiah Hardman died in 1896, but the works carried on until 1933, when the site was absorbed by the adjacent aluminium works.

The aluminium works had been built for the Cowles Syndicate Co. Ltd, a branch of an American company based in Cleveland, USA, that dated back to 1887. This company extracted aluminium from bauxite using electricity – it was a new process that had first been achieved at Neuhausen in Switzerland. At first, the Milton Works made a ferro-aluminium alloy that was used in the steel industry. A purer form of aluminium came to be made by 1888, yet Milton was disadvantaged in that it was still using steam-powered generating equipment, with the associated high costs of coal supply. With the creation of the British Aluminium Company in 1894, the Swiss process was adopted, and a new factory at Foyers beside Loch Ness was built. It obtained a supply of bauxite from Northern Ireland, and was able to cut costs by using hydro-electric power. The acquisition of the Milton Works was part of that company's prospectus. Aluminium ingots were brought to Milton by rail and the Milton Works were converted to roll this metal. The works were retained by British Aluminium until 1964.

An experimental chemical works near Milton was used for the Phoenix Process Trust to try out the Swinburne-Ashcroft process of treating zinc sulphide with chlorine and electrolysing the chlorides formed. There was an extensive outlay for an electricity-generation plant, which included a 300hp triple expansion steam engine made by Willans & Robinson.

Canal traffic in acid and related commodities, in general, was often a through trade along the Trent and Mersey Canal. It was a traffic that changed with time. Cowburn & Cowper brought acid and carbon bisulphide into South Staffordshire from their chemical works at Trafford Park in Manchester. There was also traffic in galvanizer's pickle (waste acid) to Spondon Colour Works, beside the Derby Canal, and a tar and gas liquor trade from the gasworks.

Flint

The carriage of flint by salt suppliers from London by canal was only one aspect of a complex route by which flints were delivered to the pottery industry. The use of flint from Britain and abroad for weapons and tools extends back to the Stone Age. During the eighteenth century, the need for ground flint in making pottery within Staffordshire developed as navigations improved. The supply route through Gainsborough for Chalk Pit, Gravesend and Newhaven flints, by river and road and later by river and canal, brought flints to the water mills in Staffordshire, where they were ground for pottery use.

The River Churnet provided power for flint mills at Consall and Cheddleton, located beside the Caldon Canal. The Trent had the largest concentration of mills – sometimes, they would grind flint in one part of their buildings and corn in another part. Streams that fed into the Trent also had watermills for grinding flint and used water power to grind corn at the same place. At Stone Flint Mill, as described in 1814, there was a flint mill with a 22-foot diameter wheel, but there was also a corn mill, with a 24-foot diameter overshot wheel driving '3 pairs of French Stones and 2 pairs of Derby Stones'.

Consall 'New' or Flint Mill Lock and the Flint Mill buildings.

Kings Mill on the Trent near Shardlow also had a corn mill and there was another mill owned by the Kings Mill Company (Burton Boat Company) that ground chert from Derbyshire. The Burton Boat Company carried this hard stone material to several potteries in the Stoke area. One customer was the firm of Wedgwood and Byrley of Etruria, which, in 1803, was sued by the Burton Boat Company for non-payment for the 'ground flint'. Wedgwood and Byrley's counter-argument was that the flints that had been delivered had caused a manufacturing defect, which resulted in biscuit ware being produced in a dull red colour instead of white. The court judgment was in favour of the Burton Boat Company, and this was confirmed at a second trial that year. The court case provides of an example of the importance of the quality of the ground flint that was required for pottery-making. Wedgwood contended that the limestone content in the chert had caused the problem and the lesson no doubt influenced future procurement of flint. The Burton Boat Company ceased trading a couple of years later, possibly as a consequence of the court case. The legal dispute had cost them dear, and may even have caused customers to transfer their trade elsewhere!

During the early times of flint carriage, the water-powered flint mills were to be found nearer the road transport route from the Trent. One example was the Coxshead Flint Mill at Norton Green, which was located near the turnpike road from Leek to Stoke-on-Trent. With the making of the canal, a number of watermills were converted to grind flint. Trentham Mill was converted for Thomas Griffin and William Bill and Consall Forge on the Churnet followed later. Thomas Griffin, Francis Leigh and William Bill took a lease on Consall Mill from March 1778. At Cheddleton a pair of mills were converted from grinding corn, and were grinding flint by 1815. John Leigh was then proprietor of both the Consall and Cheddleton mills. Following his bankruptcy in 1840, William Bowyers operated both groups of mills until 1862.

The process of flint grinding involved the use of large-diameter pans. At Cheddleton there were two of about 12 feet in diameter, with stones worked by waterwheels of the under-shot type. At Consall the mills had been upgraded and improved on an extensive scale. In 1862, three of the waterwheels were made of iron and there were fourteen pans each of 13 feet in diameter. The flint and other materials were landed near the kilns and the ground flint slurry, or slip, was discharged from refiners directly into narrow boats.

Near to Consall was another flint mill called Crowgutter, where flint was also ground and delivered into boats in a slurry state. Cowgutter Mill was on a stream that joined the Churnet and had a mill pool above it. The slip carried to the Potteries in this fashion was known as 'buttermilk' and the boats that carried it were nicknamed 'buttermilk boats'.

Paper Mills

In the 1820s, there was a growing need for good-quality tissue paper, which was used by the potters in the printing of their copper-plate engravings as well as, in a coarser form, for wrapping and other purposes. This led to the building of the Ivy House Paper Mill beside the Caldon Canal at Hanley, in 1827. Worked by steam power, this mill belonged to Henry Fourdrinier (1766–1854), who had transferred his business from Hertfordshire. Fourdrinier had been involved in the development of a paper-making machine that was able to make continuous rolls of paper, and had been granted a British patent for the innovation in 1801. Following various infringements of the patent, he made an application to Parliament, which granted him £7,000 in compensation. The Fourdrinier machine became a standard model and was adopted by many paper-makers in Britain.

Bone Mills

Ground animal bones were used in pottery-making to whiten the ware. Shirley's Bone and Flint Mill at Etruria, established in 1857, is a good example of the business. It was built for Jesse Shirley on the site of the former Swains crate works, to grind bone and flint using steam power. At first flints were ground dry, but later water was added to reduce levels of dust, which were causing silicosis of the lungs and premature death in the mill workers. Milling at Shirley's ceased in 1972 and the site is now a museum. There were a number of other mills located along the waterway, some steam-powered and others using water power.

There was transport in different types of ground bone, which were used both in the pottery trade and also as manure. At Tunstall, in 1873, Earp Brothers sold 'Bone Manure and Blood Manure'. George Parkhouse had the Tunstall works from 1874, supplying crushed bone and bonemeal.

Shirley's Bone Mill.

Stone

Various types of stone, for building and other purposes, were moved by canal. Mole Cop, near Lawton, was a source of four different types: grinding stone, freestone, limestone and millstone. Freestone was found on the banks of the River Trent, near Wolseley Bridge and Burton upon Trent. It was comparable in quality to Portland or Roche-Abbey stone. Not many miles from the Trent, near the River Soar in Leicestershire, were quarries of Swithland slate, durable covering for houses, and rocks of a kind of grey porphyry, which had the potential for use as paving for streets.

The Trent and Mersey Canal used a quarry at Talke for the supply of stone and had a watermill at Hoo, near Great Hayward, with wheels driven by the River Trent. There was a tramway to convey raw and finished stone from Hoo Mill Lock Wharf to this mill.

Alabaster and plaster quarried at Aston near Derby were transported by canal near Shardlow. The alabaster was used for stucco or sculpture, whist the plaster had a use in pottery-making. Henry Orton carried plaster from the Derby district to Etruria by boat.

The Trent and Mersey Canal, as first built, was intended to provide transport of limestone from Leicestershire and Derbyshire. Near that part of the Trent where the canal was to terminate there was a vast mountain of limestone, on which the village of Bredon, in Leicestershire, was situated. There were also quarries of limestone at Barrow in Leicestershire:

> [They] burnt an excellent kind of lime for building... which was conveyed to places at a great distance by land, every way; and lime is much wanted through the whole course of the canal, both for the purposes of architecture and cultivation.

All such quarries relied on the Trent Navigation and, in the case of Barrow on Soar, the subsequent development of the navigation to Loughborough and Leicester. For Derbyshire there were quarries at Ticknall, which were close to Bredon and also Crich, which came to supply canal locations with the making of the Cromford and Erewash Canals.

A principal source of limestone, as far as the Trent and Mersey Canal was concerned, was the Caldon

Froghall Upper Basin and Lock.

Froghall limestone kilns.

Quarries, linked to the Caldon Canal by tramways. They were located on land owned by the Bill and other families, but later became the property of the canal company. The stone had various uses, including building and as flux in iron smelting. Later there was a need for chemical manufacture, such as alkali.

Limestone would be burnt in kilns to make lime. The early kilns were made into the side of a bank, with a horseshoe-shaped chamber. Limestone was carried to the top and dropped into the chamber, on to a charge of coal. The front of the kiln was covered up and the limestone was left on top of the burning coal for a few days to be reduced down to lime. Later, larger structures called shaft kilns were made.

Froghall's first canal-side kiln was erected in 1786, and the site came to have a bank of shaft kilns, first four and later six, built close to the lower Froghall Basin. This basin had been created on the stub of the Uttoxeter Canal that had remained when the North Staffordshire Railway had used the canal bed for its Churnet Valley Railway, and had laid railway sidings up to the interchange with the narrow-gauge Caldon Low Railway. The kilns had a siding from the Caldon Low Railway inclines (1847/9), and Caldon Low limestone was used to make lime for mortar or agricultural use.

Other lime kilns were placed alongside the Trent and Mersey Canal, burning limestone using coal transported by canal. John Gilbert Junior had two kilns at Stonefield Wharf, north of Stone. The Cheddleton Lime Company had lime kilns at Cheddleton and Horsebridge. There was a kiln near Milton leased by Charles Hale and another at Engine Lock. At Newcastle-under-Lyme the Pool Dam Wharf lime kilns were let by the Newcastle-under-Lyme Canal Company.

The Gilberts, father and son, also owned boats in connection with their limestone business. Their Cheddleton Lime Company had seven boats in 1795 and a boat dock at Cheddleton. Sometimes their boats operating into Cheshire brought back Gilbert's salt from Marston. As a wharfinger, John Gilbert operated the Newton wharf at Middlewich.

Limestone was also carried extensively for iron-making and other uses. Lime from quarries in this region had different properties for building purposes. Transport of lime from particular lime kilns was advertised on a distance basis per boat load. This applied to lime from Breedon (George Wooten, Chellaston), Crich (Gabriel Brittain, Chirk) and Daw End (John Brawn, Daw End near Rushall). For Breedon, the quarries at Cloud Hill supplied lime to destinations in Leicestershire and Derbyshire, principally by road and turnpike at first. There was a transport link for Breedon lime to Loughborough by the short-lived Charnwood Forest Canal and later by tramroad to the Ashby-de-la-Zouch Canal. The supply of lime offered by George Wooten involved carriage by road for part of the way. The point of interchange was Cuttle Bridge, where there was a wharf on the opposite side to the towpath on the Trent and Mersey Canal. For Crich lime and Daw End lime the transit was possible by water throughout. Limestone carriage from Caldon Low Quarries to the South Staffordshire ironworks was another important trade, with services offered by carriers from South Staffordshire, such as Price & Son of Brierley Hill. It was also a trade that the North Staffordshire Railway Company considered, in 1848, to compete with lime from North Wales and the local Dudley mines.

Brick-Making

When the canal was first constructed it became clear that a great quantity of marl would be thrown up during the digging, and there were places near the banks where the marl could be delivered from the spade into the boats. Clay had an important use for lining waterways to prevent the loss of water, but it also was needed for brick-making.

Brick-making marls were often found in association with coal seams and industrial-scale brick-making was later conducted in some regions. These were however not the only places where suitable sources for brick-making were to be found. There were many other parts of Britain where bricks were made, but the marls found in the Tunstall area (Etruria Marl) were vital to the canal contractors. In the days of canal construction, the bricks were hand-made using temporary kilns. Once it had been dug, the clay was left out in the open over the winter to enable the frost and cold to make it more pliable.

The supply of bricks had been a limiting factor in making the original Harecastle Tunnel and the types of bricks found by John Rennie during his inspection were not of the best quality. By 1825, when bricks were being used to line the new tunnel, the manufacturing process had improved to include a mechanical element for the grinding and working of the clays. The bricks were also made in permanent kilns. The brick-makers at Tunstall were able to supply a larger quantity of bricks, which enabled the new tunnel to be completed in a shorter period.

There was quite a range of bricks and tiles made in the Potteries, including the hard blue bricks that came to be so useful in construction. One early supplier was Thomas Peake and Co. of Tunstall, who supplied kiln-made blue bricks, tiles, quarries and gutter pipes. Fire bricks were often brought by canal boat or railway from elsewhere, including a number of important suppliers in the Stourbridge district. Fire bricks were also made in the Potteries. Bricks made from Caldon Low clay by George Baker & Co., at Tunstall Bridge Firebrick Works, were supplied to the Shelton Bar Ironworks, among others.

Coal

The North Staffordshire Coalfield comprised three distinct seams of coal – upper, middle and lower – extending for 10 miles from Longton in the south to Harecastle and Kidsgrove in the north. It was 7½ miles in width, from Norton in the east to Leycett in the west. With the making of the canal, traffic in coal developed and increased. As the coal mines were intersected in the Potteries district, this traffic became vitally important to the existence of the canal, as well as to other waterways.

Coal was already being worked near Newcastle-under-Lyme, Burslem and Lane End (Fenton Park and Meir Heath), with the product being conveyed by road. The canal provided the opportunity for developing the mines, at and near Harecastle and Kidsgrove. At Lane End a sough was driven into the hillside, which became known as the Longton Gutter, or Longton Sough. This sough provided access to underground mines for which records exist in the year 1788. Mining of coal was also accompanied by the extraction of ironstone. Tramways provided a

> **HARECASTLE COALS**
>
> HAVING been informed that my coals are represented by interested persons not to be good, and, on consequence, several boats have left my wharf, without loading. *This is to give Notice*, That if any person will give information against such person or persons so representing them in future, they shall be handsomely rewarded by me for their troubles.
>
> I am ready to agree with any person of character who will take my Coals, or who will undertake them by commission. I charge them on the canal banks 10s per ton-others are charged 12s 6d- and I have not the least doubt, if they were tried, but that they will be approved.
>
> JOHN R HEATHCOTE
> Longton Hall, Newcastle, Staffordshire
> N.B. Mr Gilbert's lease of my Nabb's Mine, or what he calls his Banbury Coals, expired at Mid-summer last – Boats will never wait for loading.
> *Jackson Oxford Journal*, 12 August 1809

link, often through inclines, between the mines and the canal.

The two side tunnels at Harecastle were directed to mines underground for the conveyance of coal by boat. North of the tunnel there were two tramways that conveyed coal to canal-side wharves. One, to the west, brought coal from the Heathcote mines, whilst the eastern tramway brought coal from John Gilbert's mines at Clough Hall. Coal from both groups of mines were regularly sent south as far as Banbury and Oxford, and there was clearly a rivalry between the Heathcote family and the Gilberts.

Another, longer tramway was made to Trubshaw Colliery from a basin beside the canal north of Hardings Wood Lock. This tramway crossed the land of John Lawton and was held under lease from 11 June 1803. By 1829, these mines and tramways were worked by Sutton & Co., who carried the coal in their own boats to supply their salt works and wharves.

Brereton Collieries, Rugeley.

Norton Colliery.

John Sparrow & Co. leased collieries at Coxshead near Norton-in-the-Moors from C. B. Adderley. They were linked to the Caldon Canal by tramways. Boulton & Watt supplied a beam engine in 1792 and accepted an order for a crank engine in 1793. The concept of a steam engine using a crank to drive a colliery winding drum was a new development by Boulton & Watt and came after a patent was about to expire (1794) for a rival device used in a flour mill in Birmingham. Etruria Pottery had an alternative type of device called the 'Sun & Planet' design, which had been developed to avoid the crank patent. With the expiry of the patent, engineering firms across the country were entitled to supply crank engines for collieries, and flint-grinding, flour and rolling mills. The engine made for John Sparrow was an important step that encouraged steam power to flourish beside the waterways.

The Trent and Mersey Canal also passed close to the northern tip of the South Staffordshire Coalfield at Cannock Chase. A mile from Rugeley, a blazing kind of coal called cannel was found, among other types. The mines belonged to the Earl of Uxbridge, and their lower stratum was said to be a valuable one. It was believed that a navigable sough might be carried from the new canal into their heart, as had been the case at the Duke of Bridgewater's colliery in Lancashire, and that this would lay them dry. Two mines were developed there, one called Brereton and the other called Hayes. Brereton was served by a tramway to the turnpike road at first. The Hayes Colliery had a long tramway that linked the mine with a wharf on the Trent and Mersey Canal having passed through Rugeley. The Hayes Colliery was a later development made during the 1820s, it would seem.

The working of coal had been confined to mines of a certain depth, but the development of steam power enabled deeper workings to be reached. More plant was erected at the surface and mines became collieries. Pit tramways with a short-term use became colliery railways and often their coals were sent to a main-line railway company rather than to the canal. However, the canal still served a purpose, for the supply of canal-side potteries, salt works and other factories. The colliery age coincided with the North Staffordshire Railway Company taking on the ownership of the Trent and Mersey Canal, so the company had the advantage of supplying the deep-pit collieries by either canal or railway.

Infrastructure at the pit head was improved by 1860 with railway sidings, waggon loading screens, winding houses, underground haulage and pumping plant. The Kidsgrove canal side changed with the building of the North Staffordshire Railway routes there, as well as later with the Loop Line construction. Access to the early canal wharves became limited following the building of a foundry and gasworks. Although many coal mines had railway connections, there were a number close to the canal that still sent coal by boat, north and south of Harecastle Tunnel. Norton Colliery on the Caldon Canal also supplied coal using the Foxley Branch.

Coal was also loaded into boats at Tunstall and south of Stoke at Fenton. In this last example, the Stafford Coal & Iron Company retained a wharf beside the canal at Sideway. Iron was smelted at the furnaces and coal was mined at Great Fenton Colliery. From the 1920s coal was mined at Hem Heath Colliery, Trentham by the company. The mines at Hem Heath were improved by the National Coal Board and the wharf continued to supply coal by boat up to the 1950s, when the North Western fleet of British Transport Waterways would collect coal from Sideways Wharf, where it was then carried by a conveyor to the boats. It was then tipped from the conveyor end in the narrow-boat hold and delivered to Seddon's salt works at Middlewich.

Iron

Within North Staffordshire, there were three types of ironstone in the ground: argillaceous, clay band and hydrated oxide. They were found in different districts than ran from Madeley and Silverdale in the west to Froghall in the east and Lane End in the south. Iron-working began with bloomeries established in several parts of North Staffordshire. Later, charcoal smelting furnaces were built at selected sites where there was sufficient water power to work the bellows.

Several parts of the country, in the neighbourhood of the canal, yielded great quantities of a particular type of iron ore, commonly called ironstone, which was suited for making cold-short iron. Within North Staffordshire this ironstone was worked in the area north and north-west of Newcastle-under-Lyme. There were coal and ironstone mines at Apedale, Leycet and Silverdale, where the Bowyer, Crewe and Sneyd families worked the underground seams. There were also two established charcoal furnaces at Apedale and Knutton Heath (Silverdale), which used water power to provide the blast. Iron was also mined at Lane End and around Cheadle, where the hydrated oxide of iron was found. There were charcoal furnaces at Mear Hay near Longton, another near Alton, and, further south, one on Cannock Chase. Iron-working was also conducted in Derbyshire, which came to be served by inland navigation, first by the Erewash and later by the Cromford Canal.

By 1765, it had been discovered that the ironstones and ores found in North Staffordshire, when mixed with the red ore from Cumberland, made the best kind of tough, or merchant iron. It was also known that Staffordshire ironstone was necessary for working the ore in the north. Traffic was limited by the cost of land carriage, even though the Weaver had comprised part of the supply chain. The Trent and Mersey Canal promoters believed that it was highly probable that their intended waterway would allow much greater quantities of ironstone to be sent into the north, and more red ore to be sent back in return, and thereby 'greatly increase the intercourse between these two parts of the kingdom, to their mutual advantage'.

There was also the advantage of having charcoal, lime and other fluxes brought into the furnaces at a lower cost, and a saving to be made in the cost of conveying articles from the forge to the manufacturer by water. These developments must have contributed to the increase in the consumption of English iron, and enabled the iron masters of Staffordshire to compete with iron-makers in Europe and elsewhere. It was also suspected that the increased competition might reduce the price of foreign iron to the benefit of the manufacturers. A primary aim for any factory was to furnish raw materials at the lowest price, and inland navigation was seen as the means to achieve this object. With the building of the Trent and Mersey Canal main line and the branch to Caldon came the establishment of iron smelting furnaces and forges in North Staffordshire, near these waterways.

Trade in foreign iron was enabled through transport along the River Trent. Samuel and William Sketchley, of Burton upon Trent, had Russian and Swedish iron for sale in 1776, whilst a year later Eyre & Hoole advertised the fact that they had Russian and Swedish iron at the warehouse at Cavendish Bridge and at William Croby's warehouse in Derby. The expansion of the British iron trade began initially with the establishment of coke-smelting furnaces at selected locations, some close and others away from the canal. These were at first of brick construction, made in the conical form, but this changed to the iron plate cased furnace, which was characteristic of iron smelting during the age of the railway. These furnaces could be either 'cold blast' or 'hot blast'. In the latter case, the air blown into the furnace was heated.

Those who worked at these furnaces had various duties, such as the filling of the furnace from the top with calcined ore, coke and limestone. There were galleries around the top of the furnace where the workmen wheeled these constituents in barrows. Reaching the top of the furnace was achieved either by a mechanized lift or an incline. In previous times the furnaces had been made alongside a bank to facilitate the process. The iron smelted was made from a mixture of ores, obtained locally or from further afield, such as Cumberland or Furness. The canal assisted with the transport of limestone and iron ores, as well as pig iron.

Along the Trent and Mersey Canal there were a group of iron-smelting furnaces and associated ironworks south of Harecastle Tunnel at Chatterley, Etruria and Goldendale. The Goldendale furnaces were placed close to the canal, whilst Chatterley was served by a long arm to a basin. Etruria was the location for Earl Granville's complex, which included two groups of iron furnaces. The original Shelton Furnace at this complex was linked by a tramway to a wharf beside the canal, opposite the Etruria Pottery. The tramway was replaced in 1849 by standard-gauge railway sidings. At the same time, the Shelton furnaces were rebuilt as a group of four. Another group of four furnaces, Etruria, was made close to the canal, north of the pottery. There were also coke ovens there.

Forges were built at different locations where there was a suitable water supply for the finery, chafery and the hammers for working up iron into wrought iron and finished products. There were a number of pre-existing water-powered forges along the length of the Trent and Mersey Canal and the Caldon Branch. These included Marston Forge in Cheshire, which lasted long into the canal era and continued in use

Shelton Furnaces.

Etruria Furnaces before closure.

even in the age of the railway, providing metal working to the needs of the salt industry.

With the development of the puddling process, the making of wrought iron entered a new age. Pig iron was made malleable in the reverbatory furnaces and ball furnace for the shingler to shape at the steam-powered hammer. This development heralded the building of the ironworks, where, after puddling, the malleable refined iron was passed to the rolling mills, to make bar, plate, sheet and wire. It was a process aided by the use of steam engines capable of driving mills and the hammers.

Ironworks were established at different times. Records show that the ironworks at Golden Hill near Trentham were operating in 1804. Some fifty-nine years of lease remained unexpired, which might date the establishment there back to about 1764. In December 1809 the bankruptcy of William Parker led to the sale of Bucknall Forge, which was advertised as being complete with 'an excellent steam engine' driving 'two hammers (iron helves), one for shingling, or stamping iron and one for drawing out bars'. There was a puddling furnace and a balling furnace, a bloom furnace, charcoal finery and a refinery. Part of the works had been erected about 1801, with the remainder being finished by 1806.

The furnaces at Goldendale were first used in 1841 and were operated by Hugh Henshall Williamson trading as the Goldendale Iron Co. Nearby was Ravensdale Ironworks, where the old forge was built for John Bull and Sons in the 1830s and from 1862 was owned by William Bates, who built Ravensdale New Forge. Chatterley also had an ironworks complex, established by the Chatterley Iron Company, which operated for a short period during the 1870s and 1880s. North of the Harecastle Tunnel was the extensive Clough Hall Ironworks, which had been built for the Kinnersley family, from 1833, and came to include a group of forges linked by tramway to the Trent and Mersey Canal at Kidsgrove. Later, these connections were improved to join up with the North Staffordshire Railway. Hugh Henshall Williamson, in association with his brother Robert, had been involved with not only the Goldendale Ironworks and the associated collieries, but also until his death had control of the Pinnox and Chalky collieries. He operated a private railway from these mines, which conveyed ironstone to a wharf beside the Trent and Mersey Canal at Brownhills, where the ironstone was transported by boat.

There was a scrap forge at Foxley placed beside the turnpike, which was in operation by 1804. Near Norton-in-the-Moors were the Ford Green Ironworks and furnaces. These works were constructed for Robert Heath in the 1850s and were served by the private Foxley Canal, the final extent of which was five-eighths of a mile.

Some sites, such as Wychnor Ironworks, retained a water-powered mill, which in 1826 was associated with the sheet, hoop and bar iron trade. A navigable length of the Trent extended beyond the junction with the Trent and Mersey Canal at Wychnor Lock towards this mill. There was a forge at Wheelock operated by Charles Johnson. There were, in fact, water-powered mills along the length of the Trent and Mersey, including Clay Mills, near Burton, where the Dove provided the water power for the ironworks. The leat from this mill was spanned by a two-arch aqueduct and there was a wharf for the iron trade.

Traffic by canal included ironstone for North Staffordshire or elsewhere. In 1873 the amount of calcined ironstone sent out of North Staffordshire by canal was 108,939 tons and calcined ironstone used in North Staffordshire amounted to 37,421 tons. Part of this trade included the ores mined near Consall on the Caldon Canal, which started to be raised in the early 1850s. This was a declining trade as ironstones and ores came to be brought in in increasing amounts by railway. The development of mild-steelmaking after 1880 also led to change in the North Staffordshire iron trade as reliance on rail transport increased.

Alongside the trade in ironstone and ore were the foundries where iron was cast and shaped into items for domestic or industrial use, including boilers and steam engines. Among the companies involved in this industry were William Butler at Shelton, John Cope at Milton, and Rangeley & Dixson at Stone.

Gasworks

The carbonization of coal to produce coal gas for lighting and domestic heating was developed during the first decade of the nineteenth century. The technique was brought to the Potteries by the British Gas Light Company, which established a works near the canal at Shelton south of Bells Mill Aqueduct. The making of coal gas required certain types of coals, and the local supply had the benefit of falling into that category. By 1826 the company was advertising a supply of coke and coal tar that would be delivered into boats free of charge.

> **PRIVATE GAS COMPANIES ALONGSIDE THE TRENT AND MERSEY CANAL**
>
> Brownhills: British Gas Light Company
> Etruria: British Gas Light Company
> Fenton: Stoke, Fenton & Longton Gas Company
> Hanley: Hanley Gas Company
> Kidsgrove: Kidsgrove Gas Company
> Longport: Tunstall & Burslem Gas Light Company
> Middlewich: Middlewich Gas Company
> Rugeley: Rugeley Gas Company
> Stoke: Stoke, Fenton & Longton Gas Company
> Stone: Stone Gas Company

At this time these commodities were viewed as waste, but, once their commercial value had come to be recognized, the gasworks began to sell them. As the industry and the population increased in the Potteries, and elsewhere along the canal bank, new gasworks began to be established by private companies.

Other gasworks were placed near the canal where coal could be conveyed by road. Leek Gasworks was situated near the terminus canal basin.

All gasworks generated traffic in by-products and there was a works on the Caldon Branch where tar was refined. In all cases the process was the same. Coal was carbonized in retorts, located in the retort house. These were horizontal at first, but, as technology improved, so did the design of the retort, until the vertical type became more common in modern gasworks. Gas from the retorts was passed to the purifiers and then stored in a holder before distribution to the local area. Coal was also required as fuel for heating the retorts and was of a more general quality than the coal needed for making gas.

Between 1898 and 1904 the British Gas Light Company built a new works near to the railway at Etruria. With the creation of Stoke-on-Trent

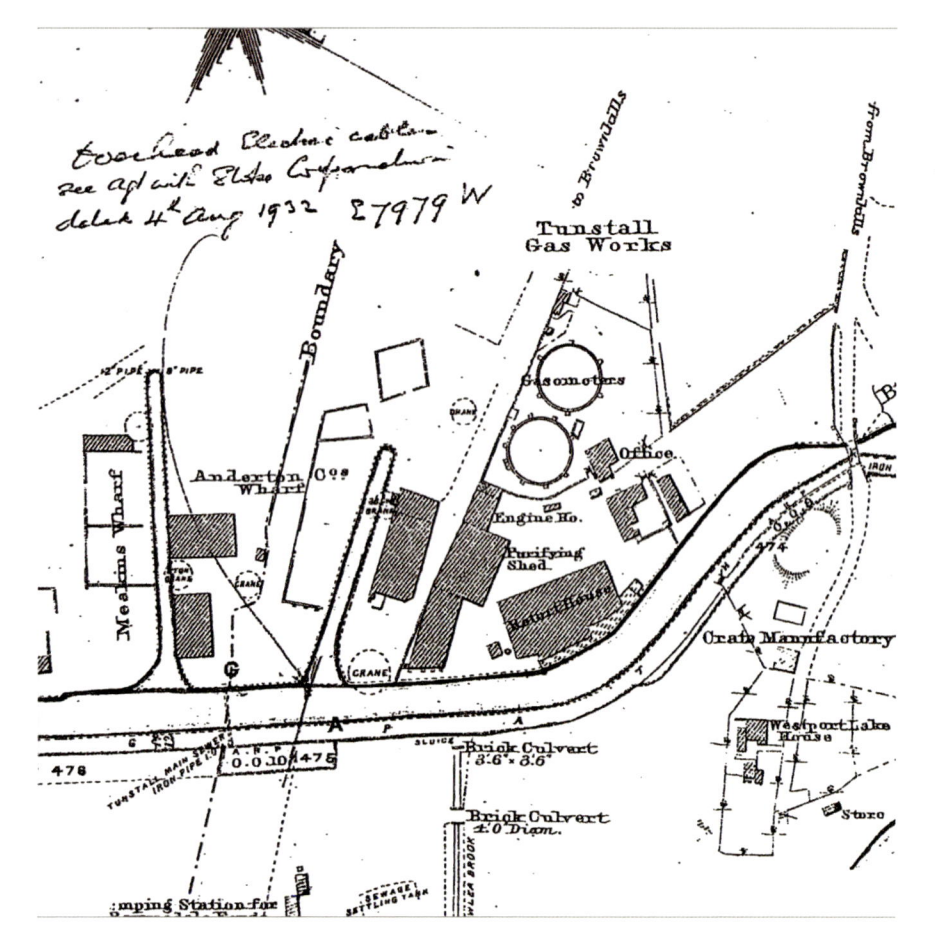

Map of Tunstall Gasworks, 1896. Otherwise known as Brownhills, these works were owned by the British Gaslight Company Ltd until 1922.

Corporation, four gasworks – at Burslem, Fenton, Longton and Stoke – became the property of that corporation. In 1922 Stoke-on-Trent Corporation purchased the modern gas works at Etruria from the British Gaslight Company at the suggestion of the Borough Engineer, Alexander MacKay, along with their other works at Tunstall. Etruria was reconstructed with modern vertical retorts and a new tar and sulphate of ammonia plant erected. Town gas production was concentrated there. When this work was completed, in 1928, the other five corporation plants at Burslem (Longport), Fenton, Longton Stoke and Tunstall were closed.

Coke

Several coal owners in North Staffordshire built coke ovens of the beehive type, producing coke that was important in the smelting of iron. Beehive ovens were located at strategic places along the private railways and tramways. There was a concentration of different kilns in the Kidsgrove area and other ironworks also had coke ovens. A bank of ovens at Etruria near the canal provided coke for Earl Granville's furnaces.

While the principal use of coke was for smelting iron, early railway locomotives also used it as fuel. Coke was transported by boat from Manchester and from the Harecastle ovens to supply the London and Birmingham Railway depot at Curzon Street in Birmingham.

The coke ovens at Kidsgrove remained and were improved over the years; indeed, they outlasted the Clough Hall Ironworks site where they had been built. The ironworks were closed in 1891 and were replaced by a coking and by-products works, which finally became the Birchenwood Gas & Coke Co. Ltd. Coke-making at the site close to Harecastle Tunnel went on until 1973. The closure of those works marked the end of the coal era at Harecastle.

Electricity Supply

The generation of electricity for domestic use, factories, public lighting and street tramways gradually gained in importance from the start of the twentieth century. In order to generate electricity for general use, a supply of coal was required to create steam for the turbines. Within the Potteries, a number of small generating stations were built, including Burslem (1905), Hanley (1894), Longport (1901) and Stoke (1904). The Stoke works was also combined with a destructor works.

With the formation of Stoke-on-Trent Corporation, in 1908, it was decided to build a central supply station. A site beside the Caldon Canal was chosen at Hanley, next to the existing station. This site was developed to generate electricity in 1913 and extended in 1922, 1925 and 1927 when the other local generating works were closed. Coal was delivered by canal boat and tenders for coal were advertised on a yearly basis. Hanley Power Station became the property of the North West Midlands Joint Electricity Authority in 1930. It was they who were responsible for the building of Meaford A Power Station (1945–1947).

Oil from Shale

There were parts of the British coalfield where petroleum could be extracted from the shale found with the coal measures. This was most notably the case in Scotland, near Edinburgh, but oil was also commercially extracted near Ruabon and at Chatterley in the Potteries.

Brass and Copper

Copper was mined at Ecton, providing considerable income for the Dukes of Devonshire, and in the Parys Mine in Anglesey. There was also copper underground in South Wales, and the works of Birmingham, Smethwick and Spon Lane had better access to water-borne transport from Swansea. Copper had many uses as a metal, once it has been refined from the ores. It was also mixed with zinc oxide to make brass. The zinc oxide was produced by roasting and grounding calamine mined in Derbyshire.

At first, copper and brass were worked using water power. There were watermills at Cheadle and Oakamoor, where members of the Patten family dealt with copper and brass to produce wire, sheets and tubing. The making of the Uttoxeter Canal provided another means of transport to supplement the traditional method of land carriage from Oakamoor Mills. The copper works at Whiston near Froghall, owned by William Sneyd, were close to the Caldon Low Tramway. The plant there comprised a chaving house, coke shed, refinery and a paved area for laying out the copper.

There was a brassworks on the side of the Trent and Mersey Canal south of Stone. Water power, acting on an over-shot wheel, was used to drive the calamine mill, a copper refinery and four melting houses, where copper and zinc oxide were combined using the traditional method of mixing in clay pots, which were heated. A steam engine (36hp) drove the rolling mill where up to 250 rings of wire might be produced.

The process of making brass using ground calamine was to be replaced with a method whereby copper and zinc, as spelter, were combined – with often pyrotechnic results. This development led to works closures at Cheadle, Oakamoor and Stone, although Oakamoor did have a new lease of life working copper for Thomas Bolton & Sons from 1852. By then, the canal had closed and all traffic in copper was by railway.

Breweries and Beer Transport

Burton upon Trent became known for the quality of the water obtained from its wells, and that reputation led to the establishment of the brewing industry in the town. The original breweries were located beside the River Trent and were served by the Upper Trent Navigation and later the Bond End Canal. Beer intended for transport by the Trent and Mersey Canal had to be taken first by road to Horninglow Wharf. Some Burton breweries had

OLD BREWERY, FROM THE HAY.

Bass & Co., the first brewery at Burton.

wharves in Stoke-on-Trent. Allsop & Sons had a wharf in Wharf Street and Ind, Coope & Co. had one in Copeland Street.

Brewing was conducted in towns and cities throughout the country to suit local needs, but Burton beer became a common cargo on canals before the railway age. Bass & Co. was one brewer that became an extensive carrier by water.

Another brewing product was porter, which was carried from London by coastal navigation to Gainsborough. Both Thrale's and Whitbread's porter was offered for sale at William Crosby's warehouse at Cavendish Bridge. Wheelock also had a porter brewery, which was close to the Trent and Mersey Canal. Beer and porter was transported by the class of canal users known as the merchandise carriers.

Flour

Canal-side flour mills in the Potteries included Burslem, Milton and Stoke-on-Trent, with canal boats bringing grain and coal to the sites and taking flour away.

Moston Mills was built during the mid-1820s, and belongs to that rare group of watermills that drew their water supply from the canal. In 1824, the landowner spoke to James Caldwell and gained permission from the canal committee to draw water from the canal into a mill pool close to the canal. That water was returned to the canal at Crow's Nest Lock beside which the watermill was constructed. The corn mill with granary above was first worked by Thomas Arden. There was also a separate bone mill there.

With the development of the crank steam engine to turn the grinding stones, more flour mills were built beside the canal. As in the water-powered mills, the stones were often Derby or French.

Waterworks

There were two waterworks built beside the Trent and Mersey Canal, at Brindley Bank and Stockton Brook, with coal being brought by canal boat. Brindley Bank waterworks was owned by the South Staffordshire Water Company. Construction started in 1902 on a site north of the canal aqueduct. Pumping was done by a Hathorn, Davey & Co. 223hp steam engine until 1969. The work had been started with the drilling of two bore holes, with the main buildings completed between 1904 and 1907. A wharf was provided at the south end of the canal aqueduct for coal transhipment and a tramway was put down by A. Kopel to convey coal and ash.

Stockton Brook was built between 1881 and 1884 for the Staffordshire Potteries Waterworks Company. It was located beside the Caldon Canal and had a basin for canal transhipment. It also used a Hathorn Davey steam engine for pumping, until 1936.

Merchandise Trade

The origins of a merchandise trade by the canal may be seen as an extension of what previously existed in land transport and river navigation. The description covers a wide range of commodities, including items that are either cultivated or manufactured. Corn transport by navigation – for local use or exportation – was seen as an important development, as were the many other facets of the British manufacturing trade. An interchange between road and canal was key to establishing a general trade on the waterways. The canal-side warehouse provided the means of interchange as goods needing cover could be stored there, whilst the wharf was used for bulkier items.

In November 1771 John Latchford of Bar Beacon conveyed goods by road from Birmingham to Bromley Common, where there was a wharf and warehouse beside the Trent and Mersey Canal for transport to Gainsborough. Nails were charged at 6d a bag and other goods were charged in proportion to their bulk and value.

Stockton Brook Pumping Station.

Another early interchange point between the Trent and the Trent and Mersey Canal was Weston-on-Trent, where there was a warehouse established during 1771. In 1820 Thomas Hall owned the wharf and warehouse and later this wharf was associated with alabaster traffic from Aston passing on to Kings Mills.

Merchandise traffic was a core business, with fly boats moving goods at speed between Preston Brook, the Potteries, the West Midlands and London. There was also the trade to Shardlow, the canal port, near Derby, where goods were interchanged with Trent boats for the journey to Gainsborough and the coastal traders there.

As part of the trade network, the canal company built warehouses for the traders and for their own carrier Henshall & Co. Generally, it was not permitted for canal companies to carry on their own waterways, but Henshall had a 'loose' arrangement that was allowed. The carrier operated merchandise traffic on the Trent and Mersey and connecting waterways until 1812, when it decided to restrict itself to its lucrative business serving the potteries.

At this time a group of private common carriers operated along the canal network using the Trent and Mersey to reach Liverpool, Manchester and London. Some carriers such as Pickford and the Anderton Company had their own establishments. When the North Staffordshire Railway took over the canal they also acted as waterways traders, developing a close working relationship with the Bridgewater Trustees. Later still, the Bridgewater business was split between a re-formed Anderton Company and Fellows Morton. Anderton became the largest fleet owner from 1894, when they took over the North Staffordshire Railway carrying business. The Shropshire Union also operated boats along the Trent and Mersey then. Canal owners had since the mid-1840s been granted rights to carry on their own account.

One important element of the merchandise carrying trade was the traffic to and from Gainsborough, and the acquisition of Trent Port Wharf by the Gainsborough Boat Company, from 1 July 1793, proved to be a milestone. This wharf had previously been held by Caleb Maulin. It was located on the Nottinghamshire side of the River Trent, where there were warehouses and cranes erected for transfer with the coastal shipping trade. There were four people in the partnership: James Soresby, Shardlow; Ralph Turner, Hull; William Brightmore, Gainsborough; and Humphrey Moore, the Trent and Mersey agent for Shardlow and Horninglow. Goods were exchanged at Shardlow with boats owned by Henshall. Traffic serving the potteries and the salt works survived through to the time of British Transport Waterways, but declined after 1963.

Carrying Companies

Whilst Henshall was the company carrier engaged in moving merchandise often associated with the pottery trade and with depots at locations on adjacent waterways, its operations were confined to specific routes. These routes were bounded by Liverpool, Manchester, Birmingham, Stourport and Shardlow. This was Henshall's domain and it used company-owned warehouses and wharves on the Trent and Mersey Canal. In addition to carrying, it also purchased and sold pottery material.

PORTS ON THE MERSEY

The first trade route along the Weaver was to Frodsham. With the development of Runcorn, goods to and from the Mersey and Liverpool had the choice of either port, although the bulk of potters' material was sent through Runcorn. The opening of the Weston Canal in 1810 provided another Mersey link with the Weaver Navigation at Weston Point and the Weaver Trustees later improved the docks there from time to time. The Ellesmere and Chester Canal made new docks at Ellesmere Port, which became popular for the iron trade to and from North and South Staffordshire. The opening of the Middlewich Branch facilitated trade from the Trent and Mersey Canal to Ellesmere Port and the Border counties. After the completion of the Anderton Lift, much of the pottery trade in clay and earthenware was concentrated on the route to Weston Point. The Weaver Trustees further improved the docks there for this purpose.

Merchandise carriage by common carriers extended beyond the realm of Henshall & Co. These operations were generally partnerships or family-owned operations and often had a finite existence. Companies with a share issue would happen much later, in the railway era. Business could be precarious and unpredictable, however, and many followed a sad path to insolvency.

One principal carrying route was that between Runcorn and Shardlow, serving Liverpool, Manchester and Hull. This provided trade for not only Henshall, but also a growing number of carriers. These carriers operated either along the whole length of the canal or on part of it, serving the salt and potteries trade in particular, but also a growing business related to iron-making. Carrying firms based themselves at strategic points along the Trent and Mersey Canal and there was also a close link with Gainsborough, where the Trent and Mersey Canal Company controlled Trent Port.

The successful firms were involved in other business interests that were intertwined with the carrying trade, including the carriage of grain, pottery, salt or timber. In this respect, the merchandise carrier was often distinct from those that carried specific commodities such as coal, limestone or lime. One group of carriers that established themselves became common carriers, with a duty to carry anything a customer put their way. The organization was complex and also involved an element of road carriage. Arrangements were made with other carriers on adjacent routes so that a more comprehensive delivery and collection service could be provided. This included road transfer to locations not on the canal network, as well as river and coastal destinations, or cross-country canal routes.

From the Midlands and the north west, carriage of merchandise to and from London had involved road waggons or coastal trading vessels prior to 1790. In that year the Oxford Canal was completed and a trading route was created to London via the River Thames. However, the problems of interchange with Thames barges provided a barrier to general merchandise trade. Carrying firms such as Pickford preferred to transport by canal and turnpike to serve London. Although some firms did provide a merchandised carrying trade to London using existing water communications, it was not until the completion of the Grand Junction Canal from Braunston to Paddington Basin, and the Thames, at Brentford, that carriage by canal to London flourished.

The Trent and Mersey Canal became part of the route for goods on the waterways that served London, Liverpool and Manchester. A trade in fly boats was established by the select group of carriers that worked the canals promising to deliver merchandise in a matter of days. The craft were worked both day and night by male crews, stopping at only selected depots. They followed a timetable of a sort, which set the day and time of departure with the calling points arranged at set days. Horses were changed at regular intervals and there was an established organization of agents and wharfingers that dealt with the trade that developed. All manner of goods were moved in this fashion and for a period of thirty years the business gave employment to

---

CANAL MERCHANDISE CARRIERS

The carriage of merchandise was conducted by carriers that can be classified into different groups:

The Early Carriers
Firms such as Henshall & Co., Worthington & Gilbert and the Burton Boat Company, which conveyed any form of goods along the Trent and Mersey Canal and adjacent waterways.

Specialist Carriers
Transported specific cargoes such as corn, salt and timber but also acted as common carriers.

Fly Boat Traders
Travelled both day and night to move goods as speedily as possible, only calling at specific wharves en route.

Stage-Boat Carriers
Conveyed goods by day and moored up for the night, and often acted as a feeder service for the fly boats. Some carriers might operate both fly and stage boats.

Later Carriers
Following the development of the railways, the remaining carriers often dealt with a more specialist type of cargo, whilst still trading as common carriers.

many boatmen. Alongside this fast trade was the slower stage-boat trade, which moved goods in craft that travelled by day only and could be operated by just a man and a boy, or by a family.

This was a trade that was affected at first by the competition that came with the completion of the Birmingham and Liverpool Canal, which provided a rival route between the West Midlands to Liverpool via Ellesmere Port. The inception of the public railways presented a new challenge for canal carrying, as the growth in railway organizations led to the creation of clearing houses, which facilitated a united form of merchandise carriage. The canal companies did not have access to such facilities, yet within the canal network the carriers did have a rival organization, which had been established over time. Through a network of agents, goods carried by water could be exchanged between canal carriers, river carriers and coastal navigation. Arrangements might also extend to road carriage, which had been improved with the making of new turnpikes. As railway competition increased, the number of canal carrying companies decreased through mergers, but a core element of traders remained. Merchandise carriers had their headquarters around the canal network.

Private carriers included James Sutton, based in Shardlow. When he stopped carrying, his trade went to the Staffordshire carrier James Fellows. During the 1860s the Shropshire Union Railway and Canal Company started to carry pottery goods, salt and general merchandise to new warehouses it had built in the Potteries. Changes with the Bridgewater organization led to the Anderton Company becoming independent again and the disposal of the South Staffordshire trade to Fellows, Morton & Co.

A big loss to the Trent and Mersey carrying trade was the decision made by Pickford to cease carrying and limit their remaining canal trade to railway interchange traffic in South Staffordshire. A large part of their business passed to the Grand Junction Canal Carrying Co., which retained a wharf in the Potteries. Eventually, Fellows, Morton & Co. took over the Grand Junction business. They, Anderton and the Shropshire Union became principal merchandise carriers on the Trent and Mersey Canal. A new carrier, the Mersey and Weaver Carrying Company, became another rival trader, once the Manchester Ship Canal had opened. They had a close association with the Salt Union and during the early years of the twentieth century were part of their organization. From 1934, after the Salt Union became part of the Imperial Chemical Industries, the Mersey and Weaver Company became an independent concern. Other carriers included John Rayner and Potter & Sons, both of Runcorn.

Merchandise Wharves and Warehouses

There were two groups of wharf and warehouse on the Trent and Mersey Canal. The first comprised the property owned by the canal company and the second group were those that were privately owned. The infrastructure included the warehouse buildings, stables, offices and cranes. In some cases, the warehouse spanned a basin so that boats could be unloaded under cover.

Warehouses are still to be found at various places along the canal and are a lasting reminder of the former trade. At Stone, these buildings have been said to have been built in 1787, but evidently had replaced earlier structures. When these buildings ceased to have a canal function in 1955, a former employee of the railway and canal companies was asked to give a statutory declaration of ownership, Trent and Mersey records being untraceable, so that the building could pass into private hands.

Warehouses were built at different times in the development of the network. Some were constructed as the canal was made, while others came later, as trade increased. Canal company warehouses were established and operated along the length of the canal, its branches and the leased Newcastle-under-Lyme Canal. The greatest concentration of company wharves was located in the Potteries where the canal company not only acted as carriers, but also as suppliers of pottery material. Space was provided by the canal company for crates, ground flint and china clay.

Wheelock wharf, warehouse and road bridge, around 1970.

Bromley wharf.

Shardlow warehouses.

London Road Wharves, Shardlow.

London Road warehouse at Shardlow.

There were a number of warehouses located at Shardlow, with some of the best examples still to be found there. Often described as an inland port, Shardlow played an important role in the interchange of goods between Trent boats and narrow boats. With navigation links established to Derby and Nottingham, the carrying trade moved away to these places, and Shardlow became a port that time forgot. By 1830, it was a place where canal craft passed through, rather than stopping to use the warehouse facilities. For the River Trent, the wharves on the Nottingham Canal at Nottingham also came to have a strategic importance.

The wharf and warehouse buildings often survived through a usefulness for other purposes and as an outpost for the Trent Navigation Company when they chose to improve their trade on the River Trent from 1920. Key warehouses belonged to the carrying companies Soresby & Flack and Sutton & Co., which took over much of the East Midlands trade from Henshall after 1812. Sutton's Wharf was a group of buildings east of the London Road, whilst Soresby had its warehouse on the east side of the Great Wharf. The earliest warehouse faced London Road and is said to have been built in the 1770s. Located on the west side of London Road, this land was previously owned by the Cavendish Boat Company, which carried to Birmingham and Stoke-on-Trent as soon as the relevant canals were completed. Bankruptcy amongst the partners, who included William Crosby and John Webster, led to the sale of the property in June 1781 and the acquisition of the wharf land by the Trent and Mersey Canal Company.

Private carriers also had a share of this trade and they might own wharves, or an independent wharfinger would own a wharf and warehouse and allow traders to use them. At the heart of all arrangements were the charges made for warehouse storage, porterage and the use of a crane. Like the canal company depots, there was a concentration of these wharfs in the Potteries, with most deployed along the length between Stoke-on-Trent and Longport. In the railway age, the Shropshire Union Railway and Canal Company, Anderton Canal Carrying Company and the Mersey and Weaver Canal Company all had warehouses in this area.

When the Shropshire Union Railway and Canal Company ceased trading in 1921, several of its Potteries trading boats were purchased by the Anderton Company, although their Trent and Mersey depots, such as Burslem, passed to the Mersey and Weaver Canal Company. During the 1930s the London, Midland and Scottish Railway estate office at Crewe started to let some of the company-owned warehouses for alternative use.

CHAPTER 7

Canal People

The Role of the Engineers

James Brindley (1716–1772) takes most of the credit for the initial surveying of and inspiration for the waterway, but he relied on the assistance of other engineers and a clerk of works for each of his canal projects. The contractors employed to cut the canal, build the bridges and locks and make the tunnels were often part of a pool of workers, a select group who worked on jobs across the various canal schemes.

Brindley was also involved in the establishment of various business ventures. The canal watershed near Ranscliff, where the land was owned by Hugh Henshall, James Brindley, John Gilbert and William Clowes, provided an opportunity for industrial development. The canal tunnel passed through coal, ironstone and millstone grit and the branch canal tunnels enabled the exploitation of the coal and ironstone measures. Later, surface railways and inclines from canal-side wharves assisted development in this area.

James Brindley was engineer to the core network of canals that joined the Trent and Mersey. With the assistance of the clerks of works, he operated at the top of a pyramid of organization associated with the canal construction. Brindley directed what needed to be done, delegating to the assistant engineers

James Brindley.

a share of the work. The organization extended across a wide region, to include the Birmingham, Coventry, Chesterfield, Droitwich, Oxford, Staffordshire and Worcestershire and the Trent and Mersey canals – although the Coventry Canal proprietors chose to dispose with his services and complete their canal under different engineers. Brindley also acted as a consultant elsewhere, for example, on the embryonic Leeds and Liverpool Canal project, which had started as a proposal to link the East and West Seas by canal in 1766. Brindley was engaged in surveying and checking the work of John Longbotham, who had suggested the canal, and made revisions to the route.

James Brindley married Hugh Henshall's sister, Ann, at Wolstanton and moved to Turnhurst Hall, where he was able to pursue his more important engineering projects. It was in the grounds of Turnhurst Hall that he constructed an experimental lock prior to using the design on his narrow canal projects.

Hugh Henshall (1734–1816) worked as a surveyor in Cheshire, Gloucestershire and Staffordshire. In 1765, he was involved with Robert Pownall on a survey from Winsford to Lawton via Middlewich for the Weaver Navigation. This experience proved of use when he was later engaged in building the Cheshire Locks. He drew up the parliamentary map for the Trent and Mersey Canal bill and generally assisted Brindley with the engineering of the new canal. Henshall replaced Brindley as principal engineer when Brindley died in 1772, an appointment that was confirmed by the General Assembly on 29 October 1772. He was recommended in the strongest terms by the canal committee 'from experience of his good conduct and attention as clerk of works'.

Henshall's skill lay in surveying waterways and he obtained contracts for a number of canal schemes. The works included the alteration of Brindley's route through Barnton and Saltersford tunnels, the survey of the Caldon Canal and the improvement of the water supply to the canal.

A number of other engineers had significant influence during the independent years of the Trent and Mersey Canal Company, chiefly John Rennie, Thomas Telford and James Trubshaw. Other consultant or resident engineers who assisted with the development of the canal through its changing roles included Thomas Dadford, Joseph Potter, James Potter and Francis Giles.

Although he later gained a reputation as an engineer, Josiah Clowes (1735–1794) is best considered in connection with the Trent and Mersey as a contractor making the canal. He advertised for labourers at Middlewich and was involved in the construction work on the waterway as it approached completion. He was also a partner in the carrying firm of Henshall & Co. As a canal engineer and surveyor, he was associated with various other canal construction projects, such as the Dudley Canal and Thames and Severn.

John Rennie was responsible for the Leek Canal Uttoxeter Branch and improvements to the canal, including Rudyard Reservoir and alterations at the

John Rennie.

staircase locks at Lawton. He also made surveys for the Burslem and Hanley branches and finally the existing Harecastle Tunnel, prior to his death.

Rennie had extensive experience in canal construction and was also the engineer for the Kennet and Avon, Lancaster and Rochdale canals as well as schemes that did not go ahead, such as the Glenkenns Canal. He was aided in a number of canal construction projects by Hugh McIntosh (1768–1840), who worked on making the Leek Canal, Burslem Branch, Uttoxeter Canal and Lawton Locks, and was employed on such work up to 1816. He married Mary Cross, the daughter of William Cross (1744–1827), a farmer and agent for the Trent and Mersey Canal, who had made early surveys for the Leek Branch.

Charles Roberts (1751–1806) assisted with the construction of the Caldon Canal and between 1796 and 1797 was involved with surveying work on the Newcastle-under-Lyme Junction Canal and the water supply to the Trent and Mersey Canal.

Joseph Potter (1755–1842) was the resident engineer on the Leek Branch and was also consulted on other Trent and Mersey projects, when James Caldwell was on the select committee. James Potter, his son, was employed as an assistant engineer to the Trent and Mersey Canal and worked with John Rennie and Thomas Telford.

Thomas Telford (1757–1834) made important changes to the Trent and Mersey Canal between 1822 and 1831. His improvements comprised four projects: the Harecastle Tunnel, Knypersley Second Reservoir, the Hall End Branch and the Wardle Branch. Telford had a long association with and lengthy experience of the building of roads and canals. By 1822 he had been engineer on many important projects. During his work on the Trent and Mersey, he was also engineer to the Birmingham Canal Navigations, the Birmingham and Liverpool Junction Canal and the Ellesmere and Chester Canal (Middlewich Branch and Ellesmere Port). Any involvement with other Trent and Mersey Canal projects is more difficult to determine. There was, it appears, a belief on the part of certain canal committee members that Telford's involvement with the Birmingham and Liverpool Junction Canal was not in the interest of the Trent and Mersey Canal. This project, with which Telford became involved in 1826, was a rival route to the Trent and Mersey Canal. The misgivings of the committee were further amplified by the problems that occurred at Knypersley Reservoir during construction. As a result of these concerns, future projects were directed elsewhere and other engineers were invited to give their input into canal affairs.

Whilst Telford's name has been linked with the concept of the Cheshire Lock duplication, this work is probably better attributed to the vision and plans of James Caldwell. It is possible that Telford gave advice on the delays to traffic caused by the single locks on the Cheshire side of the canal and the increased traffic that would result through the new Harecastle Tunnel. However, no survey by Telford has been found. There were, however, the surveys made in 1825 and 1827 by Francis Giles for the Trent and Mersey Canal, which may be relevant to the duplication of the locks from Wheelock to Lawton.

Francis Giles (1787–1847) was born in the same year as William Faram, who also worked for the Trent and Mersey. Giles was employed as surveyor and then as a civil engineer. In his witness statement in the bill for the Liverpool and Manchester Railway, he was critical of the making of the railway across Chat Moss. There were several occasions when he stayed with Caldwell, at his home in Linley Wood, discussing navigation matters. This was a period when the duplication of the Cheshire Locks was discussed, as well as a suggested link between the Trent and Mersey Canal and Acton Quay and the River Weaver near Acton Bridge.

Francis Giles's input in Trent and Mersey Canal affairs was received in at least two recorded cases. The first was the survey made for the Hall End Branch in 1825, by Giles and James Potter. Potter is credited with drawing the map for the application to Parliament. Giles's other survey was the plan, book of reference and section of 'the intended canal from the Trent and Mersey Canal near Limekiln Lock at or near Stone to the Staffordshire and Worcestershire Canal at or near Baswich and also the intended canal from near Kingston Pool to or near Lamberscote Farm House, County of Stafford'.

James Trubshaw (1777–1853) had a principal, or consulting, engineering role to the canal after Thomas Telford. There were some overlapping roles undertaken by Joseph Potter and Francis Giles during the busy reconstruction period of 1820–1840, yet it was Trubshaw who was to have a crucial input from 1833. He was associated with construction, repair or supervision on reservoirs, feeders and other works. His obituaries mention this fact, but not the detail. Some major engineering was conducted at this time, including the removal of the Etruria and Meaford staircase locks, the Stanley Reservoir dam and new locks and an aqueduct at Hazelhurst, the last Caldon Low tramway.

Like Telford, Trubshaw was associated with the masonry trade, but, unlike Telford, who hailed from a humble background, he came from a family that had built up an extensive fortune. He was born the son of James and Elizabeth Trubshaw, at Mount Pleasant, Colwich, on 13 February 1777. Elizabeth was the second wife of James Trubshaw senior. Their union produced nine children, with John the oldest and James the second oldest. James senior also had two older sons, Thomas and Richard, by his first wife Margaret. Several of the sons were trained by their father in the masonry trade and the family members were involved in many design and construction projects. James Trubshaw senior also became county surveyor. Still, financial difficulties led to the sale of Mount Pleasant and a move to a smaller house.

James Trubshaw learnt his trade with James Wyatt, an architect in Stafford. In 1799–1800, James and his elder brother John assisted their father in completing Wolseley Bridge and in 1800 James married Mary Bott. They moved to Stone and had six children between 1802 and 1811. Trubshaw built a new family house, Hawlesmore Lodge at Little Haywood, and it was from this base that he ran his business as building contractor, engineer and architect.

It is helpful to understand the Trubshaw family connections, as the names Charles, James and John Trubshaw are all associated with the Trent and Mersey Canal. The fact that there were two James Trubshaws, father and son, both architects, complicates any attribution as to who did what. For example, James Trubshaw was assisted by James Trubshaw junior and nephew John Trubshaw on the Dee Bridge at Chester. An understanding of the roles undertaken by the two James is helped by the fact that James Trubshaw junior went on to work in the foundry trade at Stafford, until bankruptcy, in 1841. After this time, he became an architect.

John Trubshaw, the nephew, was a son of John, the elder brother of James. Later, that John was an architect and a building contractor. He had two brothers, Charles and James, who also became architects. James Trubshaw, of Little Haywood, had two other sons, Thomas and Richard, who were architects. So the extended Trubshaw family had at various times seven members involved in the building trades and canal affairs, and some also acted later as railway contractors. This is another fact that makes any resolution of individual roles difficult.

John Trubshaw, brother of James of Little Haywood, was one of the surveyors employed by the Trent and Mersey Canal and was involved with works such as water supply until his death in 1834, at Endon. Charles Trubshaw, his son, offered to replace his father as surveyor. His appointment by the committee appears to have been a junior role to William Faram, yet both were engaged in surveying duties whilst Caldwell remained chairman. Thereafter, Charles Trubshaw went on to be surveyor to the Newcastle-under-Lyme Canal as well as becoming an established architect in his own right.

William Faram (1787–1854) was born in Stoke to John and Martha Faram. He was one of several brothers, including Samuel and James, who worked on canal repair, reconstruction or new work. In 1820 he was recorded as carpenter when he became a member of the Masons, and in the 1841 Census he was listed as a surveyor, living in Middlewich. He was associated with important works such as the staircase replacements and the doubling of many of the locks in Cheshire. By the time of the takeover by the North Staffordshire Railway, William Faram's association with the canal had ceased and in 1851 he was a bookkeeper in a timber yard near Wheelock. Samuel Faram lived at Thurlwood and was a brick-maker and builder.

From 1847 there were many staff changes. Company records mention a Mr Giles and a Mr Rigby as canal surveyors until December 1848, when James Forbes was appointed surveyor at a salary of £250. The resident (railway) engineer was Mr John Curphey Forsyth (1815–1879); according to company minutes, it had been agreed

> That Mr Forsyth's appointment as engineer for canal date from 15th Jan 1847 and cease 31 December 1848 and that from such date he be appointed resident engineer to company at a yearly salary of £600 until the entire line is opened and at £650 thereafter with an increase of £50 pa for every ½ per cent beyond 5½ per cent dividend paid to the proprietors.

Forsyth was resident engineer until 1865 and also general manager between 1853 and 1863. With the takeover by the North Staffordshire Railway, the canal engineers tended to be involved with repair and maintenance, although there were occasions when greater skills were required. These included the improvements to the Cheshire sections following the 1865 Act and the making of the Anderton Lift by the Weaver Trustees. In this respect, there are a number of engineers who deserve special mention.

James Forbes (1804–1866) was often involved with the day-to-day engineering issues of the canal such as pollution and subsidence. He spent much of his adult life in the Army, serving with the Royal Sappers and Miners regiment until 1843. His home was the Barracks at Woolwich until his retirement, with the rank of Sergeant Major, in 1843. It was a very different life for him with the North Staffordshire Railway, where he lived at a canal-side house at Etruria Vale. He died at Caledonian House on 15 February 1866. Richard Blundell was in the post of civil engineers' clerk when Forbes was engineer and was then employed as an engineer when he lived at Etruria House, canal-side.

Edward Blakeney Smith (1847–1907) proposed an important change to the Cheshire Locks, in which the existing locks in parts of the Cheshire flight would be reconstructed for barges. Although that work did not take place, Blakeney Smith did supervise the widening of the canal from Anderton to Middlewich between 1891 and 1893. He was also entrusted with the improvement of water supply through the enlargement of Rudyard Lake. The last North Staffordshire Railway canal engineer was Harry Curbishley (1864–1931), who deserves credit for keeping the canal in operation at a time when the North Staffordshire Railway remained intent on waterways improvement. He was involved with electric towage through Harecastle New Tunnel, the building of Planet Lock, the doubling of some of the remaining locks on the Cheshire flight, Croxton Aqueduct reconstruction and raising the dam and reservoir walls at Rudyard Lake. Curbishley was retained by the London, Midland and Scottish as engineer, but then retired on a pension after fifty years' service.

While the former operations of the North Staffordshire Railway had been based at Stoke-on-Trent, the extensive London, Midland and Scottish engineers' department had staff based at Crewe, Derby, London and Stoke. The bridge work was often dealt with at Derby, whilst reservoirs and general engineering issues were the responsibility of the local office in Stoke. Graham Wood Massey (1884–1954) became canal engineer for the Trent and Mersey Canal, based at Stoke. Massey had grown up around the waterways. His father John had been associated with the Shropshire Union Railway and Canal Company as engineer, clerk and secretary, while his older brother Frederick had become assistant to George Jebb, engineer for both the Shropshire Union and the Birmingham Canal navigations. Graham Massey also trained with and gained engineering experience from Jebb, working as a canal clerk and then as a canal engineer based in Birmingham, before moving to Stoke-on-Trent to take up the post of assistant engineer on the Trent and Mersey Canal. Massey followed Harry Curbishley in that post, and found himself there during difficult times of water shortage and reservoir improvements in the 1930s. He retired in 1944.

With the formation of the Docks and Inland Waterways Executive, most of the Trent and Mersey Canal became the responsibility of the North West Division at Lime Street, Liverpool. Alexander Muir White (1892–1961) held the post of Divisional Engineer until his retirement in 1956. He was replaced by Edward Radcliffe (1915–2003), who oversaw the last structural improvements at Marston & Thurlwood. 'Teddy' Radcliffe was an accomplished engineer and had been chief engineer for the construction of the new town at Newton Aycliffe, Co. Durham. He left the canal in 1959 to become engineer to Liverpool University, a post he held until retirement in 1980.

From 1963 the British Waterways Board reorganized the waterways again, creating a Northern and Southern region for England and Wales and leaving Scotland as a separate region. The chief engineer was based at Watford. The Trent and Mersey Canal was brought together again under the control of the Northern Region.

John Sparrow.

Canal Managers and Staff

The role of clerk to the company, at first, made a significant contribution to company affairs, as was often the case with successful canal companies. The first man to fill this post was John Sparrow, who was succeeded by his brother Thomas Sparrow. John Sparrow (born 6 February 1737, died 8 November 1822) was in many ways a primary architect of the canal. He contributed to the establishment of the company, and oversaw taking the bills through Parliament and the land purchases. He was a solicitor at Newcastle-under-Lyme and later made his home at Bishton Hall beside the canal.

During Thomas Sparrow's lengthy tenure as clerk, the post of principal agent was created, first to assist the clerk and then gradually gaining in importance and effectively taking over the management of the canal. There were three men who filled the post: William Robinson, William Vaughan and Henry Moore. Thomas Sparrow retained his position as clerk until the 1820s, but his role did change with the appointment of William Robinson as principal agent. Sparrow was also clerk to the independent Newcastle-under-Lyme Canal, which regularly had the operation let on tolls, in a similar fashion to the turnpikes.

William Robinson, the first principal agent, was involved with the affairs of the company until 1816. He died of a heart attack at Stone and was replaced by William Vaughan. Robinson was agent at the

> **CANAL CLERKS**
>
> The job of principal clerk was initially a responsible one, looking after the day-to-day organization of company affairs. Legal training or qualifications were an important requirement for the role, in order to deal with the enforcement of the Acts of Parliament and any leases and agreements. All canal companies had a clerk associated with the management of the company affairs, and clerks' names regularly appeared on the published notices and by-laws.

beginning of a period of change and consolidation, with many improvements to the navigation being planned. William Vaughan was agent to the company at Stone between 1816 and 1834. This was a period of significant change, during which new canal links were established, rivalry from new waterways had to be faced, and potential competition from the railway schemes began to be an issue.

On Vaughan's death, in 1834, the post was taken over by Henry Moore, who was agent during the last years of reconstruction and the first years of competition from the new railways. This was also a time of concern for the values and morals of those working in and around the waterways, following the murder of Christina Collins. One outcome was the stoppage, wherever possible, of Sunday trading on the canal. Henry Moore came originally from Clerkenwell in London, and returned to the city later in life to work as a solicitor's clerk.

James Caldwell (1759–1838) had several business interests. He was clerk to John Sparrow from February 1777 and later a partner in the law firm of Sparrow and Caldwell at Newcastle-under-Lyme. For many years he was Recorder for Newcastle-under-Lyme, and was later a magistrate. He was also a partner with Enoch Wood in a pottery at Burslem and had partnerships in the Macclesfield, Newcastle and Shrewsbury Breweries. His position as chairman of the select committee for the Trent and Mersey Canal came at a crucial time of the development of the canal. He guided the canal through these times of change and competition. His legal training was invaluable when dealing with the preparation of new bills for Parliament, which included a number that were successful and some that were not. His home at Linley Wood was often used as a venue for meetings to discuss canal business over the period from 1814 to 1834, and his diary provides a crucial insight into these times. People who visited Linley Wood included John Rennie and Thomas Telford.

Francis Twemlow (1783–1865) was chairman of the Trent and Mersey Canal during the final years of its independent existence. The second son of Thomas Twemlow of Sandbach, he had been trained in the law and replaced Sir Oswald Mosley as chairman of the Quarter Sessions at Stafford, a post he held for twenty-four years. Twemlow had the task of completing the arrangements of the purchase of the canal by the North Staffordshire Railway between 1845 and 1846. Both he and the select committee had the difficult task of making arrangements that would be favourable to the shareholders and at the same time ensure the continued existence of the waterway. It was a credit to him that both these objects were achieved.

William Douglas Phillipps (1839–1932) was general manager of the North Staffordshire Railway and the Trent and Mersey Canal when he gave evidence to the Royal Commission on Canals on 22 May 1906. He had previously been dock master and manager of the Llanelly Railway and Dock Company.

Other People

The potter Thomas Whieldon (1719–1795) assisted with expenses for James Brindley's 1758 survey and was joint treasurer with Josiah Wedgwood in the fund for the Act of Parliament. His pottery was at Little Fenton.

John Gilbert (1724–1795) was agent to the Duke of Bridgewater and has been credited with the principal engineering works of the Bridgewater Canal, as well as assisting with the making of the Trent and Mersey Canal (often referred to in his time as the 'Staffordshire Canal'). He married Lydia Bill, with whom he had four children, including the younger John. The association between the Gilbert and Bill families went back at least to the second half of the seventeenth century, when the Gilberts acquired an interest in Cloughead Colliery (through George Gilbert's first marriage to Ellen Whieldon). They worked the colliery with the Bill family for forty or fifty years, mainly as a source of fuel for lime burning at Caldon Low and later for the smelting mill at Alton. John Gilbert senior, partner in the carrying company of Worthington & Gilbert, died in 1795. The younger John Gilbert, the last of the Gilbert entrepreneurs, died in 1812. By the time of his death, the family were secure enough not to have to engage in employment, as they were able to live comfortably on income from their investments and rents.

Women in Canal Affairs

The role of women in the canal network was often associated with the owning of shares and property, as well as, through strategic marriage, being the means of uniting business concerns between families. Some women, however, had a more direct role in canal carrying. They were sometimes partners and more closely involved with operations. One example is Nancy Whitehouse, who took over the canal carrying business of John Whitehouse & Sons, when her husband became bankrupt. Elizabeth Swain ran a carrying operation from Birmingham to Gainsborough after the death of her husband Thomas; later, her son George managed the business with his two sisters.

Nobility Associated with the Management of the Canal

The Earls of Harrowby had a family seat at Sandon, near the Trent and Mersey Canal, with a wharf for their use. Dudley Ryder (1762–1847) was the First Earl of Harrowby; he was succeeded by his son Dudley Ryder (1798–1882).

Sir George Chetwynd (1783–1850), of Brocton Hall near Stafford, and Grendon Hall near Atherstone, Warwickshire, had strong associations with the Trent and Mersey Canal. Born the eldest son of Sir George Chetwynd, 1st Baronet of Brocton, he entered Lincoln's Inn in 1808 to study law and was called to the bar in 1813. He succeeded his father to the title in 1824. He was the Member of Parliament for Stafford from 1820 to 1826 and was appointed Sheriff of Warwickshire for 1828–29. His connection with the Trent and Mersey Canal became closer when he married Hannah Maria Sparrow, the daughter of John Sparrow. George Chetwynd gave evidence at the inquiry into the Collins murder, which questioned the morals of boat people and highlighted their lack of religion and education. He died in 1850.

Ordinary People

Many people associated with the canal fall into this category, including the toll clerks, boatmen, inn-keepers and workers who maintained the canal. Also in this group are the policemen who patrolled the towpath to ensure the safe transit of the goods and material conveyed by boat. One such was Richard Glass, who lived at Etruria and was constable for the Stoke area, keeping check on the boatmen's activities and prosecuting them for crimes such as wasting water, theft or acts of violence. The brutal assault of Emma Vaughan by her husband, Thomas, was one particular case of violence that involved Glass. Vaughan repeatedly hit his wife with a windlass on 2 July 1869 in their boat cabin. The crime began with a domestic argument and ended with the bloodied Emma Vaughan running to the nearby canal inspector's house for medical assistance. Vaughan received a fourteen-month prison sentence. After his release, he tried to sell iron that he had stolen from his employers Williamson Brothers. He was handed a seven-year prison term. Once he was free again, records show that he continued to keep the canal company constables busy, often getting involved in fights.

In the early morning light of 17 June 1839, the body of Christina Collins was discovered in the canal near Bellamour Turnover bridge (page 62). Thomas Grant, a passing boatman, noticed the body when the wharfinger from Bellamoore Wharf, John Johnson, was approaching to inspect a piece of canal bank repairs. A boatman's hook was used to bring the body to the side, the wharfinger pulled the body out of the canal and later it was conveyed to the Talbot on a hurdle (a fence part) by four men. Here an inquest was held which led to criminal proceedings against the crew of the Pickfords fly boat, in which she had been a passenger.

CHAPTER 8

Decline and Restoration

Changes in Canal Traffic

It is said that the twentieth century was the century of the people. Certainly, the identity of those who had influence in politics changed from 1920. This was also a time that saw an increased use of the internal combustion engine, which led to greater numbers of lorries on roads. At about the same time semi-diesel engines started to be used to power canal boats. Use of inland navigation was diminishing, even though there were those who wanted to improve parts of the network for the future. Unfortunately, it was a time when the hopes of the North Staffordshire Railway Company for waterway improvements came to an end.

The decline of the canal had begun with the North Staffordshire Railway abandoning part of the Newcastle-under-Lyme Canal and the Caldon Low Tramway (1920). The London, Midland and Scottish ensured the abandonment of most of the remainder of the Newcastle-under-Lyme Canal (1935) and then closed the Leek Branch by Act of Parliament, in 1944, although the first 2 miles of the Leek Branch were kept as a feeder for the water from Rudyard Lake.

Prior to 1914, there had been an inclination towards continued waterway improvements. In entering into a partnership that would work in the interest of both railway and canal, the North Staffordshire Railway was perhaps unique up to this time. Had sufficient finance been available, the canal improvements might have been more substantial. As a railway company, the North Staffordshire also made many attempts at mergers and amalgamations with other railways, but one restricting factor was the canal. Trade on the waterway was declining as traffic was diverted to rail. Unlike South Staffordshire, the transport of coal by water dwindled as the modern collieries were located away from the waterway and were therefore best served by rail.

Salt-making was another industry that was undergoing significant change. With the development of the vacuum method, many of the existing salt works had closed. Many ironworks had also closed and the canal traffic in ironstone ceased, as the mines raising the ores and ironstone closed. With the closure of the Caldon Low railway, much of the limestone traffic was limited to despatch from Endon Basin. With the takeover of Brunner Mond and the Salt Union by the Imperial Chemical Industries, a change in supply arrangements was made, which sourced limestone from elsewhere. The pottery-makers were also in decline, which reduced the need for china clay and flint.

During the First World War, the operation of the waterways had been controlled by the government.

THE TRENT AND MERSEY CANAL DURING THE SECOND WORLD WAR

As had been the case during the First World War, canals and river navigation were eventually brought under government control in the Second World War, mainly through the efforts of Frank Pick. Regional canal committees were set up from 1941, reporting to a central canal committee. For the canal carriers these were challenging times with altered traffic flows. It was also a time of worry about potential enemy invasion, and pill boxes were constructed for defence purposes. Indeed, there was some damage to property and waterways infrastructure as a result of German bombing. Bridge 117, a brick arch, at Etruria Locks, was one that was damaged, taken down and replaced after a bomb hit the structure in 1940.

Pill box at the Dove Aqueduct.

With the end of this arrangement in 1921, subsidies also ended, with significant consequences. It was decided to end canal carrying operations for the Shropshire Union Railway and Canal Company from 1 September 1921, and this would have an effect on the potteries trade, leaving other carriers to take up that business.

Some traffic related to the potteries and the salt trade remained on the waterway after the Second World War, even though it continued to diminish steadily. Firm such as Seddons of Middlewich still carried salt to the Anderton Boat Lift and there were some commercial carrying firms. During the war, commercial canal carrying had adapted to the needs of the supply of ordnance and goods for the war effort and government control of both railways and canals lasted until after the war. In 1947, the incoming Labour government had a new vision: the nationalization of the service industries of transport, coal, power and gas.

The transfer of the canals to the Docks and Inland Waterways Executive was defined by the Transport Act, which came into force from 1 January 1948 (10 and 11 Geo 6 c49, 6 August 1947). This Act created a controlling public body called the British Transport Commission. For the Trent and Mersey Canal, the

Boating near Wychnor at Bridge 40.

transfer was made instead to the Railway Executive and the London Midland Region.

The transfer of the canals to the Docks and Inland Waterways Executive took effect from 30 July 1948. The Executive then set about taking over certain carrying operations, purchasing the fleet and depots of Fellows, Morton & Clayton in the same year. However, the Anderton and the Mersey and Weaver companies remained independent for the time being.

With nationalization came a form of segregation for the Trent and Mersey. The bulk from Burton to Preston Brook was placed within the North Western Region, whilst the remainder to the River Trent became part of the North Eastern Region. The period of ownership of the Docks and Inland Waterways Executive was the first time that a large group of navigations in England, Scotland and Wales had become part of a single authority. This authority also absorbed former railway-owned ports around the coastline. The time of the Executive was a period of consolidation.

Political change, with the election of a Conservative government, led to the Transport Act of 1953 and the disposal of the Road Executive and the Railway Executive being taken over by the British Railways Board. The British Transport Commission decided, as a measure of decentralization, to separate the management of the docks and waterways from 1 January 1955. Sir Reginald H. Kerr was appointed general manager of the organization, which was named British Transport Waterways and had a London office at 22 Dorset Square. The division boundaries were retained. At the same time there was a policy to recruit new engineers. The board was confronted with a need for cost-saving, with canal closures on its agenda, along with the other tasks of finding traffic and maintaining waterways that had long been neglected in terms of maintenance.

There were limited prospects for commercial traffic on the Trent and Mersey Canal, and the future seemed to lie with improvements of the Weaver and the trade along the River Trent from Nottingham, effectively turning back the clock to the pre-Brindley era. Parts of the Trent and Mersey Canal had already closed to trade. For a long section of the Caldon Canal, the water was simply conveyed by pipe and there was talk of complete closure. Yet there was a group of users of the canal that were increasing in number by the year and the month – the leisure boaters. There had been a growing interest in boating along the canals and this increased significantly during the 1950s.

Commercial provision for boat hire began in a small way. Early hirers included the Inland Cruising Association, which in the late 1940s had a base at Rowton Bridge on the Shropshire Union Canal, near Chester. Their hire craft could reach the Trent and Mersey Canal by way of the Middlewich Branch.

Canal Subsidence

In Staffordshire, coal-mining led to subsidence in the Stoke area and a long length of the canal was affected by the problem. It led to the North Staffordshire Railway, the London, Midland and Scottish, and later owners to embank the canal to higher levels, with concrete being extensively used.

In Cheshire, the area around Marbury and Thurlwood was badly affected through subsidence into old salt workings. One of the locks at Thurlwood was replaced by a steel version made to a subsidence-resistant design in 1958. Considerable work was needed to keep the canal open. British Transport Waterways decided to construct a steel tank that would be self-supporting in the event of differential settlement, and could be jacked straight and level. Following subsidence, the lock pit would be sealed off from the canal water to prevent flooding. At first, it was necessary to replace a temporary bridge with a double-span bridge, to transport heavy civil engineering plant. The new bridge was built with pre-stressed concrete beams on concrete abutments and was completed in 1956. Demolition

Wedgwood Pottery at Etruria.

Former railway bridge at Etruria, 119B.

of the towing path started in mid-1956 with a new concrete retaining wall constructed to support the offside lock. Steel work was ordered in 1956, but there was a shortage and delivery was delayed. The lock was prefabricated at the contractor's works at Dalmarnock and sections were delivered to the site by road for erection towards the end of 1957.

The exterior dimensions of the new lock were as follows: length 106 feet, height 45 feet, width 18 feet. The lock itself was 72 feet long, 7 feet 9 inches wide and 18 feet deep. There were concrete abutments and the upper and lower ends of the lock were sealed in a bed of clay. Guillotine gates were installed at each end. These were chain-driven and had a locking device to prevent more than one gate being lifted at a time. The four sluices and sluice pipes were based on traditional lock equipment. Sir William Arrol & Co. of Glasgow was the contractor, who did the work at a cost of £61,000. This firm had a reputation for bridge-building, with a portfolio that included the Forth Railway Bridge.

At the same time, the canal at Marston was diverted along a new alignment, following subsidence near Marston Hall Rock Salt Mine. The stretch north of this spot had been affected by a breach in 1907. In 1957 British Transport Waterways chose to move the canal away from the worst-affected parts of the new slip. Work started in the summer of 1957 and was expected to be completed and open to traffic within sixteen weeks, but bad weather caused the site to be waterlogged and virtually no work was undertaken for a time. The contract was completed in March 1958, by contractors George Dew and Co. Ltd of Oldham, under the superintendence of E. W. Ratcliffe, who was engineer for the North East Division of British Transport Waterways.

The length of this section was 1,750 feet, with a width of 55 feet and a depth of 5 feet. The bed width was 20 feet and the towpath width 8 feet. Concrete walls were provided on the offside for a distance of 1,400 feet and along the towpath for 1,320 feet. The depth of the concrete walls varied from 4 feet to 12 feet. There was also a length of steel piling that amounted to 750 feet sunk to a depth of between 9 feet and 18 feet; 20,000 cu yards of spoil were excavated. The cost was £30,000, including the purchase of the land.

This new line of waterway remains in use to the present day, although the Thurlwood Lock had only a brief existence and was later removed.

The End of Commercial Canal Carrying

British Transport Waterways continued with a carrying operation, but it was in terminal decline. They absorbed the last private carrier, Mersey and Weaver, into the fold in 1958, but the closure of the canals through ice in the winter of 1962–1963 brought about the end of British Transport Waterways' ownership of the Trent and Mersey Canal.

Steel lock at Thurlwood.

The British Transport Commission was abolished through the Transport Act of 1962 (c 9 and 10 Elizabeth II, 1 August 1962). British Transport Waterways became the British Waterways Board from 1 January 1963. The icy reception for the new authority was accompanied by various other challenges of the time. Many reports into canal operation had been conducted during the 1950s, looking at profit and canal closure, and as a result the board decided, from 6 October 1964, to end canal carrying. The remaining operations were transferred to private carriers again.

In 1964, the remaining trade in raw materials for the potteries was handed over to Willow Wren, which had a northern depot at Middlewich, using a basin placed between the top and second lock at Middlewich. The company's operation as a commercial carrier had already been in existence for some ten years, but would last only for a few more. It gave up the trade in the North West in November 1967 and re-invented itself as an operator of hire boats and camping boats, using the former working narrow boats. A company trading under the name of the Anderton Carrying Company operated the commercial trade until 1970. This was the second carrier to bear the name, and was followed by a third from 2014 to 2017.

Much of the through traffic from the North West to the Midlands had been concentrated on the Shropshire Union route, by British Transport Waterways, with Ellesmere Port retaining a role. China clay and other traffic at Weston Point Docks for the Weaver

DECLINE AND RESTORATION

British Waterways motor boats at Middlewich.

British Waterways motor boats at Preston Brook.

Etruria Vale Wharf, Caldon Canal.

and the Anderton Lift declined steadily during the 1950s. At Runcorn the basins and remaining lock flight were closed by Act of Parliament in 1966 and the site developed as the Port of Runcorn. Some craft were transferred to the maintenance fleet.

Movement of clay by waterways to the Potteries lasted until the end of commercial carrying.

Abandonment of the Burslem Arm

There was a breach in the Burslem arm of the canal during 1961. It occurred on the bend near the junction with the main waterway, opposite a boat maintenance yard where craft were regularly 'side-slipped' into the water. Boats would often be moored on the opposite bank to break the wave when other craft were being launched, but this was not always done. At this point, the canal was gradually built up because of mining subsidence and along the east side was a brook course. The varying water flow created a weak area beside the canal embankment and the progressive effects of launching craft into the canal were believed to have contributed to the collapse. British Transport Waterways chose not to reinstate the branch.

The Burslem arm was one of thirteen waterways (also including the Caldon Canal) that were marked for closure, with the approval of Ernest Marples, Minister of Transport. The reasons given were mining subsidence and a need to avoid expensive remedial work. The land was destined for redevelopment for industry and, in 1962, the canal was officially abandoned.

Canal Maintenance and Restoration

British Waterways dealt with the changing situation by improving the waterways and facilities for the boater, rather than maintaining them for the working boats. Whilst some waterways did retain a commercial aspect, that age had passed for the Trent and Mersey Canal and by the mid-1960s commercial traffic was in the minority. The only new development was the short-haul trade associated with the Milton Packing Depot belonging to Johnson Brothers. These premises had been used

Working boats and steel piles at Bridge 176.

for the aluminium industry and for a time conveyed pottery between three potteries, Hanley, Imperial and Trent beside the Caldon Canal to the depot. This traffic ended in May 1986, although craft were retained for deliveries to the Eagle Pottery at Hanley. All Johnson Brothers works were closed in 2003.

For British Waterways the principal maintenance work involved improving the banks of the canal using steel piles or, in some cases wood, to protect the habitat as ecological factors came to have more importance. In the North West Region of British Waterways, a number of former working boats were retained for maintenance work, becoming a nostalgic feature of the fleet.

Caldon Canal Restoration

Whilst the Caldon Canal was never legally closed, its traffic had declined to such an extent that it became almost unusable. A survey of the canal was carried out in 1960 by the Inland Waterway Protection Society. In April 1959, the government had created the Inland Waterways Redevelopment Advisory Committee, whose responsibility was to assist schemes to redevelop canals that were no longer commercially viable. The Caldon Canal survey formed the basis of a submission to that committee. With further threats of closure in 1961, the Stoke-on-Trent Boat Club organized a public meeting in Hanley and a cruise along the canal towards Froghall in September 1961. This attracted press coverage and local council support, which led to a suggestion by the Caldon Canal Committee that the National Trust should take over the waterway. Although this did not occur, there was clearly interest in looking after the waterway. The committee became the Caldon Canal Society, and worked with the British Waterways Board towards the eventual restoration of the canal.

In 1969, Staffordshire County Council and Stoke-on-Trent City Council announced that they would make contributions towards the restoration, and in May 1971 the Inland Waterways Association held a

> **STOKE-ON-TRENT BOAT CLUB**
>
> The Stoke-on-Trent Boat Club was formed in 1957 and established its first moorings in the Newcastle-under-Lyme Canal, using the grain store buildings as its first headquarters. The person responsible for forming the club was Guy Barks, who became the first Commodore. Guy was instrumental in bringing the Inland Waterways Association rally to Stoke in 1960 as well as organizing the protest cruise along the Caldon Canal in 1961. The Caldon Canal Society was formed in 1963 and members of both groups assisted with the restoration of the Canal.
>
> Stoke-on-Trent Boat Club moved its base to Endon in 1966. The Newcastle-under-Lyme Canal junction with the Trent and Mersey Canal was removed through new roadworks being done from 1968.

boat rally at Endon, to publicize the need to restore the canal. In February 1972 the government introduced a scheme to help local authorities to fund work on local facilities that were visually unattractive. Called 'Operation Eyesore', it offered grants of up to 85 per cent for suitable projects. Plans for the restoration of the canal were officially announced on 22 August 1972 and the main line was reopened to Froghall in 1974. A short section of the Leek Branch was also reopened, creating a navigation that included both Froghall and Leek Tunnel. Boaters were able once again to experience the unique industrial heritage of the canal.

The Caldon Canal was officially opened on 28 September 1974 and British Waterways upgraded the status of the canal to a cruising waterway in 1983.

Removal of Armitage Tunnel

The underground workings of Lea Hall Colliery had undermined the foundations of Armitage Tunnel to such as extent that the tunnel had to be replaced in 1971 by a new, open, concrete-lined section.

Alteration at Harecastle Tunnel

During 1953, the Docks and Inland Waterways had introduced a system of forced ventilation at Harecastle Tunnel, covering over the entrance at the Tunstall end with the housing that provided it. In 1973 roof falls caused the closure of the tunnel, which underwent repairs and then was reopened on 2 April 1977. In 1974, British Waterways removed the towing path through the tunnel, as horse towing of boats had ceased and there was little need for it.

Replacement of Stoke Bottom Lock

During the 1970s, the canal at Stoke was affected by roadworks. A replacement lock and lock house were made at Stoke Bottom Lock during 1974. The old lock was removed and the towpath lowered from the new lock placed north of the original.

A500 Pathfinder Project

Between 2004 and 2006 the Trent and Mersey Canal was diverted through a man-made tunnel at Stoke-on-Trent, as major improvements were made to the A500. This road was locally known as the 'D' road, referring to its number in Roman numerals.

From February 2004 contractor Edmund Nuttall undertook a temporary diversion of the Trent and Mersey Canal through a tunnel and at the same time also diverted Fowlea Brook, in order to make a dual carriageway, partly in the open and partly in

> **FESTIVAL PARK, STOKE-ON-TRENT**
>
> Much of the land occupied by the Shelton Ironworks and Furnaces (which had closed in 1978) was redeveloped in the early 1980s for the National Garden Festival held at Stoke-on-Trent. British Steel's rolling mills on the west side of the Trent and Mersey Canal (part of the modernization of the Shelton site from 1961 to 1964) remained in use until 2000.
>
> Whilst the festival was open to the public, from May to October 1986, a water-bus service was operated along the canal, linking the northern end and southern end of the site. At the southern end a marina was excavated and linked to the canal. Etruria Hall, built originally for Josiah Wedgwood, became the festival headquarters. After the event closed, St Modwen Properties and Stoke-on-Trent City Council entered into a joint venture to create Festival Park, which opened in 1995. The site comprises parks and gardens, play areas, retail and various entertainment premises, and offices.

Stoke Bottom Lock.

tunnels. A large roundabout was also made. Work was completed in September 2006, after which the canal was allowed to revert as close as possible to the original line as made during 1772.

Repairs to Brindley Bank Aqueduct
The Brindley Bank Aqueduct was one of two major aqueducts to be constructed along the waterway when the canal was first opened to traffic. Over the years, flooding on the Trent had taken its toll and repairs had been necessary from time to time, including the re-facing of the southern side by the North Staffordshire Railway in 1904. The last repairs were done in the days of British Waterways.

Canal Repairs near Anderton
The proximity of salt working to the canal east of the Anderton Boat Lift meant that the waterway was badly affected by subsidence, and required special maintenance as a result. In the summer of 2002 a leak was discovered between Soote Hill and the boat lift. Work to stabilize the embankment involved the removal of silt, the installation of a waterproof membrane across the canal and the construction of a wall 325 yards long.

The Anderton Boat Lift
With the abandonment of the Runcorn Locks, the traditional and original purpose of the Trent and Mersey Canal had been removed. By this time, the Bridgewater Canal and the plans of John Gilbert were ancient history. The Bridgewater Canal was owned by the Manchester Ship Canal Company, whose directors decided to redevelop the basins at Runcorn as a new, road-served port. The only links to the River Mersey from the Trent and Mersey were either by way of the Anderton Lift, the Weaver Navigation and Weston Point Docks, or the Middlewich Branch and the Shropshire Union Canal to Ellesmere Port. Commercial traffic on these routes eventually was reduced to those people who used traditional narrow boats to supply coal, fuel oil and logs. Their customers were the remote waterside properties and the boaters who lived on the waterways.

During the autumn of 1983, the Anderton Boat Lift was taken out of operation by British Waterways – the structure had been failing for some time. More than a decade later, plans to restore it were put in place, motivated by the uniqueness of its nature and status. The restoration began in 2000 and the lift was finally reopened for use on Tuesday 26 March

2002, providing once again a link between the Trent and Mersey Canal and the River Weaver.

Restoration of the Uttoxeter Canal

The restoration of the Uttoxeter Canal began with work on the junction lock at Froghall, which was reopened in July 2005. At this point the Caldon Canal Society was renamed the Caldon and Uttoxeter Canals Trust.

The trust is active today in the restoration of the waterway, and has begun a programme of placing traditional Trent and Mersey mile posts along the route of the canal. In April 2019 a mile post was placed at the site of Uttoxeter Canal Wharf, although restoration to this point is restricted because of issues with access. At present, the principal object of the trust is to reach Denstone.

The Burslem Branch Canal

The Burslem Port Trust has plans to reopen the Burslem Branch Canal, creating new waterside facilities through a major regeneration project that will extend from Rogerson's Meadows and the Trent and Mersey Canal to Furlong Mills in lower Burslem. The completed project aims to deliver the reopened canal branch, a mooring basin in a newly constructed pool at Furlong Mills, recreational facilities in the heritage buildings on the historic wharf, and an activity centre alongside the canal.

Subsidence had led to the infilling of this waterway following its closure in 1961, following a serious breach. The Burslem Port Trust after a lengthy investigation decided to proceed with restoration with a new junction to the east of the original Burslem Branch Canal junction. The new junction is planned to align with a narrow section immediately to the north. Boats will not be able to pass in the narrow section so the intention is to make a waiting area close to the junction. As this branch was closed through a breach, the Canal and River Trust requires the installation of some type of barrier, to provide protection against a repeat event.

The new route will follow a straight line immediately to the east of a proposed development area. The canal will be made in a concrete box section, with a channel 8 feet wide. The terminus of the

Cooperative Bakery Buildings, Burslem Arm. These buildings remained after the closure of the canal arm.

new plan is intended to be the same as the original basin terminus. This part will be accessed by boaters via a new lift or swing bridge from the wharf area. The remaining warehouse buildings will be either refurbished or replaced. Because of subsidence, the original footbridge now has only 1 metre of clearance above the waterline. The canal will follow the original line beside modern warehouse building to a new basin. A smaller basin with slipway may be provided to the south end of the site, just after the bridge.

In addition to receiving grant money from Stoke-on-Trent City Council and from the Canal and River Trust, Burslem Port Trust continues with its fundraising efforts.

Reservoir Maintenance and Improvement

British Waterways continued to maintain and improve the reservoirs at Knypersley, Rudyard and Stanley, which provided water to the Trent and Mersey Canal summit level and also supplied adjacent waterways. An Act of Parliament of 1975 brought new legislation for reservoir owners.

Alterations were also made to the former canal reservoir at Bath Pool, which had come under the ownership of the ironmaster Thomas Kinnersley, according to the Staffordshire Tithe Survey. It later supplied water to the Birchenwood coking plant. It was altered in 1965 and 1966 when British Railways London Midland Region decided to divert their London–Manchester line as part of the West Coast Main Line electrification programme. The diversion took a new route through the Bath Pool Valley, following a route that was similar to that of the early canal proposal. The route was laid along part of the former Birchenwood Colliery railway track bed and required Bath Pool Reservoir to be reduced in width. In order to retain the same capacity, the reservoir was extended to the north with a new dam that was financed by the local authority and British Railways. This work was done under the supervision of the railway engineer Thomas Mills.

Knypersley Old Reservoir was taken over by Staffordshire County Council during the 1970s. It is now known locally as 'The Serpentine' and still has an earth bank dam. In 2006 important work was carried out on the dam and valves of the 'new' reservoir. The old valves installed in both the wet

Winkle Weir, River Dane.
DAVID HENTHORN BROWN

Steps down to the dry well at Rudyard Lake. DAVID HENTHORN BROWN

The spillweir at Knypersley, 2010. DAVID HENTHORN BROWN

and dry well shafts were replaced. The original Telford valves are now exhibited on the bank of the reservoir.

Rudyard Reservoir still retains the complex water supply arrangements, with the feeder from Wincle Weir, the reservoir and the feeder to the Leek Branch all being maintained to the standards of modern legislation.

With regard to Stanley Reservoir, following the major dam work of 1934 and 1935, routine maintenance included the emptying of the reservoir in 1955. Between 1991 and 1992 a new labyrinth weir was constructed at Stanley Pool.

The Canal and River Trust: Preserving the Heritage

The Canal and River Trust was established in 2012 to look after English and Welsh waterways that had formerly been owned and controlled by British Waterways. With its formation, the Trent and Mersey Canal was brought under new ownership – and it was an ownership that was based on different values, and had new objectives and aims. In particular, the Trust wanted to make the waterway more accessible to all. The organizational structure was also changed and the Trust now has strong ties with volunteers and communities, all pursuing the message that waterways bring pleasure and a sense of well-being to those who use them.

Among the many challenges faced by the Canal and River Trust, one of the most important is heritage preservation. In November 2014, for example, alterations were made to the Grade II listed locks at Hazelhurst (10–12), where leakage was causing problems to the infrastructure. The solution was to seal up chambers and outlets, but only after giving notice to and securing the agreement of English Heritage, as it then was.

Change has been a constant factor in the history of the Trent and Mersey Canal. In the 250 years since trade commenced on the waterway, there have been many modifications and significant reconstruction work. It has seen the rise of the canal age and the competition of the railway age, and it is now a waterway for leisure, where people are able to enjoy boating, cycling, fishing or walking.

With the coming of the railways, public companies erected new bridges across the canal and some private industrial lines also crossed the waterway. Many of these former crossings have been now lost as works closed and the national railway network was rationalized.

The turnpikes also made changes to canal crossings until they were disbanded and replaced by local and national government control. Road alterations were another facet of the twentieth century, as the network was improved to meet the needs of the motor car and of commercial road vehicles.

The North Staffordshire Railway, London Midland and Scottish, British Transport Waterways and, later, British Waterways have all had to deal with reconstructed or new bridges spanning the waterway. The restoration of Bridge 2 on the Caldon

Bridge 2, Caldon Canal (Bedford Street Bridge) before reconstruction.

DECLINE AND RESTORATION

PUBLIC RAILWAYS BRIDGES ACROSS THE CANAL

188A Cheshire Midland 1863
180A London and North Western 1868
158 Manchester and Birmingham 1842
151A North Staffordshire 1852
132A North Staffordshire 1848
131A North Staffordshire 1848
127A North Staffordshire 1874
119C North Staffordshire 1872
119 B North Staffordshire 1917
114 B North Staffordshire 1874
114A British Railway (LM Region)
95A North Staffordshire 1848
71A Trent Valley 1847
65B Cannock Mineral 1859
59A Trent Valley Railway 1847
22A North Staffordshire 1849
20A Birmingham and Derby Junction 1839
13A Midland Railway 1873
11A Midland Railway 1868
7A Midland Railway 1869

There are four railway crossings on the Caldon Canal where the North Staffordshire Railway crossed. These are numbered 14A, 19A, 24A and 50A.

Canal, in 2019, preserved the form of the iron bridge built there. The iron decking of the original bridge had to be replaced, but the distinctive panels were retained. This iron bridge was itself a replacement, of a brick one, and was constructed by Thomas Shore & Sons at Hanley.

Railways and former railways cross the route of the canal between Marston and Weston-on-Trent. Some of the disused crossings have bridge numbers, including two at Stoke-on-Trent. Bridge 119B is a metal bridge that was built by the North Staffordshire Railway in 1917, to bring ironstone and other minerals for use at Etruria Furnaces at Shelton Steelworks. With the building of this railway, the transport of ore by canal boat was effectively terminated.

The other bridge had been constructed as part of the railway deviation work of 1864, when the passenger line was completed to Hanley Station. It ceased to carry passengers with the closure of the loop line, but was retained for freight traffic until the principal steel and ironworks closed in 1978, and only the modern mills continued to operate.

Following the Garden Festival at Stoke-on-Trent, groundwork during 1998 altered the route of the

The former railway bridge at Shelton.

towing path, to create a pedestrian and cycle path from Bridge 117 past the demolished Wedgwood Pottery. The path used the former railway bridge to cross the canal.

The infrastructure of the canal reflects a mixture of past and present and there are some unique features, such as the mile posts and the bridge numbers that are cut into the stonework. Both features were from a time when James Caldwell had influence in canal company affairs. The survey of the canal made in 1816 shows that the bridges that were constructed across the waterway for roads or for accommodation purposes had names. Later, they carried a stone plaque with a number that related to a numbering scheme that also included the brick bridges over the tail of the lock, where such bridges were provided. Most of these numbers have disappeared, following the reconstruction of the upper half of the bridge, but a few remain. The present numbering scheme was instituted by the North Staffordshire Railway.

The distinctive mile posts show the distances in each direction to Shardlow and Preston Brook quoted, which add up to 92. The originals have the initials 'R & D' cast into each post, identifying Rangeley & Dixson, who were iron and brass founders in Lichfield Street, Stone. John Rangeley was an enthusiastic engineer who devised a method of canal haulage, but had less success in business. Stone Foundry sold a patent roller pump, fire engines and steam engines. The partnership with William Dixson Junior was dissolved from 31 October 1820, when Edward Holt Diggles replaced him. Mounting debts led to insolvency in 1822 and Dixson was forced to advertise the foundry for lease in June 1824. John Rangeley remained in the Potteries until 1834, when he moved to Camberwell, Surrey. He pursued further engineering projects there, including the Safety Rotation Railway, but his various ventures brought him into insolvency for a second time.

Whilst many mile posts have been lost, there are a number that remain. In 1977 the Trent and Mersey Canal Society erected replica mile posts to fill the gaps and complete the line once again.

Mile post near Bridge 29.

Another distinctive feature of the canal is the presence of iron footbridges across the tail of some locks, which can still be seen at Meaford Locks. These were made with a centre split, to enable the tow rope to pass through. Although variations of such bridges were adopted on other waterways, the design appears to be unique to the Trent and Mersey Canal. Etruria Top Lock also had a footbridge of this design, although this has now been replaced.

Canal-side buildings can still be found along the waterway. They were constructed at different times and the inventory even includes a Second World War pill box. Many buildings were homes for engineers, inspectors, managers, toll-keepers, wharfingers or workers. They vary in design from the functional, such as the house at Lock 4 on the Caldon that was associated with the wharf there, before the lock was made, to the towpath-side house at Bridge 26 at

Split footbridge at Lock 33, Meaford.

Eggington. The latter is a large structure, which, if it had not been modified, would probably have been a case for listing by Historic England. The façade appears to be original.

Modern Developments

Other developments in Canal and River Trust times include Oakwood Marina, Davenham Lane, which has used the sunken land adjacent to the canal north of Middlewich. These flashes were on the land of Higgins Lane Farm and were used as a place for disused canal boats to be abandoned. The proposal for the marina was first made in 2003, but there were delays with obtaining planning consent. Plans for a triangular marina were produced in May 2014 and the first part of this was opened on 11 August 2018. The marina is on the route of Phase 2b of HS2, the new high-speed railway scheme for England, and that may well affect operations in the future.

During 2018, the area around the canal at the Treble Locks, Middlewich and Brooks Lane was proposed for redevelopment. This scheme has included a marina south of Kings Lock and will include the dry dock at the Treble Locks and the former Murgatroyds salt works pump house, which still survives.

One of the biggest transformation projects on the Trent and Mersey Canal has been at Etruria, where the former steelworks site has been transformed with new buildings on much of it since the Garden Festival. The basin created there is now the base for Black Prince boat-hire business. Further north of Etruria, the remainder of the site, which was closed in 2000 and demolished during 2005, is gradually returning to nature and is awaiting the attention of future development projects.

Lift bridge at the entrance to the basin at Festival Park.

House at Hanley Wharf.

ROAD BRIDGES OVER THE TRENT & MERSEY CANAL

The road bridges that span the Trent & Mersey Canal show diversity in design and construction, which vary from the original brick arch construction to include iron girder bridges, to early concrete bridges such as Bridge 23 (B5008) at Willington, which was erected during 1933 and Bridge 24 (B5009) from 1936. The Road Traffic Act classified bridges with letters. The replacement bridge at Etruria, for the A53, (1943) was classed as 'Z' whilst the crossing of the Dane Feeder at the Royal Oak (1943) was classed as 'Y'. Later road improvements include Clay Mills (Bridge 28) where the original bridge had been altered by the North Staffordshire Railway from 1913. This had been the Roman Road Ryknield Street and became the A38. Between 1963 and 1968 the dual carriageway Burton-on-Trent Burton By-Pass was constructed between Branston and Clay Mills, which included raising the road at Bridge 28 for a flyover junction and the reclassification of the road at Bridge 28 as the A5121. The crossing of the M6 at Hassall Green, on the section opened in 1965, became bridge 147A.

Bridge 23 at Willington.

A significant engineering challenge was presented to the Canal and River Trust, Trent and Mersey Canal Section, by the planning of Phase 1 of the HS2 scheme. Near Fradley there were two locations (Trent and Mersey Canal East and West), where the railway to Birmingham would cross close to Shade House Lock and then Woodend Lock. During 2014 these crossings were abandoned in favour of making a tunnel under the concentration of roads, railways and canals in this area. With Phase 2a of the HS2 scheme to Crewe, the construction of a viaduct is currently planned at Great Hayward.

The principal reason for making the Trent and Mersey Canal originally was trade and, with the completion of the canal and the expansion of the network, the vision was successfully realized. Over time, its purpose has changed and the Trent and Mersey now plays a vital role in the leisure industry for private boat owners, boat-hire firms, marinas and boatyards.

Canal-side industries no longer use the canal for transport. In that respect, history has come full circle, as road transport provides the main means of carriage for raw material and finished products. There are also trades that have gone, including

Grade II-listed Hargate Lane House at Bridge 26.

Longport Pottery buildings.

coal-mining and iron-making. The Staffordshire pottery industry has been decimated, with only a fraction of the original number of potteries continuing in operation. Wedgwood is still busy making quality pottery at its present works, north of Barlaston. The Burleigh Pottery, Middleport, owned by Burgess, Dorling and Leigh, makes 'hand-made pottery' at its canal-side factory and nearby Steelite is also busy in the pottery trade. However, there are many open spaces where potteries have been demolished and production moved elsewhere. At Longport there are still many reminders of this trade that was once so busy. It is perhaps fitting to close with an image of a site that was occupied first by the pottery established by John Brindley, brother of James, and later by John Davenport, potter, glass-maker and one-time partner in a canal carrying concern.

Bibliography

Books

A Biographical Dictionary of Civil Engineers in Great Britain, Mike Chrimes. A. W. Skempton, 2002

A General History of Inland Navigation, Foreign and Domestic, John Phillips. Fifth Edition, B. Crosby and Co, 1805

A History of Burslem, M. W. Greenslade. Reprinted by Staffordshire County Library from the Victoria History of the County of Stafford, 1983

Agents of the Revolution: John and Thomas Gilbert – Entrepreneurs, Peter Lead. Centre for Local History at the University of Keele, 1989

Britain's Waterways: A Unique Insight, George Roberts. GEO Projects, 1999

Canals and Traders, Edwin A Pratt. P S King and Son, 1910

Canals of the West Midlands, Charles Hadfield. David and Charles, 1969

East Midland Canals – Through Time, Ray Shill. Amberley Publishing, 2013

Harecastle's Canal and Railway Tunnels, Alan C. Baker and Mike G. Fell. Lightmoor Press, 2019

Historic Waterway Scenes: The Trent & Mersey Canal, Peter Lead. Cromwell Press, 1993

Historical Account of Navigable Rivers, Canals and Railways Throughout Great Britain, Joseph Priestley. Longman, Rees, Orme, Brown & Green, 1831

Industry and Empire, the History Book Club for Penguin Books Ltd. E. J. Hobsbawn, 1968

North West Canals – Through Time (Merseyside, Weaver and Chester), Ray Shill. Amberley Publishing, 2013

Silent Highways, Ray Shill. The History Press, 2011

The Caldon Canal and Tramroads, Peter Lead. Oakwood Press, 1990

The Ceramic Art of Great Britain, Volumes 1 & 2, Virtue & Co, 1878, Llewellynn Jewitt

The Industrial History of England, Methuen & Co, 1894, H de B Gibbons

The Life and Works of James Trubshaw, Private publication, 1978 Anne Bayliss

The Trent and Mersey Canal, Jean Lindsay. David and Charles, 1979

Trent and Mersey Canal: Trade and Transport, Tom Foxon. Lightmoor Press, 2016

West Midland Canals – Through Time, Ray Shill. Amberley Publishing, 2012

Pamphlets and other Publications

Hunt's Mineral Statistics 1873
Hunt's Mineral Statistics 1878
Opening of Thurlwood Lock and Marston New Cut, Trent & Mersey Canal, British Waterways Board 1958
Seasonal Considerations on a Canal intended to be cut from the River Trent to the River Mersey 1766
The History of Inland Navigation, a combination of pamphlets, Second Edition, T Lowndes 1769

Articles

Quarterly Papers in Engineering, Volume 1, 1844
Memoirs of James Brindley, Samuel Hughes
Steam tugs on the Trent and Mersey Canal, Railway and Canal Historical Society Journal 238, 2020, Mike G. Fell

Websites

Diaries of James Caldwell: https://jjhc.info/caldwellnotes
North Staffordshire Railway Study Group: http://www.nsrsg.org.uk/
Saltscape: http://www.saltscape.co.uk/
Trent & Mersey Canal Society: https://trentandmerseycanalsociety.org.uk/

Archives

Birmingham Library Archives
Birmingham University
Chester Records Office
Derby Library Archives
Derby Records Office
Institute of Civil Engineers
Staffordshire Records Office (Stafford)
The National Archives, Kew
Waterways Archive Canal & River Trust
Wedgwood Archives
William Salt Library, Stafford

Former archive sources consulted, but now closed

British Newspaper Library, Colindale
British Waterways Archive, Gloucester
Staffordshire Records Office (Lichfield)

Newspapers

Aris's Birmingham Gazette
Birmingham Daily Post
Burton Chronicle
Cheshire Observer
Chester Chronicle
Chester Courant
Crewe Chronicle
Derby Mercury
Eddowe's Journal and General Advertiser for Shropshire and the Principality of Wales
Globe, London
Gores Liverpool Advertiser
Leeds Intelligencer
Liverpool Mercury
London Courier
London Gazette
Manchester Courier and Lancashire General Advertiser
Manchester Mercury
Morning Chronicle, London
Nantwich Guardian
Northwich Guardian
Sheffield Independent
Shrewsbury Chronicle
Stafford Mercury, Pottery Gazette & Newcastle Express
Staffordshire Advertiser
Staffordshire County Herald
Staffordshire Sentinel
Star, London
Sun, London
Wolverhampton Chronicle

Assistance has been provided by the following people: The late Harry Arnold, Alan Baker, David Henthorn Brown, Peter Cross-Rudkin, Nigel Crowe, Richard Dean, Tom Foxon, Roger Evans, Christopher Jones, Martin O'Keeffe, Victoria Owens, Allison Smedley, Howard Sprenger, Steve Wood, David Wooliscoft.

Support information for births, marriages and deaths has been checked with relevant Parish Records, the census 1841–1911, England & Wales Register (1939), Civil Registration (Birth, Marriage and Death), Canterbury Wills, Cheshire Wills, Lichfield Wills, the National Probate Calendar and trade directories for Cheshire, Derbyshire and Staffordshire.

Index

Abram & Co. 49
Acton Bridge 26
Acton–River Weaver Canal 49
Adams, George 15
alkali trade 105
Alrewas Aqueduct 14, 16
Alrewas Lock 17
Alrewas Mill 16
Alrewas–Wychnor Canal 16
Anderton 48, 49
Anderton Boat Lift 77
Anderton Carrying Company 49, 85, 88
Anson, Lord 15
Armitage 14
Armitage Tunnel 14, 15, 145
Aston Lock 22
Aston plaster quarries 109

Bagnall Reservoir 36, 46, 66, 90
Barker, John 16
Barnitt, James 41
Barton Tunnel 31
Bateman, William 59
Bath Pool 43, 46, 52
Bedford Street Bridge 150, 151
Bedford Street Locks 35
Bellamour Turnover Bridge 62
Bells Mill Aqueduct 24, 52
Bentley, Thomas 9, 11
Bidder, G.P. 74
Bill, William 34
Birchenwood Coke Ovens 118
Birmingham & Fazeley Canal 37
Birmingham & Liverpool Railway 44, 71
Birmingham & Liverpool Ship Canal 80
Birmingham Canal Navigations 37
Blundell, Richard 132
Boatmen's Missions 65
Bond End Canal 16, 43, 80
Bone Mills 108
Boulton & Watt 54, 56
Boulton, Matthew 11
Brass & Copper Works 119
Brereton Colliery 112
Brereton Sough 46
Breweries 119, 120
Brick Making Trade 111
Bridgewater Canal 8
Bridgewater, Duke of 10
Brindley Bank Aqueduct 146
Brindley, James 7, 8, 13, 22, 24, 43, 128, 129
British Transport Commission 138
British Transport Waterways 140, 141
British Waterways 141–147
Broadby, Issac 11
Broads Gutter 45
Broken Cross Bridge 81
Bromley Wharf 125
Brookes, Sir Richard 32
Broughton, Sutton & Co 49
Bullivant & Co. Ltd 85
Burslem Branch Canal 143, 147, 148
Burslem Port Trust 147–148
Burslem Pottery 95
Burton Boat Company 12, 24, 107
Burton Forge 12

Calamine 119
Caldon Canal 54–36, 144
Caldon Low 34, 70
Caldwell, James 44, 50, 53, 54, 56, 134
Canal & River Trust 86, 150–156
Canal Carrying Companies 122–124
Canal Control Committee 89
canal widening in Cheshire 80–81
Cavendish Boat Company 21, 127
cheese transport 21
chemical trade 105–106
Cheshire Locks Scheme 80
Chester Canal 57
Chetwynd, Sir George 135
Clive–Tetton Canal 75
Clowes, Josiah 30, 129
coal trade 111–114
Cobb, Francis 11
Coke trade 118
Coleman, Thomas 88
Coleshill Agreement 37–39
Collins, Christina 65, 135
Colwich Lock 19
Commercial Canal 41
Consall Flint Mills 106
Consall Forge New Lock 67
Cooper, Benjamin 11
Coventry Canal 37–39
Coventry¬–Burton Canal 43
Coxshead Engine 54, 60
Crewe Construction Syndicate 84
Crompton, Samuel 11
Cross, William 41, 46
Crown Inn (Stone) 9
Croxton Aqueduct 30
Curbishley, Harry 132
Curr, John 36
Cuttle Bridge 111

Dadford, Thomas 16
Darwin, Erasmus 11, 16
Derby & Crewe Junction Railway 73
Derby Canal 39
Derwent (Derbyshire) Navigation 42
Derwent Mouth 21
Docks & Inland Waterways Executive 137
Dunstall Roving Bridge 18
duplication of Cheshire locks 60–61
Dutton Stop Lock 66, 67

Eggington Brook Aqueduct 18
electricity generating stations 119
Ellesmere & Chester Canal 42, 57
end of commercial carrying 140–141
Engine Lock 35
Etruria back pumping scheme 52
Etruria Deviation 64
Etruria Locks 52
Etruria Vale Wharf 143
Eyes, John 7

Faram, James 50, 61, 63
Faram, John 63
Faram, Samuel 61, 132
Faram, William 50, 60–63, 131, 132
ferro-concrete bridges 155
Festival Park, Stoke-on-Trent 145, 154

Finch, John 11
Findern 52
Flint Mill Lock 107
flint trade 10, 106–108
flour mills 120
Forbes, James 132
Ford, James 11
Forsyth, John Curphy 76, 132
Fourdinier, Henry 108
Foxley Canal 79
Foxlow Brook 46
Fradley 39
Fradley Junction 37, 38
Fradley Storage Reservoir 14
Fradley Workshops 78
Froghall 70–71
Froghall Limestone Kilns 110
Froghall Tunnel 36

G. & J. Cope, iron founders 52
Gainsborough 21, 123
Garbett, Samuel 16
gas works 117, 118
Gaskell's Bridge 16
Gilbert, John (Junior) 48
Gilbert, John (Senior) 8, 10, 35, 37, 134
Gilbert, Thomas 37
Gilbert's Salt Works 48
Giles, Francis 130
Glass, Richard 155
Gower, Earl 9, 25
Grand Junction Railway 71, 72
Great Haywood Wharf
Griffin, Thomas 34

Hall End Branch 56, 57
Hall End Stop Lock 57
Hanley–Shelton Canal 42
Hardingswood Junction 56, 62
Hardingswood Lock 26
Harecastle Tunnel (1777) 14, 19, 26, 43, 83
Harecastle Tunnel (1827) 53–55, 83–86, 145
Hargate Lane House 156
Hazelhurst Aqueduct 64
Hazelhurst New Locks 64, 65
Hazelhurst Old Locks 41
Hazelhurst Staircase Locks 41, 42
Hempstones 8, 9
Henshall, Hugh 13, 16, 34, 41, 43, 44, 129
High Bridge Aqueduct 18
Hoof, William 54, 57
Horninglow 17
Hugh Henshall & Co. 21
Hunt's Lock 14

Inland Waterways Protection Society 144
interchange basins 78, 88
iron trade 114–117
ironstone traffic 117

Jebb, G.R. 84, 132
Jessop, William 40
Jones, Charles 26

Kidsgrove lock duplication 86
Kings Lock 29
Kings Mill 8, 12

159

INDEX

Knypersley Reservoir 36, 58, 149

Lawton Feeder 45, 50
Lawton Treble Locks 26, 49, 50
Lawtonwich 7
Leek Canal 40, 41
Leek Tunnel 41
Lichfield 37
limestone trade 109–111
Lion Salt Works 101
lock standardisation 19
London & Birmingham Railway 71
London, Midland & Scottish Railway 89
Long Bridge 7, 8
Longport 7
Longton Gutter 45
Lower Thurlwood Lock 60

Macclesfield & Red Bull Railway 44
Macclesfield Canal 12, 56
maintenance boats 90, 146
Malkins Bank 61
Manchester & Birmingham Canal 75
Manchester & Birmingham Railway 72
Mansfield, John 48
Marston Deviation 140
Marston Hall Mine 100
Massey, Graham Wood 132, 133
McIntosh, Hugh 42
Meaford Staircase 64
Meaford Top Lock Bridge 25
Meaford Turnover Bridge 62
merchandise trade 121–127
Mersey & Irwell Navigation 8
Middleport 9
Middlewich (3) Locks 50, 51
Middlewich Big Lock 81
Middlewich Treble Locks 50, 51
Moira, Earl of 46
Molineaux, Benjamin 11
Moore, Henry 134
Musgrave, William 11

Newcastle-under-Lyme 9
Newcastle-under-Lyme Canal 78, 79, 91
North Staffordshire Pottery 95
North Staffordshire Railway 71–75, 77–78
Northwich 7
Norton Colliery 113
Norton Green Branch 46

oil shale 119
Old Bagnall Reservoir 36, 46
Old Knypersley Reservoir, 36
Old Roebuck Inn (Newcastle) 10
Oxford Canal 37

pack horses 8, 9
Paget, Lord 16
Paper Mill, Winkle 47
Pathfinder Project 145
Peck Mill 46
Pentens (Cockshutt) Lock 24
Phillipps, William Douglas 134
Pierpoint Locks 28
Pinkerton, John 39
Planet Lock 87, 88
plateways 42, 68, 69
Pointon Mill mail coach accident 63
Pool (Limekiln) Locks 86
Pool Aqueduct 56
Poor Rates (1818) 52
Potter, James 52, 56, 59, 60, 130
Potter, Joseph 59, 130

pottery kilns 96
pottery ovens 95
pottery trade 94–98
Pownall, Robert 11
Preston Brook 13, 14, 76, 77
Preston Brook & Chester Railway 72
Preston Brook & Runcorn Railway 72
Preston Brook Tunnel 26–28, 76
Pritchard, Daniel 54, 57

Radcliffe, Edward 133
railway bridge numbering 151
Railway Executive 138
Rangeway & Dixson 152
Red Bull Aqueduct 67
Reid, Alexander 49
Rennie, George 44
Rennie, John 41, 46, 47, 49, 50, 52, 129, 130
Ricardo, John Lewis 74
River Churnett 35, 42
River Churnett Feeder 58
River Croco 29
River Dane Feeder 18, 58
River Dove Aqueducts 18
River Sections in the canal 16, 35, 43
River Severn 7, 12
River Trent 7, 40
River Trent Aqueduct (Norton) 35
River Trent Aqueduct (Stoke) 24
Roberts, Charles 130
Robinson, William 133
Rock, A.F. 85
Roe, Charles 11
Royal Commission on Canals 83
Rudyard Reservoir 47, 87, 149
Rumps Lock 32
Runcorn 33
Runcorn Docks 33
Runcorn Staircase Locks 33
Russell Bridge–Newton Canal 75
Ryder, Dudley 135

Salt Tax 48
salt trade 99–105
Salt Union 100, 103
Saltersford Tunnel 31
Sandon, Viscount 74
Saner, J.A. 84
Scotch Brook Aqueduct 22
Shade House Lock 14
Shardlow Wharf 21, 22, 123, 126, 127
Shardlow–Nottingham Canal 39
Sheasby, Thomas 39
Shelton Furnace (iron) 115, 116
Shenton Road Lock 24
Shirley's Bone Mill 108
Shobnall 16
Shropshire Union 98
Shugborough 19
Sideways Wharf 114
Silverdale Railway 79
Sitch Reservoir 46
Skew Railway Bridge (Stoke) 78
Smeaton, John 8
Smith, Abel 11
Smith, Edward Blakeney 80, 132
Smith, William (bricklayer) 54
Snapes Aqueduct 61
Sparrow & Co., Coxshead 113
Sparrow, John 10, 14, 19, 133
Staffordshire & Worcestershire Canal 13
Staffordshire & Worcestershire Canal 13, 21
Staffordshire Canal 30
Stanley Mill 46

Stanley Reservoir 46, 66
Stanley, John 48
Steam Boat experiment 63
Stoke Basin & Wharf 24
Stoke Bottom Lock 145
Stoke-on-Trent Boat Club 145
Stone 22–24, 109
Stone Boatyard 23
Stone Canal Office 23, 24
Stone–Baswich Canal 130
Stud Green Bridge 32
subsidence in Cheshire 82, 140
subsidence in Staffordshire 139
Sunday trading 65, 66
Swarkestone 29, 39, 40
Swarkestone Stop 40

Taylor, William 7
Team Aqueduct 42, 75
Telford, Thomas 54–56, 59, 130
Thomas Broade 7
Thomas Sparrow, Thomas 47, 133
Thurlwood Steel Lock 140, 141
tramroads 63–71
Trent & Mersey Canal purchase 73, 74
Trent boats 17
Trent Navigation 40
Trent Valley Railway 72, 73
Trentham Mill 46
Trubshaw, James 59, 60, 131
Trubshaw, John 60, 131
tunnel tugs 83–86
Tunstall Gasworks 117, 118
Turnpike Roads 9
Twemlow, Francis 134
Twentyman, Samuel 11
Twyford Lock 24

Upper Trent Navigation 12
Uttoxeter Canal 34, 42, 43, 75

Vaughan, William 133, 134

Wardle Branch 57, 58
Wardle Branch Junction 58
Wardle Lock 58
water supply 45–48, 52, 89
waterworks 121
Weaver Navigation 11, 43, 49
Wedgewood, John 9
Wedgewood, Josiah 9, 10, 13
Weston 19–21
Weston, Samuel 30
Wheelock 28, 29, 125
Wheelock Locks 29
Whieldon, Thomas 134
White, Alexander Muir 133
Whitmore 71
Whittington Brook 39
Wilden Ferry 16, 21
Willington Bridge
Wilton Mill 11
Wincham Brook Aqueduct 30, 82
Wincham Wharf
Winsford 12
Witton Brook–Macclesfield Canal
Wolfe-Barry, Sir John 84
Wolseley Bridge 10
women in canal affairs 135
Wood, Enoch 95
Woodend Lock 15
Worthington & Gilbert 74
Wychnor 16, 17
Wychnor Mill 16